A CENTURY OF THE
ENGLISH BOOK TRADE

A CENTURY OF THE ENGLISH BOOK TRADE

SHORT NOTICES OF ALL PRINTERS, STATIONERS,
BOOK-BINDERS, AND OTHERS CONNECTED WITH
IT FROM THE ISSUE OF THE FIRST DATED
BOOK IN 1457 TO THE INCORPORATION OF THE
COMPANY OF STATIONERS IN 1557

BY

E. GORDON DUFF

LONDON
THE BIBLIOGRAPHICAL SOCIETY
1948

FIRST PRINTED BY
BLADES, EAST & BLADES 1905
REPRINTED PHOTOGRAPHICALLY 1948
IN GREAT BRITAIN
AT THE UNIVERSITY PRESS, OXFORD
BY CHARLES BATEY
PRINTER TO THE UNIVERSITY

TO

MY VERY GOOD FRIEND

THOMAS WILLIAM RENWICK.

———

Tecum etenim longos memini consumere soles,
Et tecum primas epulis decerpere noctes ;
Unum opus, et requiem pariter disponimus ambo.

FOREWORD

GORDON DUFF's *Century of the English Book Trade* was the first, and it has proved itself one of the most valuable, of the Bibliographical Society's Dictionaries of Printers. It has long been out of print and in order to meet the continued demand for it the Council of the Society has decided to issue this reprint. As in the case of the reprint of the *Short-title Catalogue*, this is an interim measure. The preparation of new editions of the Dictionaries remains one of the Society's most important tasks.

F. C. F.

PREFACE.

M Y OBJECT in compiling this book has been to attempt to provide for England what has been so admirably done for Paris by M. Renouard in his dictionary of persons connected with the book trade in that city from 1470 to 1600.

At present there is no handy book to which we can turn to find what is or is not known about an early English printer or stationer. Every one who studies the subject knows that he is continually coming across small facts, perhaps not of use to him at the immediate moment, which he loses sight of again not knowing whether they are worth noting or not.

Herbert's Typographical Antiquities, that model of care and accuracy, is still our standard reference book, but it was published nearly a hundred and twenty years ago, and since then hundreds of sources of knowledge have been made available and much good work has been done.

The Bibliographical Society with its handlists of English printers aims to show what is or is not known about their productions; in the present work I have attempted to do the same for their personal history. I have not of course endeavoured to give full biographies of men whose career and work have been well described elsewhere. It would be out of place for instance to write detailed accounts of Caxton or Day when so many good and full accounts are readily available. In these cases I have restricted myself to the briefest account into which I could compress the necessary facts. The length of a notice in no way measures the importance of a man.   In the case of little known or hitherto unnoticed stationers I have given any piece of information I could find, but of many nothing beyond the name is known.

For many valuable notes extracted from the Oxford University Archives I have to thank my friend Mr. Strickland Gibson, of the Bodleian, while my friends at Cambridge, Mr. Charles Sayle, Mr. E. J. Worman, and Mr. G. J. Gray have also been most helpful with information.

No one is better aware than myself how incomplete this work must necessarily be, how much is still lying undiscovered in the vast mass of manuscript records in public and private hands and in unexpected places in printed books.   In its compilation the notes of many years have been brought together, and many hundreds of volumes, often without result, read through. Such as it is, it is published, and I can only ask those into whose hands it may fall to assist in correcting the errors or in adding new names or facts. New facts though seemingly unimportant should never be overlooked : it is often the little fact that makes all the difference.   Only by such help, if at any future time a new edition of the book should be called for, can it be made more useful to the student and more worthy of the subject of which it treats.

E. G. D.

PRINCE'S PARK,
      LIVERPOOL.

CONTENTS.

INTRODUCTION.

EVER since books have existed, the stationer or bookseller in some form or another must have existed also. Of the early history of the stationers in England we know little or nothing, beyond the fact that they were numerous enough to form themselves into a company in 1404. No records of this early company have been preserved, though frequent references to it are found in wills and elsewhere. No doubt its rules and regulations were on similar lines to those of other city companies, and the charter granted to the Stationers' Company in 1557 merely re-expressed and re-affirmed these rules, but did not radically change them. The invention of printing and the consequent enormous increase in the production of books brought about also a corresponding impetus to the trades of the bookbinder and the stationer. How soon after the issue of the first dated printed book in 1457 printed books found their way into this country is not clearly known. John Russell, Archdeacon of Berkshire, bought two copies of Cicero's De officiis printed by Schoeffer at Mainz in 1466, the year after their publication. An edition of the Sarum Breviary, which naturally must have been intended for the English market, was printed at Cologne about 1474, but I think we may take it that for the first fifteen years or so the importation of printed books was exceedingly small. Caxton came to Westminster in 1476 and in 1478 a press was at work at Oxford. About 1479 St. Alban's followed and in 1480 John Lettou began to print in London, but at best the output of books in England was miserably scanty. There is no doubt this want was felt by the more educated English people, and when in January, 1484, a very important act was passed to regulate and restrict the conditions under which foreigners carried on business or trade in England the following proviso was added, " Provided always, that this act or any parcel thereof, or any other act made " or to be made in this said parliament, shall not extend, or be in prejudice,

" disturbance, damage or impediment to any artificer or merchant stranger, of
" what nation or country he be, or shall be of, for bringing into this realm, or
" selling by retail or otherwise, any books written or printed, or for inhabiting
" within this said realm for the same intent, or any scrivener, alluminor,
" binder or printer of such books, which he hath or shall have to sell by
" way of merchandise, or for their dwelling within this said realm for the
" exercise of the said occupations; this act or any part thereof notwith-
" standing." *

In 1482-3 we have two documents relating to foreign stationers. The
first is a lease to Henry Frankenbergk and Barnard van Stondo, merchants of
printed books, of an alley in St. Clement's Lane called St. Mark's Alley: the
second an account of books received on sale or return by Thomas Hunte of
Oxford from two stationers, Peter Actors and John of Aix-la-Chapelle.
Though London was the headquarters of the book-trade the stationers did
not confine their attention to the city, but travelled about the country and
attended the principal fairs where, as we know from early accounts, a
considerable portion of their trade was done. This practice of selling books
at fairs continued up to quite a late date and at the end of the seventeenth
century large consignments were sent down to the great fairs by the leading
London dealers and sold by auction or otherwise. The greatest fair of all
was from a very early period that of Frankfurt and to it many scholars and
booksellers journeyed for the purpose of seeing all the new books or
purchasing fresh stock. Perhaps it is worth noticing that the books consigned
from Frankfurt to England were packed for their journey in tubs.

About 1483 the foreign printers began to issue books for the English
market. Raynaldus de Novimagio at Venice, Egidius van der Heerstraten at

---

* Purveu toutz foitz que cest acte ou ascune part dicell, ne ascune autre acte fait ou affaire en le dit parle-
ment, en null maner extende ou soit prejudiciall ascun destourbance damage ou empediment au ascun artificer
ou marchaunt estraunge, de quell nacion ou paiis it soit ou soira, de ou pur amesnance en cest Roialme ou
vendicion par retaille ou autrement dascuns maners livres escriptez ou enpressez, ou pur lenhabitacion deinz le
dit Roialme pur mesme lentent, ou au ascun escrivener alluminour liour ou enpressour autrement dit imprintour
de tielx livres, quelx il ad ou avera a vendre par voie de marchandice, ou pur leur demeure en mesme le
Roialme pur lexcercicion de les ditz occupacions ; cest acte ou ascune part dicell nient contristeant. [Statutes
of the Realm, fol. 1816. Vol. II, p. 493.]

The word liour=lieur, an old form of relieur, binder, and is not as often translated "reader."

Louvain, Gerard Leeu at Antwerp and others printed service books, grammars and such like. They do not however appear to have kept agents of their own in this country, at least we find no mention of any in the various colophons to their books. Doubtless the encouragement offered to foreigners by the act of 1484 cannot have been without some immediate result.

The first year of Henry VII is an interesting date in the history of the English book-trade, marking its official recognition by royalty, for on December 5th, 1485, Peter Actors was appointed Stationer to the King. The grant is a most interesting document. " Grant for life to Peter Actoris, born in Savoy of the office of Stationer to the King; also license to import, so often as he likes, from parts beyond the sea, books printed and not printed into the port of the city of London, and other ports and places within the kingdom of England, and to dispose of the same by sale or otherwise without paying customs etc. thereon and without rendering any accompt thereof."

At this time so little printing was done in England, almost all books being imported, that no Printer to the King was appointed, but only a Stationer to the King. Peter Actors is not heard of after 1501 and it is probable that after his death he was succeeded by William Faques who, being himself a printer, had the title altered to Printer to the King.

The terms of the grant also show that, although great privileges had been granted to stationers under the act of 1484, duties had to be paid on imported books, but what these duties were does not clearly appear, unless they were the ordinary tonnage and poundage levied on all imported merchandize.

In 1487 we have the first definite instance of an Englishman commissioning a foreign printer to print for him, for in that year Guillaume Maynyal printed for Caxton the first edition of the Sarum Missal. This production of English service books in France rapidly increased to a most important trade, and though for a few years Venice was a serious rival to Paris and Rouen, her work in this direction ceased before the close of the fifteenth century.

It is fairly evident that up to the time of Caxton's death in 1491 the book-trade in England was not important and the demand for books was not large. The revival of letters, though beginning to make itself felt, was not a strong enough power to influence the trade, and the books printed in London at this time were all of a popular character. But it cannot be supposed for a moment that at this time and to a considerably later date the products of the printing press in England represented in any way the literary wants of the people. When learned foreigners were beginning to resort to our schools and English scholarship was rising to a higher level, the demand for educational and classical books must have been large. Gibbon sneeringly remarks that Caxton never printed a classic, a fact which points eminently to that printer's common sense, for he could neither hope to rival the excellence of foreign workmanship, nor had he the facilities for obtaining, then a very important matter, good manuscripts for copy. In what he attempted he succeeded admirably, and that was to produce for England what could not be obtained elsewhere. It is a matter on which we may congratulate ourselves that, instead of printing poor editions of Virgil, of Terence, or of Cicero, which could easily be obtained from abroad, he published for us, at a time when our own language was undergoing a great change, our own classics, the *Canterbury Tales*, the *Confessio Amantis*, and the *Morte d Arthur*.

It may be roughly stated that before 1535 no classics were printed in England. It is true that Rood about 1483 issued Cicero's *Pro Milone*, and between 1495 and 1497 Pynson printed separately the six plays of Terence, but these were merely intended as school text-books and can hardly be called editions of the classics. Probably the Cicero was produced for the use of Magdalen School at the instigation of Anwykyll the head master, and doubtless William Horman was responsible for the Terence, his favourite author, as a class-book for Eton. In ordinary books it is certain, in fact we have their own word for it, that the foreigner could easily undersell us, so that it is hardly a matter for surprise that our printers confined themselves to work on which they could make a livelihood.

The absence of competition amongst the resident printers and stationers is very clearly shown by the scattered situation of their places of business; Caxton in Westminster, Machlinia in Holborn, Franckenberg in St. Clement's Alley and, later on, De Worde in Westminster, Pynson in the Strand, Notary at St. Thomas Apostle. But soon after Caxton's death foreign competition began to make itself very distinctly felt. The large supply seemed to create a larger demand, and the foreign printers awoke to the fact that England with so few printers of her own was a very desirable country to exploit.

The position held by the foreigner in the English book-trade may easily be gauged from the fact that, with the exception of William Caxton and Thomas Hunte the Oxford bookseller, we find no English name in the colophon of any book printed in or for England as printer or bookseller until about the year 1516. The school-master printer of St. Alban's was doubtless also an Englishman, but his name is not known. That there were many English booksellers and stationers at this time is certain, but for some reason or other the foreigner took the lead and the native workman lagged well in the background.

He was however distinctly and aggressively jealous of this foreign competition and endeavoured by every means in his power to hinder and restrict the alien in his work. Some of the more important early printers, such as Wynkyn de Worde, who had lived much of their lives in England and had become denizens in the reign of Henry VII when foreign immigration was encouraged, were practically Englishmen and became citizens and free of the stationers. It was the humbler undenizened alien, who worked often in the liberties where he could not be touched, that was the most objected to and against whom the "customs of the trade" were more especially directed.

From the year 1500, when the older printers and stationers began seriously to feel the new foreign competition and concentrate their forces in London, there appears to have been endless trouble between them and the aliens. It was no doubt at this time that the Stationers' Company which had existed since 1404 began to bestir itself, but unfortunately all records before

1554 are lost, so that our knowledge of the "customs of the trade" can only be learned from accidental references, and the relative positions of the foreign and native craftsmen judged from acts of Parliament.

The position of the alien, at that time hardly a pleasant one, could be made more or less secure in two ways. He could either by act of Parliament become naturalised or else take out letters of denization. In the first case he became practically a native and obtained all the rights and privileges of a free born Englishman. In the second, though he obtained the privilege of living and trading as a native, he remained an alien, subject to the heavy taxes levied on strangers and seriously handicapped in the succession, possession and bequeathment of real property. Any outbreak on the continent which threatened the peace of England resulted at once in the taking out of a large number of letters of denization, since all foreigners belonging to the nation involved were ordered out of the country. In 1535, for instance, when Henry, without allies, was threatened by the Pope and the Emperor, special attention was attracted to the inhabitants from the Low Countries over whom the Emperor might be supposed to have considerable influence. A commission was formed to inquire into the foreign element, and as a result 127 persons belonging to the Low Countries were denizened, a number almost as large as the total of all foreigners during the preceding years of the reign.

In spite of all repression the alien element increased and the beginning of the sixteenth century saw much of our book-trade in the hands of foreigners.

At an early date St. Paul's Churchyard seems to have been the great resort of booksellers and before the close of the fifteenth century we have notices of several stationers such as Nicholas Lecomte who had shops there. No doubt it was a central and convenient place for doing business and one much frequented for marketing, as is even now the case in many continental towns where booths and stalls still cluster round the cathedrals. Again it was probably a place where foreigners had liberty to trade unhampered by the rules of the various city companies. Certainly the foreigners who were not denizened congregated there in numbers, bookshops and bookstalls multiplied, and in 1500 in the Sarum Missal printed by Dupré we first meet the general statement, which becomes so familiar in later books, that it was to be "sold by the booksellers in St. Paul's Churchyard."

The native printers whose business premises were situated in other parts of the city soon saw the necessity, brought about by the competition of these foreign booksellers, of themselves setting up shops in the churchyard. Thus Wynkyn de Worde who printed at the Sun in Fleet Street had a shop by the cathedral with the sign of Our Lady of Pity. Notary also had a small shop there (cellula he calls it) though his main place of business was outside Temple Bar. Richard Faques who lived and printed in the Strand had a shop in the churchyard called the A.B.C.

The shops in St. Paul's Churchyard, it must be borne in mind, were of two distinct classes. There were the substantial houses situated all round the churchyard in which the printer could both reside and carry on his business, and there were also a large number of booths clustered around the cathedral which were merely shops and had no accommodation for either living or printing. A very good idea may be obtained of one of these from the description of the shop which John Day, much against the will of the other book-sellers, put up in 1572. "Whereupon he got framed a neat handsome shop. It was but little and low and flat-roofed and leaded like a Terrace, railed and posted, fit for men to stand upon in any triumph or show, but could not in any wise hurt and deface the same. This cost him forty or fifty pounds."

There seem also to have been ordinary bookstalls in the churchyard, for Thomas Symonds, a stationer, giving evidence in a lawsuit in 1514 speaks of himself as "standing before his stall," and it is worth noting in passing that this was at seven o'clock in the morning, perhaps not a very early hour at a period when witnesses were summoned to appear before the Privy Council at eight !

Even the most important booksellers had stalls before their houses, for in an account of another lawsuit in 1536 occasioned by an assault on some

Frenchmen in Fleet Street, a witness mentioned in his evidence that one of the victims endeavoured to conceal himself under the King's printer's [*i.e.* Berthelet's] stall.

As regards the signs of the shops they could doubtless be changed at will. As an example take Rastell's sign of the Mermaid. He first printed under this sign at the south side of St. Paul's. When he moved to Cheapside, next St. Paul's gate, he still used the same sign and was succeeded in business by Goughe. When this latter again moved and went to Lombard Street near the stocks, he still kept to the sign of the Mermaid. Doubtless a good sign was a valuable asset, so that a printer who purchased or inherited a well known shop would retain the sign, as in the case of the Sun and the George in Fleet Street, which both housed a long succession of printers. On the other hand it is clear that the sign was the property of the lessee and that when he moved he could, if he so pleased, set up his old sign over his new house. In 1510 Notary had not only a house outside Temple Bar with the sign of the Three Kings, but he had also a little shop in Paul's Churchyard with the same sign which in its turn was transferred to a substantial house, previously known by the sign of St. Mark, when Notary moved into this with his whole plant from the Strand.

There does not seem to have been any kind of copyright in the signs themselves, for instance we have three persons living at the sign of the George at the same time,—Pynson in Fleet Street, Redman outside Temple Bar, and Reynes in St. Paul's Churchyard. But a man would naturally choose some sign different from others to prevent business intended for himself finding its way to someone else.

A certain number of printers seem not to have used, at least they never mention, any sign, and this will often be found to be because they did not print on their own account, but always for some other person.

Before passing on again to the historical side of the subject a word or two may be said as to the status of some of the persons employed in a printing office. The master of the establishment himself was probably little actively engaged in the press work, which would be done by his "servants" or "journeymen" (a word occasionally used in Acts of Parliament) and apprentices. The apprentice was a lad put to learn the trade and bound for as many years as would allow of his issuing from his apprenticeship at the age of twenty-four. After this he could become free of the Stationers and either set up on his own account or stay as an assistant to his old master or some other printer. In this case he was called a servant and shared that name with the journeymen, in many cases foreigners, who had not served any apprenticeship. In fact the word servant covered everyone employed in a printing office with the exception of the apprentices. It is the more necessary to draw attention to this point as the confusion between apprentices and servants in many bibliographical books has led to many blunders.

In the period between 1500 and 1523 there are few historical facts to be noticed. About 1503 William Faques, a Norman, succeeded Peter Actors in the Royal appointment and being himself a practical printer assumed the title of Printer to the King in place of Stationer to the King. The office was at first for life and was not changed on the accession of a new king, for R. Pynson who succeeded Faques in 1508 and therefore in Henry VII's reign, continued in office until his death in February, 1530, when Berthelet was immediately appointed in his place. With the death of Henry VIII the custom of appointing the king's printer for life fell into abeyance, for Edward VI upon his accession deposed Berthelet and appointed Grafton who was in turn superseded by Cawood on Mary's coming to the throne. The list of Royal printers given by Mr. Rivington and printed in the fifth volume of Arber's Transcripts [p. lix] is entirely misleading. William Caxton who heads it was never King's printer. William Faques (printed in the list Faynes) preceded not succeeded Pynson. Whitchurch was never officially King's printer though associated with Grafton. Reyner Wolf was King's printer only in Latin, Greek and Hebrew, just as Gaultier (not mentioned) was King's printer in French. Neither printed official work. Besides the King's printer there appear to have been other appointments of a semi-official nature. W. de Worde was printer to Margaret, Countess of Richmond, and Grafton to Edward, while Prince of Wales, but these appointments so far as we know carried no special privileges.

In 1507 printing was introduced into Scotland under the direct protection of the King and fortunately the official documents relating to it have been preserved. In 1509 it was introduced into York, and here again our documentary history is abundant.

In 1523 an act was passed which must have very materially affected all foreign born printers and binders, though, as it does not like the act of 1534 specifically mention them, it has been passed by without notice. This act which was passed by Henry as a set-off to the levying of a subsidy, enacted that no alien, whether denizen or not, practising any handicraft should take any apprentices except English born and that he should not keep more than two foreign journeymen. It also put him under the search and reformation of the wardens of his craft. It seems already to have been the custom of the trade that no freeman of the Stationers should take any foreigner as an apprentice, so that this act did away with foreign apprentices altogether and as a consequence prevented them, with one or two rare exceptions, from ever becoming members of the Stationers' Company. A very few were admitted by special favour, Reyner Wolfe for example was made a freeman at the request of Anne Boleyn, and Simon Martynson at the request of the King.

In February, 1529, a more stringent act was passed which beside repeating the provisions of the earlier act enacted "that no stranger artificer not a denizen which was not a householder the 15 of February last past shall not set up nor kepe any house, shop or chambre wherein they shall occupy any handy craft within this realm."

The restrictions concerning the taking of apprentices did not hold good however in Oxford and Cambridge which had special privileges of their own.

The ten years or so following 1525, when the first English New Testament was printed, are peculiarly interesting ones about which much has yet to be learned. This period saw floods of controversial books published and those attacking the party for the time in power had either to be secretly printed at home or printed abroad.   The number of the latter is I think considerably smaller than usually supposed and many books with foreign imprints were produced in this country.   In some cases we can only suppose these foreign imprints some mild form of jest, for the books containing them are printed in type and have initials or borders which could not have deceived the youngest apprentice as to their place of origin.   Proclamation after proclamation was issued against Lutheran books and it is much to be regretted that these proclamations have never been reprinted in some available form, since they contain much information valuable to bibliographers.   There is no doubt that the war waged against heretical and pernicious books was a fierce one and vigorously carried out.   Taking the case of the New Testament it would not be too much to say that of the editions which can from sound evidence be proved to have been printed before 1532, of not one quarter does the slightest trace remain.

The history of the people who smuggled over and sold these Testaments and controversial books, their adventures, their misfortunes and their persecutions, though deeply interesting must be passed over.   Though they sold books they cannot be called booksellers and though some, when up for trial and entered under their trades were called "sellers of seditious books," the very word seditious shows that they were not ordinary booksellers.   When the selling of these books was a hazardous task and rendered those engaged in it liable to fine, imprisonment, or worse, we can quite understand that those engaged in the ordinary book-trade would avoid so dangerous a speculation.

The act which came into effect on Christmas Day, 1534, has always obtained far too prominent a notice owing to the fact of its being the first definitely called an act concerning printers and printing.   It was in no way arbitrary or crushing, but manifestly just.   All it did was to put the alien printer on a level with every other alien craftsman and annul the protective clause which had been appended to the act of 1484.   Two new enactments were made, however, to protect native trade.   The first relates to binding. " And further be it enacted by the authority aforesaid, that no persons resiant

c

or inhabitant within this realm, after the said feast of Christmas next coming, shall buy to sell again any printed books, brought from any parts out of the king's obeysaunce, ready bound in boards, leather, or parchment upon pain to lose and forfeit for every book bound out of the said king's obeysaunce and brought into this realm and bought by any person or persons within the same to sell again, contrary to the act, 6s. 8d."

This enactment put an end to all dealing in foreign bound books. The second relates to printing. "And be it further enacted, by the authority aforesaid, that no person or persons inhabitant or resiant within this realm after the said feast of Christmas shall buy within this realm of any stranger born out of the King's obedience, other than of denizens, any manner of printed books brought from any the parts beyond the sea, except only by engross and not by retail, upon pain of forfeiture of 6s. 8d. for every book so bought by retail contrary to the form and effect of this estature."

Now this clause did not affect the native or denizen, but only prevented an undenizened alien retailing foreign-printed books, and its object is quite clear. It did not affect general trade in any way, for the denizened foreigner could still sell his books in this country as before, but it prevented other foreigners coming over and retailing seditious books, peddling them about the country.

This act, though only coming into force at Christmas, 1534, was passed before April and in July special letters patent were issued giving certain special privileges to Cambridge. In May of the same year a charter was granted to the Company of Stationers of Chester.

The native stationers were clearly not yet satisfied and it is evident that further efforts were made to stop the importation of foreign books. Though no official documents are in existence relating to this subject, there are in the Record Office two private letters relating to François Regnault, the Paris printer, of extraordinary interest in this connexion. The first is from Regnault himself to Cromwell and written in 1536. In it he states that he lived in London forty years ago and had since returned to Paris continuing his trade as a bookseller in London and likewise printing missals, breviaries, and hours of the use of Sarum, and other books. He goes on to say that he had entertained at his house honourable people of London and other towns of England. He understands that the English booksellers wish to prevent him printing such books and to confiscate what he has already printed, though he has never been forbidden to do so and his books have been well received. He asks permission to continue to sell the said "usaiges" and other books in London and the environs. If any faults have been found with his books he will correct them. The second letter written on September 12th, 1538, by Coverdale and Grafton to Cromwell on Regnault's behalf, runs "Where as of long tyme he hath bene an occupier into England more than xl yere, he hath allwayes provyded soche bookes for England as they moost occupied, so that he hath a great nombre at this present in his handes, as Prymers in Englishe, Missoles with other soche like: wherof now (by the company of the Booksellers in London) he is utterly forbydden to make sale, to the utter undoying of the man. Wherfore most humbly we beseke your lordshippe to be gracious and favourable unto him that he may have lycence to sell those which he hath done allready, so that hereafter he prynte no moo in the english tonge, onlesse he have an english man that is lerned to be his corrector." The ostensible reason for this prohibition was the careless printing of the books, a censure not without truth, but the most interesting point of the letter is the evidence it affords of the power of the Stationers' Company as then existing. Just at this time a stronger element was at work against these Parisian printers and that was the rapid disuse or suppression of Service books. No Sarum Missal, for instance, was printed between 1534 and 1554.

The remaining years of Henry VIII's reign were an unsettled period for printers. Opinions were changing year by year and controversial books were pouring from the press. The printers themselves seemed hardly to know what might or might not be printed and even the most important were continually in trouble. In October, 1535, the first English Bible was printed at Zurich, an undertaking in which Edward Whitchurch was perhaps concerned. He and Richard Grafton, neither being stationers, assisted by Anthony

Marler, a wealthy haberdasher, turned their attention to producing Bibles. In November, 1539, a proclamation was issued forbidding anyone to print the Bible except such as should be permitted by Cromwell, who was evidently the patron of Whitchurch, Grafton, and Marler. The last named, who presented a splendid copy on vellum of the April, 1540, Bible to Henry VIII, no doubt saw his large expenditure of capital jeopardised by the fall of Cromwell and consequently obtained for himself early in 1541 a monopoly of Bible printing for four years. Much curious information on this subject will be found in the acts of the Privy Council, especially as to the way Marler got rid of his stock by getting a proclamation issued in 1541 compelling every church to buy a "bible of the largest volume," which cost ten shillings unbound, and twelve bound. In 1540 a number of broadside ballads for and against Cromwell were written by William Gray and Thomas Smyth and these came under the notice of the Privy Council. The proceedings relating to them show a curious state of affairs and add a new terror to bibliography. Richard Banks was "noted to be the prynter," as might be expected since his name occurs in the colophon of several, but when examined "denied the same and layed the faulte to Robert Redman, decessed, and Richard Grafton." Redman there was no possibility of examining, but R. Grafton confessed to having printed "part of the sayd invectives" and was committed to the Fleet during the King's pleasure. This shows that colophons, especially those to ephemeral publications, are not to be implicitly trusted and emphasizes the value of a careful study of type.

In 1541 under the Act of Six Articles we find many printers getting into trouble, but this was mainly on account of their religious opinions and not often in connexion with the printing or publishing of books.

In April, 1543, some very interesting proceedings were taken against printers. Whitchurch, Byddell, Grafton, Middleton, Mayler, Petit, Lant and Kele were all brought up in a body before the Privy Council for printing "suche bokes as wer thought to be unlawfull" and were imprisoned. Five were released after a fortnight, but Whitchurch, Grafton and Petit were still confined. Those who were released were bound to send in a true declaration of what number of books and ballads they had bought within three years, what they had sold, and what merchants they knew to have brought in prohibited books, which lists they produced in three days.   On April 25th, twenty-five booksellers appeared, bound in £100, to give a list of the books they had bought or sold in gross for the last three years.   It must be remembered that by the act of 1534 no person could buy books printed abroad from a stranger except in gross, so that these proceedings of the Privy Council were aimed against the importation of foreign books.   These lists supplied by the eight printers and twenty-five booksellers, perhaps still hidden away in the mass of documents in the Rolls Office, could they only be discovered, would throw a wonderful light on the book-trade of the time.

The accession of Edward VI in 1547 placed the Protestant party strongly in the ascendant and in November the Six Articles were repealed.   Many refugees of high standing came over to England and several important printers such as Stephen Mierdman and Gellius Ctematius, came with them.   Owing to the uncertain political relations with France but few Huguenot refugees seem to have come over until 1550, when peace was made between France and England.   After 1550 England became the dumping ground for all the religious persecuted poor of Europe, trade stagnated, the coinage was debased, and to such a state of poverty were the native workmen reduced, entirely, as they considered, by reason of this foreign immigration, that they signified to the Lord Mayor their intention of a general slaughter of aliens, who then numbered in London alone over 40,000.   In 1549 proclamations were issued against papistical books and also, owing to the appearance of the first prayer book, to order the destruction of all the old service books.   The licensing of books was also strictly enforced and on August 13th the Privy Council ordered "that from hensforth no prenter sholde prente or putt to vente any Englishe booke butt suche as sholde first be examined by Mr. Secretary Peter, Mr. Secretary Smith and Mr. Cicill or the one of them, and allowed by the same."

In February, 1552, Scotland woke up to the necessity of licensing books and a statute was passed "Anent Prentaris.   Forsamekill as thair is divers

Prentaris in the Realme that daylie and continuallie prentis bukis concerning the faith, ballatis, sangs, blasphematiounis, rymes, als weill of kirkmen as temporale, and others Tragedeis, alsweill in latine as in Inglis toung, not sene, vewit, and considderit be the superiouris, as appertenis to the defamatioun & sclander of the liegis of this Realme, and to put ordour to sic inconvenientis : It is devisit, statute and ordanit be my Lord Governour, with avise of the thre Estates of Parliament, that na Prentar presume, attempt or take upone hand, to prent ony bukis, ballatis, sangis, blasphematiounis, rymes or Tragedeis, outhir in latin or Inglis toung in ony tymes to cum, unto the tyme the samin be sene vewit and examinit be sum wyse and discreit persounis depute thairto be the Ordinaris quhatsumever. And thairefter ane licence had and obtenit fra our Soverane Lady, and my Lord Governour for Imprenting of sic bukis, under the pane of confiscatioun of all the Prentaris gudis, and banisshing him of the Realme for ever."

The accession of Queen Mary in 1553 altered considerably the position of many printers and stationers. England at once ceased to be a refuge for persecuted foreigners and many refugees were forced to fly the country. Early in 1554 an Act was passed commanding all foreign refugees not being denizens to depart out of the realm and it was specially directed against preachers, printers, booksellers and other artificers. The act does not seem to have had much effect and the native artificers were so reduced to poverty by the general employment of foreigners that in 1555 the Mayor and Commonalty of London issued an order that no citizen should employ a foreigner in any business except in certain stipulated trades, amongst which neither printing nor bookselling was included. In June, 1555, two proclamations were issued, the first against seditious and heretical books printed abroad or secretly printed in this country, and the second against the writings of the reformers and the service books of Edward. The inefficiency of the various acts and the continued production and importation of seditious books called for some powerful remedy and resulted in the incorporation of the Stationers' Company on the 4th of May, 1557. "Know ye" begins the charter "that we considering and manifestly perceiving, that several seditious and heretical books, both in verse and prose, are daily published, stamped and printed by divers scandalous, schismatical, and heretical persons, not only exciting our subjects and liegemen to sedition and disobedience against us, our crown and dignity, but also to the renewal and propagating very great and detestable heresies against the faith and sound catholick doctrine of holy mother the church:" etc. This shows clearly that the object of Philip and Mary was not so much to benefit the stationers as to have a greater control of the trade. In fact they put power into the hands of the Stationers' Company to control and crush all outside and unauthorised trade, well knowing that they could easily control the Company itself. The various clauses of the charter relate almost entirely to the government of the Company, but the twelfth is of more general interest and importance. "XII. Moreover we will, grant, ordain and constitute for ourselves, and the successors of our foresaid queen, that no person within this our kingdom of England, or dominions thereof, either by himself, or by his journeymen, servants or by any other person, shall practise or exercise the art or mystery of printing or stamping any book, or anything to be sold, or to be bargained for within this our Kingdom of England, or the dominions thereof, unless the same person is, or shall be, one of the society of the foresaid mystery or art of a stationer of the city aforesaid, at the time of his foresaid printing or stamping, or has for that purpose obtained our licence, or the licence of the heirs and successors of our foresaid queen."

From a misunderstanding of the way in which the regnal years of Philip and Mary were expressed the date of the grant of this charter has always, from the time of Herbert onwards, been given as May 4th, 1556, in place of 1557. Even Mr. Arber in his great Transcript has fallen into the same error and consequently obscured the early history of the revived Company. The charter was granted by the King and Queen on May 4th, 1557, enrolled on June 3rd, and the full and formal registers begin on July 19th. Very fortunately, moreover, a series of miscellaneous entries, accounts, subscriptions, enrolments of freemen and such like from December 9th, 1554, to July 18th, 1557, were copied from an earlier account book into the beginning of the first register, and these give most valuable information on the position of the Company for nearly three years before the charter.

The list of names of the hundred or so freemen enrolled in the charter shows how effective had been the acts against aliens. The act of 1523 prevented any alien from having a foreign apprentice and the custom of the trade of stationers in London had laid a like prohibition on its members. Whereas in the first forty years after the introduction of printing into England the majority of persons connected with the book-trade were foreigners, the second forty years saw this state of things entirely changed, all the important men of business being Englishmen, and the foreigners decreasing in number and status.

Though we know of no foreigner admitted as a freeman of the Stationers' Company after about 1540, yet they appear to have been received into the Company in some honorary capacity under the name of Brothers. We find at the time of the incorporation several important stationers, such as Arnold Birckman, giving large subscriptions towards the objects of the Company, and we can hardly suppose that such generosity was without reciprocal advantages received from the Company, though what form these took is not very clear. Apparently permission to take English apprentices was one of them.

The original list of stationers as entered in the charter offers some points which are difficult to explain. Mr. Arber suggests that they stand in some order of seniority, but though this may be roughly the case the order is by no means exact. We know the exact dates of their taking up their freedom in the case of six men: S. Kevall in 1535, R. Wolfe in 1536, R. Lant in 1537, A. Hester in 1538, T. Devell January 18th, 1541, and R. Jugge October 4th, 1541, and the order of these in the list is 9, 7, 35, 37, 38, 20. Perhaps other causes were at work and Jugge's place above so many senior men may be due to the importance of his position in the trade. Again the last man in the list was senior to the ten who preceded him. Another very curious point is the insertion of three men, Thomas Powell, Anthony Croste and Richard Hill as numbers 30, 31, 32 when all three had only taken up their freedom in the latter half of 1556. That they did not properly belong where they are placed is clear from the fact that in the list of subscribers to Bridewell, which follows very closely the list in the charter, these three are omitted from this position.

No doubt the charter would take some time to prepare, so that those who joined just before it was passed could not be included in the list, but the last person inserted, Richard Hill, was made free November 26th, 1556, and many made free before this date are omitted. It may be too that many persons qualified to take up their freedom at an earlier date only did so when the incorporation of the Company was determined on.

It seems probable that the list of members does not contain the names of many more than half the existing freemen of the Company, and amongst these freemen were many of other trades, such as joiners, chandlers, and others, so that although a man was officially described as a stationer he might have nothing to do with the business as we now understand it. This probably accounts for the occurrence of many names which so far as we know have no connexion with books. Thirty-five only out of the ninety-seven stationers mentioned in the list are known to have printed or published books.

Again the converse must be remembered. Many important printers and booksellers were members of other companies. Grafton and Kingston belonged to the Grocers; Barker, Veale, Wight and Kitson to the Drapers, and others were members of other companies, so that of course they would not be found in the list of Stationers, though by royal licence they were permitted to print.

A few names not in the original list are found later in the registers, and these, not having occurred in the lists of freemen made since the passing of the charter, may be considered as those of freemen made before that date. Another small point to be noted is that no man could be made a freeman by patrimony unless his father had been a freeman at the time of his birth, and no man could be made a freeman before he was twenty-four years of age. Therefore the father of any person made a freeman by patrimony before 1581 must have been a member of the Company before the passing of the charter.

With the incorporation of the Stationers' Company in 1557 my work comes to a close. I do not for a moment suggest that its registers furnish a full guide to the subsequent history of the book-trade in England, for this is certainly not the case. But they supply a vast amount of official information which before 1557 was entirely wanting. Information on the preceding hundred years can only be gathered, fragment by fragment, from very numerous sources often unexpected, frequently almost inaccessible; but every fact, unimportant perhaps in itself, when put in its right place helps to build up a surer foundation for the future historian.

LIST OF THE PRINCIPAL BOOKS QUOTED.

Accounts of the churchwardens of the parish of St. Martin-in-the-Fields. 1525–1603.
Edited by J. V. Kitto.   8⁰. London, 1901.

Acts of the Privy Council. Proceedings and Ordinances of the Privy Council of England.
Edited by Sir Harris Nicolas.   7 vols. 8⁰. London, 1834–7.

Acts of the Privy Council of England. New Series.
                                  28 vols. 8⁰. In progress. London, 1890, etc.

Ames (J.). Typographical Antiquities: being an historical account of Printing in England.
                                                  4to. London, 1749.

Arber (E.). A transcript of the Registers of the Company of Stationers of London, 1554–
1640.   5 vols. 4to. London, 1875–1894.

Archaeologia; or miscellaneous tracts relating to Antiquity.
                         Vols. I–LX. 4to. In progress. London, 1770, etc.

Bannatyne Miscellany. [Bannatyne Club. Vols. 19, 52, 105.]
                                  3 vols. 4to. Edinburgh, 1827–55.

Bibliographer (The). A journal of book-lore.   6 vols. 4to. London, 1881–84.

Bibliographica.   3 vols. 4to. London, 1895–97.

Bibliographical Society. Transactions. Vols. I–V. 4to.   London, 1893, etc.

Bibliographical Society. Handlists of English printers, by E. Gordon Duff, H. R. Plomer
and R. Proctor.   2 parts. 4to. In progress. London, 1895–6.

Bibliothèque de l'Ecole des Chartes.   8⁰. In progress. Paris, 1839, etc.

Biographie Universelle ancienne et moderne. Rédigé par un société de gens de lettres et
de savants.   71 vols. 8⁰. Paris, 1811–36.

Blades (R. H.). Who was Caxton?   8⁰. London, 1877.

Blades (W.). The life and typography of William Caxton.
                                          2 vols. 4to. London, 1861-3.

Bloxam (J. R.). A register of the Presidents, Fellows, etc., and other members of St.
Mary Magdalen College, Oxford.   5 vols. 8⁰. Oxford, 1863–81.

Boase (C. W.). Register of the University of Oxford. Vol. I. [Oxford Historical
Society.]   8⁰. Oxford, 1885.

Bradshaw (H.). Collected papers.   8⁰. Cambridge, 1889.

British Museum. [B.M.] Catalogue of books in the library of the British Museum printed
in England, Scotland, and Ireland, and of books in English printed abroad to the
year 1640.   3 vols. 8⁰. London, 1884.

Brunet (J. C.). Manuel du libraire et de l'amateur de livres. Avec supplement par P. Deschamps et G. Brunet. 8 vols. 8º. Paris, 1860-80.

Calendar of Wills proved and enrolled in the Court of Husting, London. Edited by R. R. Sharpe. 2 vols. 8º. London, 1889-90.

Cambridge Antiquarian Society. Proceedings and Communications. 8º. In progress. Cambridge, 1851, etc.

Churchwardens' accounts of the town of Ludlow. Edited by T. Wright. [Camden Society. Vol. 102.] 4to. London, 1869.

Clark (A.). Register of the University of Oxford. Vol. II, Part I. [Oxford Historical Society.] 8º. Oxford, 1887.

Davenport (C.). Thomas Berthelet, royal printer and bookbinder to Henry VIII. [Caxton Club.] 4to. Chicago, 1901.

Davies (R.). A memoir of the York press. 8º. Westminster, 1868.

Demaus (R.). William Tyndale, a biography. New edition revised by R. Lovett. 8º. London, 1886.

Descriptive catalogue of ancient deeds in the Public Record Office. Vols. I–IV. 8º. In progress. London, 1890, etc.

Dibdin (T. F.). Typographical Antiquities. Begun by Joseph Ames, augmented by William Herbert. 4 vols. 4to. London, 1810-19.

Dickson (R.) and Edmond (J. P.). Annals of Scottish printing, from the introduction of the art in 1507 to the beginning of the 17th century. 4to. Cambridge, 1890.

Dix (E. R. M'C.). The earliest Dublin printing. 12º. Dublin, 1901.

Duff (E. Gordon). Early printed books. 8º. London, 1893.

Duff (E. Gordon). The printers, stationers and bookbinders of London and Westminster in the fifteenth century. [Sandars Lectures.] 8º. Privately printed. 1899.

Duff (E. Gordon). William Caxton. [Caxton Club.] 4to. Chicago, 1905.

Dugdale (W.). History of St. Paul's Cathedral. Second edition. fol. London, 1716.

Egerton Papers (The). Edited by J. P. Collier. [Camden Society.] 4to. London, 1840.

Enzinas (F. de). Histoire de l'estat du Pais Bas et de la religion d'Espagne. 8º. [Geneva.] 1558.

Fabric Rolls of York Minster. Edited by J. Raine. [Surtees Society. Vol. 35.] 8º. Durham, 1859.

Foxe (J.). Acts and monuments. Edited by J. Pratt. 8 vols. 8º. London [1877].

Freemen of York. Register of the freemen of the city of York, from the city records. [Surtees Society. Vols. 96, 102.] 2 vols. 8º. Durham, 1897-9.

Frère (E.). De l'imprimerie et de la librairie à Rouen dans les xv et xvi siècles. 4to. Rouen, 1843.

Frère (E.) Des livres de liturgie des Eglises d'Angleterre imprimées à Rouen dans les xv et xvi siècles. 8º. Rouen, 1867.

Gentleman's Magazine (The). 228 vols. 8º. London, 1731-1868.

Gibson (S.). Early Oxford bindings. [Bibliographical Society Monographs, X.]
4to. Oxford, 1903.

Gray (G. J.). The earlier Cambridge stationers and bookbinders and the first Cambridge printer. [Bibliographical Society Monographs, XIII.] 4to. Oxford, 1904.

Griffiths (J.). An index to wills proved in the Court of the Chancellor of the University of Oxford. 8°. Oxford, 1862.

Hain (L.). Repertorium Bibliographicum. 4 vols. 8°. Stuttgart, 1826–38.

Hain (L.). and Copinger (W. A.). [H. C.] Supplement to Hain's Repertorium Bibliographicum. 3 vols. 8°. London, 1895–1902.

Handlists of English printers. *See* Bibliographical Society.

Heber (R.). Catalogue of the library of the late Richard Heber.
13 parts. 8°. London, 1834–7.

Heitz (P.). Die Kölner Büchermarken. fol. Strassburg, 1898.

Heitz (P.). Die Zürcher Büchermarken. fol. Zürich, 1895.

Herbert (W.). Typographical Antiquities. Begun by Joseph Ames.
3 vols. 4to. London, 1785–90.

Historical Manuscripts Commission. fol. and 8°. In progress. London, 1870, etc.

Hoskins (E.). Horae Beatae Mariae Virginis, or Sarum and York Primers.
8°. London, 1901.

Inquisitiones post mortem, for London. [Index Society.]
8°. In progress. London, 1879, etc.

James (M. R.). Sources of Archbp. Parker's MSS. at C.C.C. Cambridge. [Cambridge Antiquarian Society.] 8°. Cambridge, 1899.

James (M. R.). Ancient Libraries of Canterbury and Dover. 8°. Cambridge, 1903.

Leadam (I. S.). Select cases before the King's Council in the Star Chamber: edited for the Selden Society. 4to. London, 1903.

Letters and Papers, Foreign and Domestic, of the reign of Henry VIII. (Calendar of). Edited by J. S. Brewer and J. Gairdner. 4to. In progress. London, 1862, etc.

Letters of denization and acts of naturalization for aliens in England, 1509–1603. Edited by W. Page. [Huguenot Society.] 4to. Lymington, 1893.

Library (The). 10 vols. 8°. London, 1889–99.

Library (The). New Series. Vols. I–V. 8°. In progress. London, 1900, etc.

Machyn (H.). Diary from 1550 to 1563. Edited by J. G. Nichols. [Camden Society. Vol. 42.] 4to. London, 1848.

Madan (F.). The Day-book of John Dorne. [Oxford Historical Society, Collectanea. Vol. I.] 8°. Oxford, 1885.

Madan (F.). The early Oxford press. 8°. Oxford, 1895.

Madden (J. P. A.). Lettres d'un Bibliographe. 6 vols. 8°. Paris, 1868–86.

Magdalen Registers. A register of the members of St. Mary Magdalen College, Oxford, by W. D. Macray. 3 vols. 8°. Oxford, 1894–1901.

Maittaire (M.).   Annales Typographici.   6 vols. 4to. The Hague, 1723–89.

Marriage Licenses. Allegations for Marriage Licenses issued by the Bishop of London. Vol. I. 1520–1610. [Harleian Society. Vol. 25.]   8°. London, 1887.

Marriage Licenses. Allegations for Marriage Licenses issued from the Faculty Office of the Archbishop of Canterbury at London 1543–1869. [Harleian Society. Vol. 24.]
8°. London, 1886.

Materials for a history of the reign of Henry VII, from original documents preserved in the Public Record Office. Edited by W. Campbell.   2 vols. 8°. London, 1873–7.

Moes (E. W.).   De Amsterdamsche boekdrukkers en uitgevers in de Zestiende eeuw.
4to. Amsterdam, 1900.

Monumenta Franciscana. Edited by J. S. Brewer. [Chronicles and Memorials.]
2 vols. 8°. London, 1858–82.

Nichols (J.).   Illustrations of the manners and expenses of ancient times in England.
4to. London, 1797.

Nicolas (Sir N. H.).   Privy purse expenses of Henry VIII.   8°. London, 1827.

Nicolas (Sir N. H.).   Privy purse expenses of Elizabeth of York : wardrobe accounts of Edward IV ; with a memoir of Elizabeth of York, and notes.   8°. London, 1830.

Olthoff (F.).   De Boekdrukkers, Boekverkoopers en uitgevers in Antwerpen.
8°. Antwerp, 1891.

Original letters relative to the English Reformation. Edited by H. Robinson. [Parker Society.]   2 vols. 8°. Cambridge, 1846–7.

Pellechet (M.).   Catalogue général des incunables des bibliothèques publiques de France. Vol. I.   8°. Paris, 1897.

Plomer (H. R.).   Abstracts from the Wills of English printers and stationers from 1492 to 1630. [Bibliographical Society.]   4to. London, 1903.

Plomer (H. R.).   A short history of English printing, 1476–1898.
4to. London, 1900.

Plomer (H. R.).   Robert Wyer, printer and bookseller. [Bibliographical Society.]
4to. London, 1897.

Proctor (R. G. C.).   Jan van Doesborch. [Bibliographical Society Monographs, II.]
4to. London, 1894.

Proctor (R. G. C.).   An index to the early printed books in the British Museum, from the invention of printing to the year MD. With notes of those in the Bodleian Library.
2 vols. 8°. London, 1898.

Register of the Guild of Corpus Christi in the city of York. Edited by R. H. Skaife. [Surtees Society. Vol. 57.]   4to. Durham, 1872.

Renouard (P.).   Documents sur les imprimeurs, libraires, etc., ayant exercé a Paris de 1450 à 1600.   8°. Paris, 1901.

Renouard (P.).   Imprimeurs Parisiens, libraires, fondeurs de caractères et correcteurs d'imprimerie, 1470–1600.   8°. Paris, 1898.

Returns of Aliens dwelling in the city and suburbs of London from the reign of Henry VIII to that of James I. Edited by R. E. G. Kirk and E. F. Kirk. [Huguenot Society.]
2 vols. 4to. Aberdeen, 1900-2.

Rudolphi (E. C.). Die Buchdrucker-Familie Froschauer in Zürich. 8°. Zürich, 1869.

Rymer (T.). Foedera. 20 vols. fol. London, 1704-35.

Sayle (C. E.). Early English printed books in the University Library, Cambridge.
Vols. I–III. 8°. In progress. Cambridge, 1900, etc.

Schickler (Baron F. de). Les Eglises de Refuge en Angleterre. 8°. Paris, 1892.

Scottish Antiquary (The), or Northern Notes and Queries.
17 vols. 8°. Edinburgh, 1890-1903.

Stow (J.). A survey of London and Westminster. Sixth edition.
2 vols. fol. London, 1754-5.

Strype (J.). Ecclesiastical memorials relating chiefly to religion.
3 vols. fol. London, 1721.

Timperley (C. H.). A dictionary of printers and printing. 8°. London, 1839.

Transcript of the Registers of the united parishes of St. Mary Woolnoth and St. Mary Woolchurch Haw. 8°. London, 1886.

Turner (W. H.). Selections from the records of the City of Oxford. 8°. Oxford, 1880.

Van der Meersch (P. C.). Recherches sur la vie et les travaux des imprimeurs Belges et Néerlandais établis a l'etranger. 8°. Ghent, 1856.

Van Havre (G.). Marques typographiques des imprimeurs et libraires Anversois.
2 vols. 8°. Antwerp, 1883-4.

Weale (W. H. J.). Bookbindings and rubbings of bindings in the National Art Library, South Kensington. 2 parts. 8°. London, 1894-8.

Welch (C.). History of the Tower Bridge. 4to. London, 1894.

Wiffen (B.B.). Bibliotheca Wiffeniana. Spanish reformers of two centuries, from 1520. By E. Boehmer. 2 vols. 8°. London, 1874-83.

ABBREVIATIONS.

B.M. - - - - - -	British Museum.
BODL. - - - - - -	Bodleian Library, Oxford.
D.N.B. - - - - -	Dictionary of National Biography.
HUNTERIAN - - - - -	Hunterian Museum, Glasgow.
J.R.L. - - - - -	John Rylands Library, Manchester.
R. OF A. - - - - -	Returns of Aliens.
SOC. OF ANT. - - - -	Society of Antiquaries, London.
T.C.D. - - - - - -	Trinity College, Dublin.
U.L.C. - - - - -	University Library, Cambridge.

A CENTURY OF
THE ENGLISH BOOK TRADE.

ACTORS (PETER), stationer in London, appears to have travelled about the country to supply books with his partner Joannes de Aquisgrano. In 1483 they were at Oxford and supplied a number of books to Thomas Hunte the Oxford stationer on sale or return. [Madan. *Day-book of John Dorne*, p. 142.] In 1485 he was appointed the royal stationer. "Grant, for life, to Peter Actoris, born in Savoy of the office of stationer to the King; also licence to import, so often as he likes, from parts beyond the sea, books printed and not printed into the port of the city of London, and other ports and places within the kingdom of England, and to dispose of the same by sale or otherwise, without paying customs, etc. thereon and without rendering any accompt thereof." 5th December, 1485. [*Materials*, Hen. VII, p. 211.] Peter Actors was the father of Sebastian Actors the Oxford stationer and had a daughter Margaret married to John Hewtee, another Oxford stationer. He was still alive in 1501, but probably died soon after for by 1504 his privilege had been granted to William Faques who, being a practical printer, styled himself Printer to the King.

ACTORS (SEBASTIAN), stationer in Oxford, lived in the parish of St. Mary the Virgin. The record of a grant of administration after his decease dated 23rd April, 1501, is preserved in the University Archives. [Madan, p. 272. Griffiths' *Index*.] After his death a number of claims were made against his estate. John Hewtee who had married his sister, claimed on behalf of her father, Peter Actors, the tools used for binding. John Aler, procurator for Cyprian Relia, claimed money on behalf of his master. The final administration was granted on June 25th, and what little remained after all claims were settled was given to his daughter. [Univ. Arch., Reg. Ⓠ f. 94.]

D

ADAM (JEAN), stationer, printer and typefounder in Paris, was in business between the years 1516 and 1529. He was associated for a time with J. Bienayse and also with J. Kerbriant. His name occurs in the colophons of two editions of the Sarum *Missal*, one of 1516 with J. Kerbriant, J. Petit, and J. Bienayse, the other of 1521, with J. Petit and J. Bienayse. [Renouard, p. 1.]

ADAM (RICHARD) was an apprentice to Richard Kele who, in his will, proved 19th October, 1552, left him forty shillings in "ware." [Plomer, Wills, p. 10.]

AE (REINAERDT VAN DER) is mentioned in the list of members of the Dutch church in London in 1550 as an assistant to Stephen Mierdman. He was no doubt one of the many refugees from the Low Countries who came over during Edward VI's reign and returned when Mary came to the throne. [R. of A., I, 209.]

ALARD, bookbinder in London, was an assistant to W. de Worde who left a legacy in his will "To Alard book-binder, my servant vi £ xiii s. iv d." [Herbert, I, 120.]

ALDAYE, *see* Allde.

ALDE, *see* Allde.

ALEXANDER, bookseller in Scotland, is mentioned in a letter, 31st July, 1536, from Alexander Alesius to John Epinus, saying he had sent to Epinus "by his countryman Alexander a bookseller." [*Letters and papers of Henry VIII*, vol. xi., p. 79.]

ALLDE, ALDAYE, or **ALDE (JOHN)**, printer in London, was an apprentice to Richard Kele who, on his death in 1552, left him "fyve pounds in wares." Allde took up his freedom in January, 1555, and shortly afterwards started work in his old master's shop, the "long shop in the Poultry at the stocks beside St. Mildred's church." He is mentioned continuously in the Stationers' Registers, often for bad behaviour, but it is not until 1560 that he entered any copies. From this time onwards he printed busily. In October, 1568, Allde was imprisoned in the Counter in the Poultry for printing a book about the Duke of Alva. [Arber, II, 745.]

Numbers of books continued to be issued up to about 1582, when Allde appears to have given up business. His son Edward became a freeman by patrimony in 1584, and in August of the same year his father's name is found for the last time. [*Bibliographica*, II, pp. 72-8. D.N.B.]

AMAZEUR (JEAN), printer in Paris, was in business between the years 1544 and 1555-6. He lived at the sign of the Soleil d'Or, in the Rue Alexandre-Langlois, and was succeeded by his son-in-law, Jean le Blanc. [Renouard, p. 4.] He printed some Sarum service books in 1555 for Guillaume Merlin.

ANDREWE (LAWRENCE), printer in London, was born or lived some time in Calais. He translated *The valuation of Gold and Silver* and *The wonderful shape and nature that our Saviour Christ Jesu hath created in beasts, serpents, fowls*, etc., which were printed at Antwerp by Jan van Doesborch. Though these are the only translations with Andrewe's name printed by Doesborch, it is very probable that several more of that printer's English books are also translations made by Andrewe. In 1527 he published two editions of his own translation of the *Vertuose boke of Distyllacyon*, by H. Braunschweig, which are remarkable. Though dated on two succeeding days, April 17th and 18th, they vary throughout. He appears to have been connected in business with P. Treveris, for his device is found in some copies of the latter's *Grete Herball*, of 1529. Andrewe printed four undated books, *Esop's Fables*, and the *Directory of the Conscience*, both known only from imperfect copies, and the *Mirror of the World* and the *Debate and stryfe betwene Somer and Wynter*, this last being printed about 1530 for Robert Wyer. The *Mirror* contains a curious selection of miscellaneous woodcuts, one of which was used in 1539 as a device by James Gaver. Some initials which Andrewe used were cut specially for him, as they contain small reproductions of his mark. His device consists of his mark on a shield surrounded by some florid renaissance ornament. He lived in Fleet Street at the sign of the Golden Cross. Leonard Andrewe, a printer about the same time, may have been a relation.

ANDREWE (LEONARD), printer in London, was an assistant to John Rastell, and is mentioned in the report of the lawsuit which took place relating to Rastell's printing office in 1534-5. [*Bibliographica*, II, p. 440.]

ANDREWES (WILLIAM), stationer in London, was made free on the 18th May, 1534. The Lord Mayor made him a present of twenty-six shillings and eight pence, "because the said Andrewes can write very well, and shall bring up youth virtuously." [Bibl. Soc. Trans., VI, 24.] In 1555 he changed from the Stationers' Company to the Vintners'. [Arber, I, 34.]

ANONIMUS (ADAM), pseudonym. This name is found in the colophon of Coverdale's *Shorte recapitulacion or abrigement of Erasmus Enchiridion*, which runs, "Imprinted at Ausborch by Adam Anonimus In the moneth of May. Anno 1545." [Herbert, III, 1559.]

ANTOINE (JEAN), stationer in Paris, came originally from Venice. He is mentioned by Renouard as having been in business in Paris during the years 1501 and 1502. From the titlepage of the Sarum *Missal*, printed in 1500 by Jean du Pré, we learn that at a slightly earlier date he had been in England, for Du Pré speaks of his edition as enlarged, with some new prayers " a Johanne anthonio bibliopola parisiensi ex anglia noviter allatis."

APPLAY, or **APPLE** (RICHARD), stationer in London, was an original member of the Stationers' Company, though not entered in the charter, having been made free on April 27th, 1557. [Arber I, 37.] He is mentioned several times in the Registers as taking apprentices and paying fines, and once in 1563 had a license to print a ballad. He died before 1566, when mention is made of his widow.

AQUISGRANO (JOHANNES DE), *see* Joannes.

ARNOLDT (HENRY), printer in London, is mentioned in the list of members of the Dutch church in London in 1550, "Henry Arnoldt, in de Teemstraete & Smyt vylt, een boucprenter." [R. of A., I, 204.] It is probable from the address that he was an assistant to H. Singleton, who employed several natives of the Low Countries.

ASCENSIUS (J. BADIUS), *see* Badius (J.).

AURIK (JACOB), printer in Emden, is mentioned in the colophon to *The subversion of Moris faulse foundation*, by George Joye. "At Emdon by Jacob Aurik." Herbert gives the date as 1534. [Herbert, III, 1543. Panzer, VI, p. 493.]

AWDLEY [or SAMPSON] (JOHN), printer in London, was a younger son of Sampson Awdley verger of Westminster Abbey who died in 1559-60. He was admitted a freeman of the Company of Stationers between October 1st and November 26th, 1556, under the name of John Sampson but his name is not found in the charter of 1557. From 1559 onwards he printed a very large number of books and is entered very frequently in the Stationers' Registers up to the year 1570-71, after which he entered no more copies though he continued to print. He died in 1575 and his will dated June 22nd was proved on September 16th. He left a widow Elizabeth, a son Sampson, and five daughters, one married to John Simpson a stationer. [Plomer, Wills, p. 23.] His place of business was in Little Britain Street by Great St. Bartholomew's without Aldersgate. [D.N.B.]

AWEN (WILLIAM), printer in London, is known from one book only, *A christian meditacion or praier to be sayed at all tymes whensoever God shall vyset us wyth anye mortall plague or sicnesse.* [B.M.] The imprint runs: "Imprynted at London By William Awen 1551."

AYLTON (ROBERT), stationer in London, is mentioned in the City Archives under the date 11th July, 30 Henry VIII. [1538.] "Item Robert Aylton, because he hath sett over his apprentice one Hester to a foreigner to lerne his crafte, whiche is ageynst the liberties of this citie, agreed that the said Hester shall be fre of the stacyoners. And the said Aylton to agree with master chamberlayn for his admission." [Bibl. Soc. Trans., vol. vi., p. 19.]

B. (I.), one of the two persons for whom J. Higman and W. Hopyl printed a Sarum *Missal* in 1500, "I. B., G. H., me fieri fecerunt."

BADIUS (CONRAD), printer in Paris and Geneva, was the son of J. Badius Ascensius. He began to print at Paris in 1545, but left about 1549 for Geneva, where he printed from 1550 onwards. In 1555 he became a citizen of Geneva, but returned to France in 1562, dying in that year at Orleans of the plague. [Renouard, p. 13.] He printed for the English market William Lily's *Short introduction of grammar* in March, 1557, and an edition of the *New Testament* later in the same year. He used two devices, one a picture of a printing press, the other a figure of Time leading out a female figure [Truth] from a cave.

BADIUS (JODOCUS), printer in Paris, was a native of Assche and was usually known as J. Badius Ascensius. He learnt to print in the office of John Trechsel, of Lyons, and left there for Paris in 1498. He edited a very large number of books, and in 1503 started as a practical printer, continuing in business up to his death in December, 1535. He was one of the most important printers of the time and the rival of Aldus in the issue of classical publications. [Renouard, pp. 11-13.] He never printed liturgical books, but issued several other books for the English market, beginning with a *Terence* in 1504, printed for W. de Worde and others. He also printed in 1510-11 some works of Savonarola for Henry Jacobi. A very considerable number of the educational works issued at this time in England contain prefaces written by him.

BAKER (JOHN), stationer in London, was an original member of the Stationers' Company, having been made free on October 24th, 1555. He is not entered in the charter nor is he known to have been in business.

BAKER (THOMAS), bookbinder in York, is mentioned in 1518-19 in the *Fabric Rolls of York Minster* [p. 99]. "Thomae Bakar pro coopercione duorum librorum Epistolarum et Evangelistarum, et pro coopercione iiij les whissinges cum les damask pro choro et pro plumis et aliis, 38.s. 8d."

BALDUINUS (JOANNES), *see* Boeidens (J.).

BALDWYN (RICHARD), stationer in London, was an original member of the Stationers' Company. He does not appear to have been in business on his own account, but is entered several times in the Registers as taking apprentices. The last reference made to him is in the year 1590.

BALDWYN (WILLIAM), printer in London, was educated at Oxford and took a degree in 1532. Coming later to London, he became an assistant to Edward Whitchurch, correcting for the press and doing original work. In 1549 he himself printed with Whitchurch's type *The Canticles or Balades of Salomon*, of which he was the versifier. During the reigns of Edward and Mary he superintended the production of plays at Court. Later he became a minister and schoolmaster. At the time of the incorporation of the Stationers' Company he was entered in the original list, but his name is never found in the Registers. The date of his death is unknown. [D.N.B.]

BALE (JOHN), Bishop of Ossory and publisher in London, was well known as an author and antiquary. He seems to have had some of his books printed for him and sold them himself. Leland's *Laboryouse Journey*, printed apparently by R. Jugge in 1549, was to be sold by Bale in Fleet Street at the sign of the Crown next to the White friars gate, and the *Actes of the Englyshe votaries*, printed by A. Veale in 1551, was to be sold by Bale within Paul's Chain at the sign of S. John Baptist. In spite of these colophons it is very doubtful whether he sold them himself. [D.N.B.]

BALIGAULT (FELIX), printer in Paris, carried on business between the years 1492 and 1506. At first he lived at the sign of the Corne-de-Cerf in the Rue St. Jacques, but in 1494 moved to the sign of St. Stephen in the Rue des Sept-Voyes. [Renouard, p. 14.] He printed in August, 1494, an edition of the *Multorum vocabulorum equivocorum interpretatio* [B.M.], which was also issued with a variant colophon omitting the printer's name and date. [U.L.C.] It contains translations in English and was intended for sale in England. His device, which is on the titlepage, consists of two monkeys, between whom is a tree (baliveau) supporting a shield with the name Felix.

BANKES (RICHARD), printer in London, is first mentioned in 1523, when he issued a curious little book called *The IX Drunkardes*. [Bodl.] His place of business was the "long shop" in the Poultry, next to St. Mildred's Church, and six doors from the Stock's Market. Here he continued to print until 1528, issuing a few popular books, but for the next ten years he appears to have been idle, for none of his books are dated in that period. In 1539 and 1540 he began to print again, publishing several works by Richard Taverner. In some of these books he speaks of having printed them next to the sign of the White Hart, in Fleet Street, in others it is said that they are to be sold at the White Hart by Anthony Clerke. A book entitled, *A compendyous olde treatyse shewynge howe that we ought to have the Scripture in Englyshe*, ascribed in the British Museum catalogue to 1530, but probably later, was printed by Bankes "dwellynge in gracious strete, besyde the cundyte." Towards the end of 1540 a number of broadsides, written for and against Cromwell by Thomas Smyth and William Gray, were issued in London, and came under the notice of the Privy Council, who, on the 30th December, 1540, issued letters to Bankes, Grafton, and Gray to appear before them on the following Sunday at eight o'clock in the morning.

"Richard Banks noted to be the prynter of the sayd invectives and examyned thereof, denyed the same, and layed the faulte to Robert Redman decessed and Richard Grafton, the which Richard Grafton confessyng that he had not onely printed part of the sayd invectives, but alsoo had in his keping a certain sedicious epistle in thenglishe tongue writen by Melancton, contrary to thacte of vi articles for Christian religion, was committed to the porters warde." [*Acts of the Privy Council*, vol. vii, pp. 103–106.] Now four of these broadsides [Soc. of Ant.] have clear colophons stating that they were printed by Richard Bankes, and he is therefore certainly "noted to be the prynter," but his evidence appears to show that his name had been put to them falsely. John Redman printed for him about this time a broadside upon the burning of Barnes. In 1541 and 1542 he issued four books, of which three were printed by Wyer, and the fourth contains Grafton's device, so that it appears that the only practical printing which he undertook after 1528 was confined to books by Taverner who, perhaps, subsidised his press. Bankes issued his last book, the *Book of Cookery* [Hunterian], in 1545, but the date of his death is not known. The number of books at present known published or printed by him is thirty-four. [Bibl. Soc. Handlists.] In a few he used a device consisting of his shield containing his mark and initials, surmounted by a half-length figure of St. John, and supported by a unicorn and another fabulous beast. Below the mark on the shield is a snail.

BARBANSON (JOHN), probably from his name a native of Normandy, was an apprentice to W. de Worde, who left him in his will two pounds in printed books.

BARBIER (JEAN), printer in London and Paris, began to print in London at St. Thomas Apostle about 1496, in company with I. H. and Julyan Notary. Here they printed two books, a *Questiones Alberti* and a Sarum *Horae*, and in 1498 Barbier and Notary had moved to Westminster, where they printed a folio Sarum *Missal* for W. de Worde. In 1502 he was at Paris in partnership with Pierre Levet and Francois Foucher at St. Germain-des-Prés. In 1510 he was at the Three Crowns in the Rue St. Jacques. He died in 1516. In 1504 he printed an edition of the *Ortus Vocabulorum* for Joyce Pelgrim, and about 1512 a *Legenda Francisci* for the Trinity booksellers. [Duff, *Early printed books*, pp. 143-4. Renouard, pp. 17-18. *The Library*, 1889, pp 102-105.]

BARLOW (JOHN), stationer in London, was an original member of the Stationers' Company, having been made free on August 19th, 1556. He is not mentioned in the original charter nor, beyond the fact of his making free, is he again mentioned in the Registers.

BARREVELT (GERARDUS), stationer in London (?), was partner for a short time with Frederick Egmont, and in 1494-5 they commissioned Joannes Hertzog, of Venice, to print several Sarum service books for them. [*The Library*, 1890, pp. 211-12.]

BARS (JOHN), stationer in London, was associated with George Chastelain about 1500 in the publication of an edition of the *Informatio puerorum*, printed by Pynson. [Bodl.] The colophon runs, "Here endeth the accidence made at the instaunce of George Chastelayn and John Bars : Emprynted by Rycharde Pynson."

BAUDUYN (PIERS), stationer in London, is mentioned in the wardrobe accounts of Edward IV, under the year 1480, "To Piers Bauduyn, stacioner, for binding, gilding and dressing of a booke called Titus Livius, xxs. ; for binding, gilding and dressing of a booke of the Holy Trinite, xvjs. ; for binding, gilding and dressing of a booke called Frossard, xvjs. ; for binding, gilding and dressing of a booke called Le Gouvernement of Kings and Princes, xvjs ; for binding and dressing of thre smalle bookes of Franche price in grete, vjs. viijd. ; for the dressing of ij bookes whereof oon is called La Forteresse de Foy, and the other called the Book of Josephus, iijs. iiijd. ; and for binding, gilding and dressing of a booke called the Bible Historial, xxs." [Nicolas. *Wardrobe accounts of Edward IV*, p. 125.]

BAXTER, stationer in Cambridge, is mentioned in Mere's diary of the Visitation of the Commissioners in February, 1557, "Sente for Baxter the statyoner first and after for his wyffe." [Gray, *Cambridge Stationers*, p. 70.]

BAYLEY (WILLIAM), stationer in London, is mentioned in the accounts for building the King's palace at Westminster. "For iiij forrell skynes occupied in covering of books bought of Wm. Bayley, of London, stationer." [*Archæologia*, Vol. 47, p. 335, note.]

BECKENETH (BALTHASAR), printer in Strasburg, is known only as the printer of the translation of Isaiah by George Joye, dated 1531, of which a copy is in the Baptist Museum, Bristol. [Maittaire, *Index*, I, 522. Herbert, III, p. 1540.] The name is probably a pseudonym, and the book appears to have been printed at Antwerp, probably by Martin de Keysere.

BEDFORD (THOMAS), stationer in Oxford, was a University stationer, and as such valued the goods of Christopher Coke, bookbynder, in 1501. [Arch. Univ. Oxon. Registrum Ǫ.]

BEKEN (ROWLAND VAN DER), stationer in London, was a brother of the Stationers' Company at the time of the incorporation. One of the same name was made a brother in 1559. [Arber, I, 70, 125.]

BENET (JOHN), stationer in London, appears as one of the parties in a Chancery suit, brought between 1465 and 1471, or 1480 and 1483, relating to an attachment, by the custom of London, at the suit of Hugh Wharton and Michael Berne, of goods in complainant's possession belonging to William Herbert, complainant's debtor. [Early Chancery Proceedings, Bundle 31, No. 510.]

BERCULA (THOMAS), *see* Berthelet (T.).

BERGHE (NICHOLAS VAN DE), *see* Hill (Nicholas).

BERGHEN (ADRIEN VAN), printer in Antwerp, spoken of in the colophons of his English books as Adryan of Barrowe, began to print about the beginning of the sixteenth century. He first began business at the sign of the Great Golden Mortar in the Market, but by 1507 he had moved to the Cornmarket behind the Town Hall, and later still he settled in a house by the Cammerpoorte Bridge, with the sign of the Golden Missal. He printed at least three English books, of which the most celebrated is the first edition of Arnold's *Chronicle*, famous as containing the ballad of the "Nut-browne Maid." He printed also an edition of Holt's *Lac Puerorum* and an English *Almanac* for 1529. In 1535 he became involved, by his own account unjustly, in religious troubles and was accused of keeping and selling Lutheran books. After a lengthy trial he was found guilty, and on January 3rd, 1536, was sentenced to leave the state within three days and undertake a pilgrimage to Nicosia, in Cyprus. After this date nothing further is heard of him.

BERNAERDT (DAVID), printer in London, was a native of Antwerp. He is mentioned in the Returns of Aliens [vol. 1.,-p. 203] as belonging in 1550 to the Dutch Church, and working as a printer with Thomas " Reinot." [Raynald.]

BERNARD (GUILLAUME), stationer in Rouen, worked from early in the sixteenth century up to about the year 1517. As early as 1506 he began to issue Sarum service books, issuing four editions of the *Missal* and one of the *Horae*, as well as a York *Missal* and *Horae*. His earlier books were printed for him by M. Morin, his later by Olivier. About 1517 he was in partnership with Jacques Cousin. He lived near the cathedral, opposite the " portail des Libraires." In his device his name is spelt Benard.

BERTHELET (THOMAS), printer in London, was probably at one time an assistant to Pynson and may be identified with the Thomas Bercula who printed Pynson's edition of the *Vulgaria* of Whitinton, issued in 1520, and one or two other books. On August 23rd, 1524, a Thomas Berthelet, of St. Dunstan in the West, probably the printer, married Agnes Langwyth, widow. [*London Marriage Licenses*, p. 4.] In 1528 Berthelet was in business on his own account, issuing in that year Paynell's translation of the *Regimen sanitatis Salerni*, which was followed the next year by another work of Paynell. Berthelet's address was given as in Fleet Street, " nere to ye cundite at ye signe of Lucrece." The two books, one by Wakefield on the divorce, the other the edition of the *Statutes* dated by Herbert, 1529, which are quoted as before 1530, cannot be earlier than that year. On February 15th, 1530, immediately after the death of Pynson, Berthelet was appointed printer to the King with an annuity of four pounds. His work after this was to a great extent official, though he issued many books of general interest and published all the works of Sir Thomas Elyot. On the accession of Edward VI Berthelet was deprived of his position as King's printer and Richard Grafton was appointed in his place, this being the first occasion on which a royal printer had lost his office before his death. For the succeeding eight years of his life we lose the familiar " Regius impressor " of his colophons, and this often helps in dating undated books. After the loss of his privilege he became much less active and no doubt left much of the work of the printing office to his nephew, Thomas Powell. Besides being royal printer Berthelet was also bookseller and bookbinder to the King, and it would be hard to speak too highly of his taste and skill in bookbinding. It is evident that he had been much impressed with the beautiful gilt work issued by the great Italian firms, such as Aldus, and it is supposed that he brought over to England some Italian workmen, both to work for him and to teach his own men. Berthelet's bindings are almost the first gilt tooled bindings produced in England and he himself speaks of them as worked in the Venetian manner, and many of the tools used are identical with those found on contemporary Italian bindings. Fortunately, several of Berthelet's yearly accounts have been preserved and reprinted [Arber, II, 50-60], and these give full details of the books purchased and bound for the King, and the titles of the books which Berthelet himself printed and the number of copies struck off. All bibliographers appear vague as to the date of Berthelet's death. He died on September 26th, 1555. [Inq. p. m., 2 and 3 Philip and Mary, p. 2, No. 8.] His funeral is described by Henry Machyn. [*Diary*, p. 95.] "The sam day at afternone was bered master Barthelett sqwyre and prynter unto King Henry; and was bered with pennon and cote-armur and iiij dozen of skochyons and ij whytt branchys and iiij gylt candyllstykes, and mony prestes and clarkes, and many mornars, and all the craftes of prynters, boke-sellers and all stassyoners." His will, dated 24th September, 1555, was proved on the 9th November. [Plomer, Wills, p. 11.] To his elder son, Edward, who was born on July 24th, 1553, he left his estate in Hereford and house property in London. To his younger son, Anthony, more property in London, with reversion to Thomas Powell, his sister's son. To his wife, Margaret, his own dwelling-house in Crokhorne Alley and other property. There are also legacies to god-children, apprentices, and charities. The trustees were John Abingtone and John Wekes, a goldsmith, probably the father of Henry Wekes the printer, who was an apprentice of Berthelet's at the time of his death. Margaret was Berthelet's second wife, whom he married in or shortly before 1550. Edward, the son, became a lawyer and was a member of Lincoln's Inn. Berthelet's property was valued at over £125 per annum. Berthelet's widow married Richard Payne, early in 1556. [Davenport, *Thomas Berthelet*. Plomer, *English Printing*, pp. 61-67. *The Bibliographer*, 1881-2, pp. 13-15.]

BIENAYSE (JEAN), printer and stationer in Paris, first appears in 1506. Renouard gives 1511 as his earliest date, but a Sarum *Breviary* was printed for him in 1506 at Rouen by P. Violette. By 1510 he was in partnership with Jacques Ferrebouc, and in 1511 with W. de Worde and R. Faques they paid for the printing of a Sarum *Missal*. Soon after they started as printers at the Lion d'Argent, in the Rue St. Jacques, a house lately vacated by J. Petit, and continued in partnership until 1516. After this Bienayse issued books with J. Kerbriant and J. Adam, and in 1521 we find him joining with J. Petit and J. Adam in the publication of a Sarum *Missal*. After this time his name is not found, and he certainly died before 1529.

BIGNON (JEAN), printer in Paris, appears to have commenced business about the year 1516, and continued to about 1544. He lived first at the sign of La Heuze, in the Rue St. Jacques, and later on in the Rue Judas. [Renouard, p. 29.] About 1521 he printed an edition of the Sarum *Horae* for R. Faques. [Bodl.]

BILTON, *see* Bylton.

BIRCKMAN (ARNOLD), stationer in London, was a native of Cologne, and one of the large family of stationers of the name who had establishments in various cities. He is first mentioned in 1541 in the Returns of Aliens [I, p. 67], when he kept a shop in charge of Henry Harman, his factor, and his goods were valued at 100 marks. In 1544 their value had risen to 80 pounds [R. of A., I, p. 93], and in 1549 to 100. [R. of A., p. 159.] At the time of the incorporation of the Stationers' Company in 1557, Arnold Birckman is entered as giving large subscriptions and a window to the Hall, so that he was probably a brother of the Company. A letter from Sir W. Cecil to the Marquis of Winchester, dated April 21st, 1564, gives some curious information about the importation of tubs of books from the Frankfort Fair by Birckman. [Arber, II, 63.] As late as 1571 Arnold and Agnes Birckman had a shop in London, with Andreas Fremorshem and Reynolde Mercator as servants. [R. of A., I, 411; II, 12.] The last entry of his name is in 1576, but this may refer to another Arnold, son of the former. A third Arnold Birckman died about 1540-41. All these Arnolds are much confused and it is hardly possible at present to separate them exactly. The whole family, though very important as traders, bore anything but a good reputation. Erasmus was especially bitter against them and the reformers repeatedly wrote of them as dilatory and untrustworthy.

BIRCKMAN (FRANCIS), stationer in London, was a native of Cologne, and one of a large family of booksellers who had shops in many cities. Francis is first mentioned in 1504, when in partnership with Gerard Cluen of Amersfoordt, presumably a relative of his wife, Gertrude van Amersfoordt, he issued a Sarum *Missal*. For the next few years he disappears, but about 1510 commenced a career of great activity, issuing numbers of Sarum service books, remarkable for their fine printing and decoration. His place of business was in St. Paul's Churchyard; no sign is ever mentioned, but it was on the east side somewhere near Colet's school. No book is known printed for him after 1529, and he probably died about that time, as his place was taken in 1530 by his son Francis. In 1531 an action was brought against the guardians of his children to recover money for a large consignment of English *New Testaments*, so that Birckman was mixed up in their dispersal in England. The devices which he used always contained his mark and the arms of Cologne, and these are introduced in many of the ornamental borders which were engraved for the books which he published.

BIRCKMAN (FRANCIS), II, stationer in London, was apparently the son of the elder Francis. His name is found only in the colophon of one book printed for sale in London, an edition of the Sarum *Processional*, printed at Paris by Prevost in 1530. This colophon runs "Venundatur Londonii in edibus junioris Francisci Byrckman apud cimiterium divi Pauli." The device in this book is the hen with her chickens, in reference to the sign of the Birckmans at Antwerp and Cologne of the Fat Hen, the printer's mark is identical with that of the elder Francis. This Francis probably returned abroad and is not found again in England.

BIRCKMAN (HENRY), stationer in London, was a native of Culemburg, and took out letters of denization, February 19th, 1535. [Pat. 26 Hen. VIII, p. 2, m. 41.]

BIRCKMAN (JOHN), stationer in London, is mentioned first in 1541, in which year he was keeping shop with John Cawood in St. Paul's Church-yard, and his goods were valued at 100 marks. [R. of A., I, 67.] In 1544 he was valued at £20, and in 1547 at £30. [R. of A., I, pp. 93, 134.] In 1549 he was still valued at £30, and was living in St. Paul's Churchyard with Andrew Hester, and many letters written about this time by him to Dryander were preserved in the University of Strasburg. He seems to have been associated in business with Arnold Birckman, for Reynes, in his will, written in 1542, speaks of books to be valued "after the price as Arnold and John Bryckman doe sell them to London to the booksellers."

BLONE (NICHOLAS), *see* Leblonde (N.).

BLYLEVEN (SIMON), *see* Cock (S.).

BLYTHE (ROBERT), stationer in London, was an original member of the Stationers' Company.

BOCARD (ANDRÉ), printer in Paris, was a native of Poitou, and carried on business from 1491 to 1531. [Renouard, p. 33.] In 1502 he printed an edition of the Sarum *Hymns and Sequences.* "Ab Andrea Bocardo impendio Joannis balduini seu boudonis in inclyta Parrhisiorum Lutecia." [B.M.] John Boudins was a London stationer who died in 1503.

BOEIDENS, or BOUDINS (JOHN), stationer in London, was a native of Antwerp and lived in the parish of St. Clement's, Eastcheap. Only one book is known printed for him, an edition of the Sarum *Expositio Hymnorum et Sequentiarum,* printed at Paris by A. Bocard at the commencement of 1502. Boeidens died in 1503, and his will, dated October 11th, 1501, was proved March 30th, 1503. [Arber, II, 7.]

BOLE (WILLIAM), printer in London, was an assistant to William Tylly the printer, dwelling in the parish of St. Anne and Agnes, Aldersgate Ward. He is entered in the Subsidy Roll of 1549. [R. of A., I, 173.]

BONHAM (JOHN), stationer in London, was an original member of the Stationers' Company, but is never mentioned again in the Registers. He was most probably the son of William Bonham, who died in 1557. [Plomer, Wills, pp. 13-14.]

BONHAM (WILLIAM), printer in London, was born in 1497, and was the second son of Thomas Bonham who died in 1523. As early as 1520 Bonham had started as a bookseller and was twice a sub-tenant of John Rastell in part of the house called the Mermaid in Cheapside. [Plomer, *English Printing,* p. 74.] In 1539 Bonham, accompanied by H. Pepwell and

H. Tab, went down to St. Albans to enquire about the printing there of a seditious book. In 1542 three books, a *Primer*, a *Chaucer*, and *Fabyan's Chronicles* were issued in his name, though it is improbable that he was the printer. In 1545, with Tab, he was overseer of the will of Edward Ylle, for which he received six shillings and eightpence. In 1549 he and his first wife sold some property in London. "Demise by William Bonham, stationer, and Joan, his wife, of their messuage called Holmes College, on the south side of St. Paul's." August 1st, 3 Edward VI. [Hist. MSS. Commission, IX Report, p. 13.] His last dated book was an edition of the *Bible* issued in 1551. His address in 1542 was the King's Arms in St. Paul's Churchyard, and in 1551 the Red Lion in the same place. Bonham's will was dated July 4th, 1557, and was proved on the 27th September the same year. To his second wife, Margery, who was a widow when he married her and whose first husband's name was Mayatt, he left his lands at Cliff, in Kent, and after her to his daughter Johane, wife of William Norton, the mother of Bonham Norton. Other lands were left to his daughter Alice Savage. To his son John he left but little, and that little was to be forfeited should he attempt to dispute the will. He left also bequests to the poor of Colchester where he desired to be buried. [Plomer, Wills, pp. 13-14.] Bonham lived just long enough to be enrolled in the original list of the Company of Stationers, and made several gifts to them.

BONHOMME (YOLANDE), printer in Paris, was a daughter of Pasquier Bonhomme, and wife of Thielman Kerver. After the latter's death in 1522 she carried on the business at the same address until her death, July 15th, 1557. [Renouard, p. 39.] She printed a very large number of service books for the use of the English Church.

BONIFANTE (RADULPHE), pseudonym. This name is found in the colophon of Bibliander's *Godly Consultation*, "Basill by Radulphe Bonifante, August 1542." The book was probably printed at Antwerp. [Sayle, III, p. 1362. Herbert, III, p. 1552.]

BORRELL (JOHN), printer in London, was an assistant to Thomas Reynoldes, the printer living at Hallywell, near London, some time before 1540. He is mentioned in a deposition dated August 20th of that year as late servant to T. Reynoldes. [Bibl. Soc. Trans., VI, p. 20.]

BOUDINS (JOHN), *see* Boeidens.

BOURMAN (NICHOLAS), printer in London, commenced work in 1539 when he issued an edition of Stanbridge's *Accidence* [J.R.L.], identical, except for the colophon, with one issued by James Gaver. In the same year he issued *An introduction for to lerne to reckon with the penne.* [Bodl.] His latest book was *Newes of an horryble earthquake* of 1542, and besides these he issued five other works. His address was in Aldersgate Street, and he used as a device a geometrical design containing his initials, almost identical with that used by John Hertford. Bourman was probably a relative of Richard Stevenage, or Boreman, last abbot of St. Alban's, whose initials R.S occur in Hertford's device and who was the patron of the St. Alban's press. It seems probable that Bourman took up Hertford's work in the interval between the latter's leaving St. Alban's in 1539 and recommencing in Aldersgate Street in 1544. Bourman, after ceasing to print, continued as a stationer and on the incorporation of the Stationers' Company in 1557 was twenty-seventh on the list. He subscribed to the collections made for the hall and joined with William Hill in presenting a window. In 1558 he was an assistant and one of the renters and continued in that office until 1560, after which date his name does not occur.

BOURSETTE (MADELEINE), printer in Paris, was the widow of Francois Regnault. On his death in 1541 she carried on the business at the sign of the Elephant in the Rue St. Jacques, and issued a number of English service books up to the time of her death in 1556.

BOYDEN (THOMAS), stationer in London, was an original member of the Stationers' Company, but there is no further reference to him in the Registers.

BOYS (MICHAEL), *see* Wood (M.).

BRACHIUS (JOANNES), stationer in London, is mentioned only in the colophon to the *Terence* [U.L.C.] printed at Paris by Badius Ascensius in 1504. "Venundantur Londonie in edibus Winandi de Worde, Michael Morin, et Joannis Brachii."

BRAY (JOHN), bookbinder in Oxford, is mentioned in 1475 in a charter relating to a tenement in Cat Street. He also bound books in 1482 for the library of Magdalen College. [Gibson, *Oxford Bindings*, p. 46.]

E

BRETTON (WILLIAM), publisher in London, was a wealthy merchant, a member of the Grocers' Company and of the Staple of Calais. He was interested in the publication of liturgical books and others relating to Church matters, for which he was praised at length by the editor of the *Pupilla Oculi.* He paid altogether for the publication of six books. Three of these, the *Psalterium cum hymnis,* the Sarum *Horae,* and the *Constitutiones* of Lyndewode and Athon, were printed in 1506 by W. Hopyl at Paris and sold in London by H. Jacobi and J. Pelgrim. The last three, the *Pupilla Oculi,* the *Speculum Spiritualium,* and another edition of the Sarum *Horae,* were also printed at Paris in 1510, the first two by Hopyl, the last by Th. Kerver, and were to be sold in London by Jacobi at the sign of the Trinity. Bretton used a very fine device, containing his coat of arms supported by two unicorns, which, after it had been used in the first books, was found to be wrongly engraved, and a new shield with the correct arms had to be cut and inserted in the block. A copy of this device was used later by E. Gourmont, the Paris printer. [*Bibliographica,* I, pp. 93–113.]

BREY (LAMBERT), printer in London, is mentioned in the Registers of the Dutch Church as an assistant to Stephen Mierdman in 1550. [R. of A., I, 207.]

BREYNANS (PETER), bookbinder in Cambridge, is mentioned in the Grace book as having bound two books in 1502-3. He lived in the parish of St. Mary the Great, and died about 1504. By his will, which is undated, he left legacies to his children, Baldwin, John, and Margaret, and to his wife, Katherine, who died in 1526. One of his executors was Garrat Godfray, the stationer, who received four shillings. [Gray, *Cambridge Stationers,* pp. 26–28.]

BRIGHT (PETER), stationer in Cambridge, took a lease of some land in St. Sepulchre's Parish from St. John's College in 1527. His will was proved in the University Court, February 1st, 1545-6. [Gray, *Cambridge Stationers,* pp. 64, 65.]

BRODEHEAD (GREGORY), stationer in London, was an original member of the Stationers' Company, having been made free on October 8th, 1555. He does not seem to have been in business on his own account, but was perhaps with Luke Harrison, as they jointly gave a subscription in 1559. Brodehead is last mentioned in 1562, when he and John Harrison were both fined for quarrelling.

BROKE (ROBERT), stationer in London, was an original member of the Stationers' Company, but beyond giving subscriptions at its foundation is not mentioned again in the Registers.

BROWNE (EDWARD), stationer in London, was an original member of the Stationers' Company, but is not mentioned in the Registers.

BRYGGES (JOHN), was an assistant in 1549 to John Growte, the bookseller. [R. of A., I, 160.]

BUKETON (WILLIAM), stationer in London, was party to a suit in Chancery in 1467–72 relating to the will of John Dowgo. [Early Chancery Proceedings, Bundle 45, Nos. 348, 356.]

BURTOFT (JOHN), stationer in London, was an original member of the Stationers' Company. He is last mentioned in the Registers in 1561, when he presented an apprentice.

BURTON (ROBERT), stationer in London, is mentioned twice in the Accounts of the churchwardens of the parish of St. Michael, Cornhill [p. 35], under the year 1467. "Payde to Robert Burton, Stacyoner for new byndyng and new helyng of a grayell and an antyphoner of the chirche xvjs iiijd." "Payed to Robert Burton Stacyoner for new byndyng and new helyng of the new prikked song boke. ijs. viijd."

BUTLER (JOHN), printer in London, was said by Ames, on the authority of Maurice Johnson, to have been a judge of the common pleas. He was, however, probably an apprentice, certainly at one time an assistant to Wynkyn de Worde. By 1529 he had started in business on his own account, issuing in that year an edition of the *Parvulorum institutio ex Stanbrigiana collectione*. Wynkyn de Worde, at his death in 1535, left a bequest of six pounds in printed books to "John Butler late my servant." Besides the one dated book of 1529, eight undated books by this printer are known, the *Jeaste of Sir Gawayne* [Lambeth], the *Doctrynale of good servantes*, and the *Convercyon of Swererers* [Huth], and five grammatical works. An edition of the *Expositiones terminorum legum Anglorum*, dated 1527, is generally ascribed to Butler, but was apparently the work of Rastell. Butler printed in Fleet Street, at the sign of St. John Evangelist,

E 2

and sometimes made use of a small woodcut of St. John, apparently taken from a Horae series, as a printer's device. He appears to have had some business connection with John Skot, some of whose printing material he made use of.

BYDDELL, or SALISBURY (JOHN), printer in London, was for some time an assistant to Wynkyn de Worde. The first four books which he issued were all printed by De Worde between November 15th, 1533, and March 21st, 1534, but after this he printed for himself. In 1535 he was one of the executors of De Worde who, in his will, remitted all his debts. In the same year he left his former house in Fleet Street with the sign of Our Lady of Pity and moved to De Worde's house, The Sun. Here he printed steadily until 1544, issuing altogether, as far as is known at present, fifty different books. In 1543 he was imprisoned in the Poultry Compter for printing unlawful books [*Acts of the Privy Council*, N.S., vol. i, pp. 107, 117], but was liberated after a fortnight's detention. Byddell probably died in 1545, for his last dated book was issued in November, 1544, and he was succeeded at the Sun by Edward Whitchurch before June, 1545. Byddell used several devices, all containing a heart-shaped mark with his initials. The most ambitious was copied from a device of Jean Sacon, of Lyons, which, in its turn, was copied from an illustration in a work by Bernardino Corio printed at Milan by Alexander Minutianus in 1503. [Bibl. Soc. Handlists.]

BYLTON (THOMAS), stationer in London, was an original member of the Stationers' Company. He is last mentioned in 1566, when he paid a fine of fourpence.

BYLTON (WILLIAM), stationer in London, was an original member of the Stationers' Company, though not mentioned in the charter. He was made free on March 29th, 1557. He is last mentioned in 1581, when his apprentice, David Ward, was made free.

BYRCKMAN, *see* Birckman.

C. (H.), bookbinder in England, used a broad ornamental roll with his initials interlaced and surmounted by his mark, besides flowers and fabulous animals.

CAESAR, DE KEYSER, LEMPEREUR, EMPEROR (MARTIN), printer in Antwerp, began to print about 1524, and was admitted as a member of the St. Lucas Gilde in 1528. In 1525 he lived in the street called Bucsteech, and used as a device a shield with his initials and emblems, supported by two lions, with the motto "Sola fides sufficit" and the engraved date, 1525. This motto, which was apparently dangerous, was changed in 1530 to "Spes mea Jesus." From about 1531 to 1535 Caesar printed several English books, including the *Mystik sweet Rosary* of 1533. a Stanbridge's *Accidence* for John Toy in 1534, and a *New Testament* in the same year. Martin Caesar disappears after 1536, and in 1537 his widow, Françoise Larouge, was at work at the sign of St. Jerome in the Lombarde-straet. She printed an edition of Colet's *Grammar* for John Cockes in 1539. [Bradshaw, *Collected papers*, pp. 361, etc. Olthoff, p. 55.]

CAILLARD (JEAN), stationer in Rouen, lived in the parish of St. Michael, near the sign of the Four Sons of Aymon. In 1517 he issued an edition of the *Ortus Vocabulorum* [J.R.L.], which was to be sold at Hereford by J. Gachet. He also published a Sarum *Missal* in 1518 and 1521, and a *Manual* in 1522.

CALY (ROBERT), printer in London, commenced business there in 1553. He was a strong Catholic and was probably abroad during Edward's reign. There are some reasons for believing that he printed abroad. The copy of Gardiner's *Explication and assertion of the true Catholique fayth*, 1551, in the Bodleian, has a printed slip with the following words pasted on the title, "And nowe aucthorised by the Queens hignesse Counsale. Imprinted at Roan by Roberte Calye, and are to be solde in Paules churcheyard at the signe of the Byshoppes head." This looks as though the book, previously without name of place or printer, had been acknowledged immediately on Mary's accession. From 1553 to 1558 Caly printed continuously, issuing a large number of books all on the Catholic side. The accession of Elizabeth, and consequent change of religion, caused the cessation of his press. In 1557, although not a member of the Stationers' Company, he was fined for printing a book without license. In 1559, after giving up printing, he took the freedom of the Company, but is only once mentioned afterwards in the registers, when he paid a fine in 1565-66. Caly printed "within the precincte of the late house of the Grey Friars, nowe converted into an hospital called Christ Hospitall." This was the address which Grafton also used, so that Caly may have succeeded him there, a surmise rendered more probable by Caly's having used Grafton's device with monogram.

CAMPION (EDMUND), bookseller in London, was father to Edmund Campion, the Jesuit, who was born in 1540. [D.N.B.]

CAMPION (E.), stationer in Canterbury, is known only from the colophon of a book entitled *Newes from Rome concerninge the blasphemous sacrifice of the papisticall Masse*, printed at Canterbury about 1550 by John Mychell for E. Campion.

CANDOS (GUILLAUME), stationer in Rouen, occupied, in 1504 and 1505, a shop at the "portail des Libraires." [Frère, *Livres de Liturgie*, p. 26.] In 1509 he issued an edition of the Sarum *Missal*, printed for him by Pierre Violette.

CAR (ROGER), printer in London, printed in 1548 an edition of the *Psalms* for Anthony Smith. [B.M.] Herbert mentions [II, p. 707] an edition of Herman's *Institution of Baptism* of about the same date. He also suggests that Car may be the R. C. who printed *Five sermons of Bernardine Ochine* for William Riddell, but it is more probable that these initials stand for Robert Caly.

CASE (JOHN), printer in London, lived in St. Peter's College rentes in St. Paul's Churchyard, at the sign of the "Baule." He printed about 1550 an edition of T. Sternhold's *Certayn chapters of the proverbes of Salomon drawen into metre*, for W. Seres. [B.M.] About the same time Nicholas Hyll printed for him *The Pleasaunt, Playne and pythie Pathewaye*, by V. L. In 1551 R. Crowley printed for him *Poore Shakerley his knowledge of good and evil*, and Herbert [II, 763], on the authority of Maunsell, quotes two other books. He was an original member of the Stationers' Company.

CATER (EDWARD), stationer in London, is mentioned by Strype [Memorials, III, 219.] "May 28, 1555 Edward Cater of London, Stationer, for falsifying and razing of a Dispensation granted by the Cardinal, was adjudged to be set on the Pillory." He was an original member of the Company of Stationers, though he printed and published nothing. He is last mentioned in 1563, when he supplied some vellum to the Company. [Arber, I, 222.] He died before September, 1564, for in that year his widow, Grace Cater, took an apprentice. [Arber, I, 254.]

CAVYE (CHRISTOPHER), stationer in Oxford, is mentioned as binding a City account book in 1556-7. [Oxford City Archives, Audit book.] He was admitted a university bookseller October 6th, 1570, and in 1574 the Chancellor recommended that he should have a monopoly of second-hand books, since he was in difficulties. [Clark, I, p. 321.] He probably died about 1578. [Gibson, *Oxford Bindings*, p. 47.]

CAWOOD (JOHN), printer in London, was born in 1514. He was apprenticed to John Reynes, and by 1541 was working on his own account in St. Paul's Churchyard, and John Byrckman was with him. In 1546 he began to print, his office being in St. Paul's Churchyard at the sign of the Holy Ghost. In 1553 he was appointed Royal printer by Mary in place of Grafton and had the reversion of Wolfe's patent for printing books in Latin, Greek, and Hebrew. At the time of the incorporation of the Stationers' Company he was one of the Wardens, and was Master in 1561, 1562, and 1566. Under Elizabeth he was made Royal printer, jointly with Richard Jugge. Cawood died in 1572, and had been three times married. His device consisted of his mark and initials. [Plomer, *English Printing*, pp. 109-112. D.N.B.]

CAXTON (WILLIAM), printer in Westminster, was born in the Weald of Kent about the year 1421. In 1438 he was apprenticed to Robert Large, a leading member of the Mercers' Company and Lord Mayor in 1439-40. Large died April 4th, 1441, and in his will left a legacy of twenty marks to his youngest apprentice, Caxton. Caxton had still a few years of apprenticeship to run, but seems to have gone abroad almost at once, for, in 1471, he wrote, "I have contynued by the space of xxx yere for the most part in the contres of Braband, Flandres, Holand and Zeland." In 1450 Caxton was settled in Bruges and in the same year was a party in a lawsuit, which he lost. In 1453 he paid a visit to London and was received into the livery of the Mercers' Company. On returning to Bruges he carried on business with increasing success, and from 1463 to 1469 was Governor of the Merchant Adventurers. In 1469 Caxton entered the service of the Duchess of Burgundy and, having more leisure, turned to literature and made several translations. On a visit to Cologne in 1471 Caxton saw the new art of printing being practised and, being struck with its obvious advantages, obtained some practical knowledge of the art by assisting to print an edition of *Bartholomaeus de proprietatibus rerum*, which was then in

preparation. On returning to Bruges in 1471 and presenting his translation of the *Recueil des histoires de Troyes* to the Duchess, he found that
many others of high rank wished for copies, and that the labour of
transcribing them was very great. On this account he determined to start
a printing press, and about 1473-4 took as a partner Colard Mansion, an
illuminator, and set to work to obtain the necessary material. When
Caxton had learnt the art in 1471, Cologne was the nearest town to Bruges
where it was practised, but in the interval presses had been set up in the
nearer towns of Utrecht, Alost, and Louvain. A study of Caxton's first
types clearly shows that they very strikingly resemble those of John de
Westphalia who printed at Alost in 1473 and moved to Louvain in 1474.
Between 1474 and 1476 Caxton and Mansion printed three books in partnership, but some time in 1476 Caxton, leaving his first fount of type with
Mansion, who continued to use it at Bruges, set out for England with a
newer fount, and on his arrival settled with his material in a house with the
sign of the Red Pale in the precincts of Westminster Abbey, and started
the first printing press in England. From the Westminster accounts we
learn that for his first shop Caxton paid a rent of ten shillings. In 1483 he
paid for two houses, and in the next year for an additional room over the
gateway to the Almonry. As Robert Copland tells us, Caxton began by
printing small books, and examples of these are still in existence. It was
not until November 18th, 1477, that he issued his first dated book, *The
dictes or sayengis of the philosophres*. About 1480, owing, perhaps, to the
rivalry of John Lettou's press, established in London in that year, Caxton
introduced several improvements. He cut smaller and neater type, commenced to use signatures, and in 1481 issued a book with illustrations. In
December, 1487, Caxton commissioned an edition of the Sarum *Missal*,
which was printed for him at Paris by Guillaume Maynyal, who apparently
printed also for him a Sarum *Legenda*, now known only from fragments. In
the *Missal* Caxton's mark occurs for the first time, no doubt added by Caxton
after the book arrived in England. The device consists of his trade mark
and initials, with a deep ornamental border at top and bottom, and it was
evidently engraved in England. In 1489 Caxton issued an *Indulgence* in a
very small type, but neither the *Indulgence* nor the type has been recorded
by Blades. The number of books actually printed by Caxton in England,
counting separate editions, is ninety-six, and with the three printed at

Bruges, and the *Missal*, he issued exactly one hundred books. There is no doubt, however, considering the number only known from fragments, that very many must have entirely disappeared. Blades, in his Life of Caxton, described ninety-nine books, but amongst these he includes two which were certainly printed at Bruges after Caxton had left, and three printed by W. de Worde after Caxton's death, so that the number of genuine books which he described is ninety-four. The number of Caxton bindings which have been preserved is small. His usual method of ornamenting the sides was to make a large panel by means of a framework of dies. This panel was divided into lozenge-shaped compartments by diagonal lines running both ways from the frame, and in each compartment thus formed a die was impressed. The die most commonly found has the figure of a winged dragon, another a conventional flower. The border was often made up with a triangular die pointing alternately right and left, also having the figure of a winged dragon. These bindings are invariably of calf, no genuine Caxton binding in vellum being known. The exact date of Caxton's death is unknown, but from the position of the entry in the parish registers it probably occurred towards the end of 1491. In a copy of Julian Notary's edition of the *Fructus Temporum* of 1515, which belonged at one time to a Mr. Ballard, of Cambden, in Gloucestershire, there was written in an old hand the following epitaph : "Of your charitee pray for the soul of Mayster Willyam Caxton that in hys time was a man of moche ornate and moche renommed wysdome and connyng, and decessed fel crystenly the yere of our Lord M.CCCC.Lxxxxi.

"Moder of Merci shyld him from thorribul fynd
And bryng hym to lyff eternall that neuyr hath ynd."

This may very well be a copy of a genuine inscription. Caxton's will has never been discovered, nor is it among the huge collection of deeds in Westminster Abbey. We know, however, that he had a daughter, Elizabeth, who obtained a separation from her husband, Gerard Croppe a tailor, in May, 1496. In the records of St. Margaret's, Westminster, are entries relating to the burials of William Caxton in 1479 and Maud Caxton in 1490, and these entries are often supposed to refer to the printer's father and wife, but beyond the names there is no evidence to support the conjecture. Caxton apparently left no son, and on his death all his printing material passed to Wynkyn de Worde. [Blades, *Life of Caxton*. Duff, *William Caxton*. R. H. Blades, *Who was Caxton*. D.N.B.]

CERVICORNUS (EUCHARIUS), printer in Cologne and Marburg, began to print in the former town about 1517. In 1520 he printed *Richardi Croci Britanni introductiones in Rudimenta graeca* for Joannes Lair de Siborch, the first printer at Cambridge.

CHANDLER (GILES), stationer in London, was an original member of the Stationers' Company, though not entered on the charter. He was made free on March 5th, 1555, and beyond giving subscriptions at the time of the incorporation, is not mentioned further in the Registers.

CHARLEWOOD (JOHN), printer in London, commenced business early in Mary's reign in partnership with John Tisdale, in Holborn, "nere to the Cundite at the signe of the Sarsins head." Two ballads are known printed at this address. [Soc. of A.] Charlewood was a member of the Grocers' Company until about 1574, though he took out licenses to print books. From 1562 to 1593 he printed continuously, and issued a very large number of books. His address was the Half-Eagle and Key in the Barbican, and in one of the Marprelate tracts it is stated that as printer to the Earl of Arundel he had a press in the Charterhouse. Charlewood's widow, Alice, married again James Roberts, who thus succeeded to the business.

CHARLTON (RICHARD), stationer in London, is thus entered by Herbert [II, p. 771], "Had printed for him *A treatise of the argumentes of the old and new Testament*, by John Brentius; translated by John Calcaskie. Maunsell, p. 23. Octavo."

CHASTELAIN (GEORGE), stationer in London and Oxford, is first mentioned in the colophon of an edition of the *Informatio puerorum*, printed at London by Pynson, about 1500, for him and John Bars. In June, 1502, he was admitted to the liberties of the University as a "servant" of Eliseus Ruthyn. In December of the same year he acted as deputy for Jean Richard in a dispute concerning the debts left by William Lesquier. In 1506 Pynson printed for him an edition of the *Principia* of Peregrinus de Lugo. He is described on the titlepage as living in Oxford in the street of St. Mary the Virgin, at the sign of St. John the Evangelist. In 1507–10 he bound books for Magdalen College. [Magd. Reg., I, pp. 64–6.] He died in 1513, and on October 3rd his goods were valued by William

Howberch and Richard Pate at £24. The administrators of the estate were Richard Wutton, a bedell, and Henry Jacobi, a stationer. [Madan, *Oxford Press*, p. 11. Gibson, *Oxford Bindings*, p. 46.]

CHAUDIERE (REGNAULD), printer in Paris, commenced business as a bookseller in 1514. In 1546 he succeeded to the printing office of Simon de Colines "sub sole aureo e regione gymnasii Bellovacensis," where he worked in partnership with his son Claude. [Renouard, p. 63.] He printed Richard Smith's *Confutation of a certen booke called a defence of the true and Catholike doctrine of the Sacrament*, without date, but about 1550. [U.L.C.]

CHAUNTER (PETER), is mentioned in the returns of aliens in 1549 as an assistant to H. Singleton. [R. of A., I, 159.]

CHEPMAN (DAVID), merchant in Edinburgh, son of Walter Chepman, appears to have practised as a bookbinder, for in 1539 he was paid by the king's treasurer ten shillings for "binding and laying about with gold the queen's matin buke." [Dickson and Edmond, *Annals*, p. 21.]

CHEPMAN (WALTER), printer in Edinburgh, was a successful merchant of that city who, in conjunction with Andrew Myllar, introduced the art of printing into Scotland. At the commencement of the sixteenth century he supplied Andrew Myllar with funds and sent him to Rouen to learn the art and bring back material. After Myllar's return a press was set up at Edinburgh in the Southgait and a series of small poetical tracts printed, the first of which, *The maying and disport of Chaucer*, is dated April 4th, 1508, the remainder being all issued within a few days of each other. Previous to this, in September, 1507, the printers had obtained a privilege from James IV for printing law books, service books, "and al utheris bukis that salbe sene necessar." In 1510 the Aberdeen *Breviary* was issued, the Pars Hyemalis in February, the Pars Aestivalis in June or July, but after this Chapman does not appear to have printed anything more. He still carried on business as a merchant and rose to a high position. In September, 1528, he endowed a chapel in St. Giles' cemetery, having previously built an aisle in the church, but before April, 1529, he was dead, as his wife, Agnes Cockburn, and his son David, appeared as claimants to his goods. [Dickson and Edmond, *Annals*, D.N.B. Duff, *Early printed books*, pp. 174-6.]

CHEVALLON (CLAUDE), stationer and printer in Paris, was born in 1479. He carried on business from 1511 to 1537, first at the sign of St. Christopher in the Rue S. Jehan de Latran, and, after his marriage in 1520 to Charlotte Guillard, widow of Berthold Rembolt, also at the Golden Sun in the Rue S. Jacques. [*Renouard*, pp. 71–72.] Soon after commencing business Chevallon issued an edition of the *Legenda Francisci* which was to be sold in the office of Claude Chevallon, where it was printed, or in London, in St. Paul's Churchyard, at the sign of the Trinity. The colophon, however, states that the book was printed by Jean Barbier. [*Bibliographica*, I, p. 112]. He published in 1531, for the English market, in partnership with F. Regnault, an edition of the Sarum *Breviary* in folio [the Great Breviary with the long lessons]. He was also a bookbinder, and used a very handsome roll on which occurs a rebus on his name, the figure of a horse with, on one side, CLAUDE, on the other, LON.

CHILDRYN (JOHN), stationer in London, was party to a suit in Chancery between 1475 and 1485 in an action of trespass. [Early Chancery Proceedings, Bundle 64, No. 742.]

CHRISTOPHER, stationer in Oxford, was a workman with Garret Pilgrim, who, in 1536, left in his will "to stofull my Seruaynt a bed and vis viijd." [Arch. Univ. Oxon. Registrum E E E.]

CHURCHYARD (BALTHASAR), stationer in Oxford, was a Dutchman by birth and is thus mentioned in 1524 as paying the alien tax. [Madan, p. 273.]

CLARKE (JOHN), stationer in London, was an original member of the Stationers' Company. He is mentioned in the Registers in 1563–64 as taking two apprentices.

CLERKE (ANTHONY), bookseller in London, was in business about the year 1540. He seems to have been in some way associated with Richard Bankes and he lived next to him at the sign of the White Hart in Fleet Street. He issued two editions of the *Epistles and Gospels* in 1540 with the colophon, "Imprinted at London by Richarde Bankes, and solde in Fletestrete at the sygne of the whyte Harte by Anthony Clerke." [Herbert, I, 408, 410.] Nothing is heard of him until 1561, when there is an entry in the Register of the Stationers' Company, " Recevyd of Anthonye Clerke for his fyne and for his quarterages which he was behynde for xvj yeres the vj of maye. xx⁵." His son Michael was made free by patrimony in 1564.

CLESTON (NICHOLAS), stationer in London, was an original member of the Stationers' Company. He is mentioned several times in the Registers up to 1564 mainly as being fined for various offences.

CLUEN (GERARD) de Amerfort, stationer, is mentioned only in the colophon to one book, an edition of the Sarum *Missal*, printed by W. Hopyl at Paris in 1504 for Gerard Cluen and Francis Birckman. Very probably both stationers were in London at the time, and no doubt Cluen was a near connection of Birckman, whose wife's name was Gertrude van Amersfoordt.

CLUSEN (CORNELIUS VAN), is mentioned in the Register of the Dutch Church as an assistant to Stephen Mierdman in 1550. [R. of A., I, 203.]

COCK, or BLYLEVEN (SIMON), printer in Antwerp, was the son of Cornelius Cock, and was born in 1489. He began to print in 1511, and in 1557 was admitted a member of the St. Lucas Gilde. He lived on the Lombard wall opposite the Golden Hand. He died August 17th, 1562. [Van Havre, p. 109.] He printed " *Storys and prophesis out of the holy scriptur*," 1536, and may also have printed one or two of the quarto editions of the English *New Testament* issued the same year.

COCKES (JOHN), stationer in London, is entered in the lists of aliens in 1541 and 1544 as a denizen. [R. of A., pp. 67, 93.] He was evidently in a good position, as his goods were valued at a hundred marks, and he had an assistant John Gybken. In 1539 an edition of Colet's *Aeditio* was printed for him at Antwerp by the widow of Martin Caesar, and in 1541 an edition of the Sarum *Hymni cum notis*, by the widow of Christopher van Endhoven. He lived in St. Paul's Churchyard.

COFFYN (MARTIN), stationer in Exeter, was a native of Normandy. Two books, both undated, were printed for him. One, the *Vocabula* of Stanbridge, was printed at Rouen by Lawrence Hostingue and Jamet Loys, the other, the *Catho cum commento*, was printed at the same place by Richard Goupil. These books were described by Ames and the latter is noted by Bagford

[Harl. MS., 5974], but their present whereabouts is not known. Coffyn took out letters of denization April 28th, 1524, and is described in them as a bookbinder. [Pat. 16 Hen. VIII, p. 1, m. 40.]

COIPLETT (JACQUES), bookbinder in London, was a native of Normandy, and took out letters of denization on July 1st, 1544. [West. Deniz. Roll, 36 Hen. VIII.]

COKE (CHRISTOPHER), stationer in Oxford, is mentioned in 1484 as a bookbinder in the accounts of the keepers of the Chantry of St. Thomas. [Gibson, *Oxford Bindings*, p. 46.] A record of a grant of administration after his decease, with an inventory dated 13th December, 1501, is preserved in the University Archives. [Madan, p. 272.] His goods were handed over to his wife Matilda.

COKE (HENRY), printer in London, was an assistant to Stephen Mierdman, and is entered in the Parish of St. Mary-at-Hill, Billingsgate Ward, in the Subsidy Roll of 1549. [R. of A., I, 161.]

COKE (WYMAN), printer in London, was probably a brother of Henry Coke, and, like him, was an assistant to Stephen Mierdman in 1549. [R. of A., I, 161.]

COLE (THOMAS), printer in London, was an apprentice to Richard Kele, who, in his will, proved October, 1552, left him "fourtie shillings in ware." [Plomer, Wills, p. 10.]

COLSON (ROBERT), stationer in London, was party to an action for debt between 1475 and 1485, having become surety for William Moreton, vestment maker. [Early Chancery Proceedings, Bundle 64, No. 255.]

COMES (NICOLAUS), *see* Lecomte (N.).

CONSTANTIUS (MARCUS ANTONIUS), pseudonym. This name is found in the colophon of W. Turner's *New book of spirituall Physik*, 1555, which runs, "Imprented at Rome by the vaticane church by Marcus Antonius Constantius: otherwise called thraso miles gloriosus." [Herbert, III, pp. 1581–2.]

COOKE (HENRY), stationer in London, was an original member of the Stationers' Company. From his position as third on the charter and one of the Wardens, he must have then been of considerable age. He gave various donations to the Company, but is not mentioned in the Registers after 1560.

COOKE (WILLIAM), stationer in London, was an original member of the Company at the time of the incorporation. He was received on the livery in 1561 on payment of fifteen shillings. He does not appear to have been either a printer or publisher, but presented a number of apprentices. He was frequently renter and auditor to the Company and was one of the Wardens in 1574-5. He died shortly before 1598, in which year his widow presented one of his apprentices. His son William was also a member of the Stationers' Company. A daughter, Sarah, married, September 3rd, 1586, Andrew Feilde, a grocer. [*London Marriage Licenses*, p. 153.] W. Cooke lived in the Parish of St. Dunstan's-in-the-West.

COPLAND (ROBERT), printer in London, was for long an assistant to W. de Worde, and it has been suggested, from his reference in the prologue of *King Apolyn of Tyre* to his "mayster" Caxton, that he may have been with him also, but as he lived until about 1548 this seems improbable. He was apparently a good French scholar, and from 1508 onwards made many translations for De Worde and also composed verses for introductions and endings of books. About 1514 he printed an edition of the *Modus tenendi curiam Baronum* [U.L.C.], in which his address is given as the sign of the Sun in Fleet Street, W. de Worde's house. In this he used his earliest device, copied from a French model. Two animals, crowned round the neck, one being a stag, support a shield hanging from a tree. On the shield is Copland's mark and round it a garland of roses. Round all, on a black back-ground, runs a ribbon inscribed "Melius est nomen bonum quam divitie multe. Prov. XXII." The presence of the garland round the shield has reference to the sign of his shop in Fleet Street, where he began to print in 1515 at the Rose Garland. In that year he issued the *Boke of Justices of Peace*, which also contains his first device. His next book, Barclay's *Introductory to French*, did not appear till 1521, and after that there is another gap of seven years. Up to 1535 he had only printed twelve books. The real fact seems to be that his press was largely employed by W. de Worde, and just as is the case with John Skot, he printed many books which appeared with De Worde's imprint and mark. Several books issued by De Worde, and reissued by others, contain introductory verses by Robert Copland, "the boke-prynter," and there is nothing in that opposed to the fact that they were issued by others, though printed by him. The theory that all such books are merely reprints of editions issued by Copland and now lost is hardly probable. Though they were issued by others, he was the printer and as such wrote the "envoy," or prologue. It is certain that Copland's press almost ceased in 1535, the date of De Worde's death, though he did a little work some twelve years later. By De Worde's will Copland received in 1535 "as manny printed bookes as shall amounte to the value of tenne markes sterling," and was appointed one of the three executors. [Plomer, Wills, p. 4.] About 1540 he made a new translation of the *Questionary of Cyrurgyens* at the request of Henry Tab, for whom Wyer printed it. The last book which Copland appears to have printed is Andrew Boorde's *Pryncyples of Astronomye in maner a pronosticacyon*. In this book the author mentions his "Breviary of Health which is printed at William Mydyltons in Flet stret" [1547], and also his *Introduction to knowledge*, "now a pryntyng at old Robert Copland's the eldest printer of England, which do print this year my prognostications." The *Principles of Astronomy* may therefore be dated about 1548, and it is probable that Robert Copland died about this time and that the *Introduction to Knowledge* was finished by William Copland. Besides the French-looking device, only used in his earliest books, Robert Copland made use of two others. One is a garland of roses surrounding his mark, with his name below on a ribbon, the other is a narrow device containing his mark, with a long ribbon running behind it, on which is his name.

COPLAND (WILLIAM), printer in London, was most probably the son of Robert Copland, and succeeded him at his death in 1548 at his shop in Fleet Street with the sign of the Rose Garland. William Copland had married, November 19th, 1546, Joanna Tyddeswell, of St. Bride's parish. [*London Marriage Licenses*, p. 10.] From 1548 to 1557 Copland printed on steadily at the Rose Garland, though in March, 1556, he was brought before the Privy Council and bound to deliver up to Cawood all copies which he had printed of Cranmer's *Recantation*, to be burnt. [*Acts of the P.C.*, vol. v., N.S., pp. 247-8.] Some time before 1561 Copland moved to the "Three Crane Wharfe in the Vintree," in St. Martin's Parish, where he printed a few books and in 1562 he had moved again to Lothbury, against S. Margaret's Church. He seems to have fallen into poor circumstances, though he continued to enter copies of ballads and small pamphlets. He died in the latter half of 1568 or first half of 1569 and his funeral expenses were defrayed by the Stationers' Company, of which he was a member. He used as a device the Rose Garland of Robert Copland, with his own name on the ribbon below.

CORNELII DE MATGRE or VAN METEREN (JAMES), stationer in London and his son Emmanuel took out letters of denization, March 10th, 1552. [Pat. 6 Edw. VI, p. 6, m. 10.]

COSTE (PHILIPPE), stationer in Rouen, lived near the "Pont de Robec." He with others issued a Sarum *Missal* in 1506 and an undated *Manual*. He was in business after 1510, as he published a Rouen *Horae* [Brunet V. p. 1635], whose calendar begins with that year.

COSTON (SIMON), stationer in London, was an original member of the Stationers' Company, and sixth on the list in the charter. He died in 1564.

COTS (THOMAS), stationer in London, is mentioned in Repertory 6 in the Archives of the City of London : the entry dated September 6th, 1519, runs as follows : "Item. At this court was redde the letter directed to the mayor and aldermen from the University of Cambrigge, concerning divers boks to be bought and sold and seased by one Thomas Cots, stacioner, whereuppon the seyd Thomas had in comandment to bring in such proofs as he hath concerning the premises upon Tuesday next. And afterwards on the 11th day of September yt ys agreed that my lord mayor shall cause to be delivered to the Doctor of Honey Lane all such books as be specyfied in the letters as he hath from Cambridge." [Bibl. Soc. Trans., VI, p. 25.]

COTTESFORD (HUGH), stationer in London, was an original member of the Stationers' Company and was made free on October 8th, 1555. He is last mentioned in the Registers in 1562, when he presented an apprentice.

F

COUSIN (JACQUES), stationer in Rouen, was in business from 1503 to 1537. He lived in the Parish of St. Vincent and had a shop at the "portail des Libraires." In 1512 he issued a Sarum *Missal* printed by Morin. In 1517, in partnership with G. Bernard, he issued a Sarum *Horae* and a York *Missal* and *Horae* printed by Olivier, who also printed two Sarum *Missals* for him in 1519 and 1521. He issued a *Hymni cum notis* in 1518, a *Manuale* in 1537, and two editions of the Sarum *Horae*. He issued two English books, an *Ortus Vocabulorum* in 1520 and Stanbridge's *Gradus comparationum* without date. His device contains a shield with the arms of Rouen, supported by two rams, with his initials and name in full. [Frère, *Livres de liturgie*, p. 29.]

COUSTURIER, or SUTOR (RAOUL), printer in Paris, was in business between the years 1499 and 1512. He printed in the Rue Judas, and in 1511 produced a Sarum *Missal* [Jesus Coll., Camb.] for W. de Worde, R. Faques, J. Bienayse, and J. Ferrebouc.

COWELANCE (PHILIPPE DE), stationer in Paris, was no doubt a son of Jean de Cowlance [Cobelens, Confluentinus], and succeeded him at the sign of L'Asne rayé, in the Rue de la Vieille-Bouclerie. His name occurs only in one book, a "*Donate and accidence for children*," printed at Paris in 1515. The Latin imprint on the title sets out that the book was to be sold at Paris at the sign of the Striped Ass by Philip de Couuelance, and in St. Paul's Churchyard at the sign of St. Katherine or of the Holy Trinity. It is not known who lived at the sign of St. Katherine; the sign of the Trinity was occupied up to about 1512 by H. Jacobi, and from 1518-39 by Henry Pepwell. The device used by P. de Cowelance, with the motto "Inicium sapiencie timor domini," is the one used at an earlier period by A. Bacquelier. [*Bibliographica*, I, p. 113.]

CRESPIN (JEAN), printer in Geneva, was born at Arras, and studied law at Paris with Dumoulin, to whom he was secretary. He went to Geneva in 1548, and there started a press to print books in the learned languages, in which he was well skilled. He died of the plague at Geneva in 1572, and was succeeded by his son-in-law, Eustace Vignon. [*Biographie Universelle.*] He used as a device a serpent and anchor, of which he had several sizes. He began to issue books in English in 1556, when he published the *Forme of prayers used in the Englishe congregation at Geneva*. He also issued the *Bible* and *Book of Psalms*, as well as several works by John Knox.

CROKE (ADAM), stationer in London, was an original member of the Stationers' Company, having been made a freeman on November 5th, 1555. He died shortly after, leaving some money to the Company, which was paid by William Croke, his executor, in 1559.

CROM (MATTHEW), printer in Antwerp, began to print about 1537, and was admitted a member of the S. Lucas Gilde in 1542. He lived first in the Cammerstraet, at the sign of the Kettle, then at the House of Delft, and lastly, near the Place de Poids de fer. As a device he used a reproduction of his signature. [Van Havre, p. 133.] Crom printed two editions of the English *New Testament* in 1538 and 1539.

CROSSE (RICHARD), stationer in London, was an original member of the Stationers' Company. He is last mentioned in 1559, and appears then to have been one of the "ancients."

CROST (ANTHONY), stationer in London, was an original member of the Stationers' Company, having been made free on October 1st, 1556. He paid several subscriptions at the incorporation, but is not mentioned afterwards in the Registers. The reason for this is that in July, 1557, he went as one of the four soldiers sent from the Stationers' Company, levied for the army sent to Philip in Flanders.

CROWLEY (ROBERT), printer in London, was a native of Gloucestershire, and was educated at Oxford, becoming a fellow of Magdalen in 1542. Coming to London in the reign of Edward VI, he set up a printing press in Ely Rents, Holborn, and printed a number of books between 1549 and 1551, including the earliest editions of *Piers Plowman*, and several books in Welsh, printed for William Salesbury. On Mary's accession he fled to Frankfurt. On his return in the reign of Elizabeth, being in holy orders, he was presented with several livings, becoming finally rector of St. Giles, Cripplegate. In 1578 he was made a freeman of the Stationers' Company by redemption, and though he does not seem to have actively engaged in printing, he is found taking apprentices in 1580 and 1584. In 1586 he gave the annual sermon before the Company. He died June 18th, 1588, and was buried in St. Giles' Church. [D.N.B.]

CTEMATIUS (GELLIUS), *see* Erve (E. van der).

CUPERE (PIETER DE), printer in London, was an assistant to Nicholas Hill. He is mentioned in the register of the Dutch Church in 1550, "Pieter de Cupere, van Ipre, met Nicolais de prentere." [R. of A., I, 208.]

CUTTIER (PHILIPE), bookbinder in Oxford and London, came to England about 1551. He is entered in the two returns of aliens of 1571, "Philippe Cuttier, a denison, bokebynder, and his wife, in England xx^{ti} yeares, and in the said warde [Blackfriars, Farringdon Without] viij yeares; one servaunt a Frenchman, and two children." [R. of A., I, 413.] "Philippe Cuttier, howsholder, bookbynder, came into this realme about xx yeares paste." [R. of A., II, 14.] His name is not found in the lists of Denizations. He was apparently settled first at Oxford, for, on October 28th, 1558, "Philip Cutture bookbinder of Oxford" was bound over in £10 not to reveal State secrets to the French king. [Turner, *Records*, p. 274.] Immediately after this he went to London, becoming a journeyman with Thomas Purfoot, and was sworn a brother of the Stationers' Company in 1559. [Arber, I, 100.] He was fined by them fourpence in 1567–68. [Arber, I, 367.] He probably died in 1578, for an apprentice who was bound to him in March to learn bookbinding was transferred in August to Lewis Seignor. [Arber, II, 83.]

D. (M.), bookbinder. These initials are found on five panels, used by two, if not three, different binders. The two earliest are, first a panel containing a shield with the arms of England and France supported by a dragon and greyhound, above this is a Tudor rose, and at the sides a portcullis, and the binder's initials below. The other panel has a half-length figure of a saint holding a sword in a medallion, and at the corners the symbols of the Evangelists with their names on scrolls. [Weale, p. 128.] The second pair contain in the centre two medallion heads of warriors, surrounded by a border in the Renaissance style, and with the binder's initials on a tablet in the base. [Weale, p. 146.] The last panel has a Renaissance border and the interior blank save for a shield containing the binder's initials.

DABBE (HENRY), *see* Tab (H.).

DANVILLIER, DUBLIER, or DUBLE (HUBERT), letterfounder in London, came to England about 1551. In 1562 he was living in Blackfriars, and is entered as Hubertus Danvillier, fondeur de lettres. [R. of A., I, 290.]

In 1571 he is entered as Hubarde Duble, Frenche, beinge a howsholder, a denizon, of occupacion a founder of lettres hathe bene in this realme xx^{tie} yeres, and in this warde [Shoe Lane, Farringdon Without] vii yeres. [R. of A., I, 421.] In the other list of 1571 he is entered Hubert Dublier, borne in France, a denizon, came into this realme about xx yeares past: he is a founder of lettres for printers, he came to get his lyvinge. [R. of A., II, 5.] In 1582–3 he is entered as Hubert Devel, founder of letters, of the French Church. [R. of A., II, 300.] In 1562 an Anthony d'Anvillier, also a typefounder, is mentioned in the list of members of the French Church. He took out letters of denization May 30th, 1567.

DARBY (ROBERT), was an assistant to Wynkyn de Worde, who left him three pounds in printed books in his will. [Plomer, Wills, p. 4.]

DATHENUS (PETRUS), stationer in London, was born at Mont Cassel in Flanders, in 1531, and having been educated by the Carmelites joined the reformed religion and went to London in the reign of Edward VI, where he took up the business of a bookseller. He was afterwards a minister at Heidelberg, and died in 1590. [Schickler, I, 178. *Den Gulden Winckel* (Baarn) Derde Jaargang, No. 1, 15th January, 1904, p. 10.]

DATURE, DATIER, or DOTIER (MARTIN), bookbinder and stationer in London, is mentioned with others as having been granted pardon in January, 1527. [*Letters and papers of Henry VIII*, IV, pt. ii, p. 1270.] He appears to have been admitted a brother of the Stationers' Company, and presented his apprentice, William Pore, in 1556. He also gave twelve pence towards the collection for Bridewell. [Arber, I, 41, 48.] In 1543 he commissioned an edition of the Sarum *Manual*, which was printed for him at Rouen by Nicolas le Roux, and his name, Martinus Datier, is printed in small letters at the bottom of the titlepage.

DAUBET, printer in Rouen, is mentioned as the printer of a Sarum *Missal* in 1517 for P. Guerin. [Frère, *Livres de Liturgie*, p. 27.] The authority for the existence of this book is doubtful, and no copy appears to be known. The name Daubet does not occur anywhere else as a printer.

DAVIDSON (THOMAS), printer in Edinburgh, began to work some time before 1540, and the first actual mention of his name occurs in a deed of 1536. Before 1540 he issued an edition of the *Chronicles of Scotland*, for one copy [Innerpeffray Library] is known containing an inscription dated 1540. At the end of 1541 he was chosen to print some Acts of Parliament which were issued in the following year. Besides these, he is known to have issued three other works, none of them dated. He appears to have obtained some of his material from Peter Treveris, and his device, a shield with his arms hanging from a tree and supported by wild men, is copied from that of the English printer. His address is given in the *Chronicles* as "fornens the frere wynd," and in the Acts as "abone the nether bow on the north syde of the gait." [Dickson and Edmond, pp. 105-135.]

DAVIT (WILLIAM), mentioned by Herbert [I, 314] and Dibdin [III, 21] as being the publisher of a *Horae* in 1510 is fictitious. The mistake arose from the fact that in the copy in the Bodleian of the *Horae*, printed by Th. Kerver for William Bretton, the Bretton has been erased and the name Davit substituted in ink.

DAY (JOHN), printer in London, was born in 1522, at Dunwich, in Suffolk. At an early age he was apprenticed to Thomas Reynoldes, or Raynold, the printer, but by 1540 he had left him. In 1546 he began to print in partnership with William Seres, at the sign of the Resurrection, a little above the Conduit in Holborn, and shortly after this they had another shop, with the same sign, by the little Conduit in Cheapside. In 1549 John Day moved to Aldersgate, but still kept the shop in Cheapside. On the accession of Mary, Day ceased printing, and is generally stated to have gone abroad. An entry in *Machyn's Diary* [p. 72] throws a different complexion on the case. "1554. The xvi day of October cam rydyng owt of Northfolke on John Day prynter and ys servand, and a prest and anodur prynter, for pryntyng of noythy bokes, to the Towre." How long he was imprisoned is not known, but he did not begin printing again until 1557. On the incorporation of the Stationers' Company in that year Day is entered fifty-sixth on the list, which would about agree with the belief that he transferred himself from the Stringers' to the Stationers' Company in 1550. When Elizabeth came to the throne Day commenced printing on a much more ambitious scale, and his work showed a very marked improvement. The excellence of his work for the rest of his life was not due, as some suggest, to his having gone abroad and studied the art during Mary's reign, but to the great influx of refugee skilled workmen, many of whom he took into his employ. The patronage of Archbishop Parker was also of material assistance to Day who, owing to his generosity and encouragement, was enabled to cut new founts. About 1566 he issued a book printed in Saxon character, and in 1572 printed in a new Italic letter, at the private press at Lambeth, the work of Parker, *De antiquitate Ecclesiae Britannicae*, the first privately printed book issued in England, and limited, some say to fifty, others to twenty-five copies. In 1572 Day desired to build a little shop by St. Paul's Cathedral, a proceeding bitterly opposed by the other booksellers, but after considerable trouble, and with the aid of the Archbishop, he carried his point. In 1573 Day's life was threatened by an apprentice named Asplyn, who had been concerned in printing prohibited books. In 1580 Day was Master of the Stationers' Company, and shortly after was concerned in several lawsuits relating to his patent for printing the *A. B. C.* and *Catechism*, which had been infringed by others. Day died on July 23rd, 1584, at Walden, in Essex, and was buried at Bradley-Parva. He was twice married, and had twenty-two children, one of whom, Richard, was a printer. He used three devices. One shows two men looking at a skeleton on a tomb, from which springs a tree, upon which is the motto " Post funera virtus, vivet tamen." Another has a picture of a sleeper being awakened, with the inscription, " Arise, for it is day." The third has a tile supported by two hands, on which is a crucible in which a heart is burning; from a chain suspended from the wrists of the hands hangs a globe, below which is the sun, on either side are Day's initials and, on a ribbon between, the words " Horum charitas." [Plomer, *English printing*, pp. 79-100. D.N.B. *Gentleman's Magazine*, 1832, pp. 417-21.]

DE BRUGES or DEBURGES (ISAAC), bookbinder in London, is entered in the returns of 1571 "Isaac Deburges householder, dennyzein and a bookebynder by his trade, and his wyfe borne in Douchelande, he hath byn in Englande twentie yeares." [R. of A., II, 61.] He dwelt in St. Katherine's Parish, Aldgate Ward. Two people of the name took out letters of denization, one on December 13th, 1549 [Pat. 3 Edw. VI, p. 10, m. 6], the other on October 29th, 1550. [Pat. 4 Edw. VI, p. 4, m. 1.]

DE TOLNA (ADRIAN), *see* Turner (A.).

DEVELL (THOMAS), stationer in London, was living in 1549 in St. Paul's Churchyard, in which year a foreigner who lived with him, Dr Adrian, paid taxes. [R. of A., I, 59.] He was an original member of the Stationers' Company, but is not mentioned after the year of incorporation in the Registers. It appears from the Records in the Guildhall [Rep., 10., f. 189] that he was made free of the Company of Stationers January 18th, 1541.

DIXON (NICHOLAS), printer in London, was an assistant at one time to Lucy, widow of John Reynes. She left by will six shillings and eightpence to Nicholas Dixon, "sometyme my servant." [Plomer, Wills, p. 9.]

DOCKWRAY (THOMAS), stationer and first Master of the new Stationers' Company, was by profession a notary. He was a strong Catholic, and as early as 1533 was employed by Bishop Stokesley in his crusade against English religious books printed abroad. In August of that year Vaughan wrote to Cromwell, "The bishop of London, Stokesley, has had a servant in Antwerp this fortnight. If you send for Henry Pepwall a stationer in Paul's Churchyard who was often with him, he will tell you his business. The bishop of London's servant is one Docwraye, a notary public." [L. and P. of Henry VIII, vol. iv., p. 407.] In 1539 he was living in St. Paul's Churchyard. At the time of the incorporation of the Stationers' Company in 1557 he was Master, but did not long survive, dying on June 23rd, 1559. His will, a lengthy document, leaves bequests to Anne his wife, his brothers, sisters, and nephews, and also a considerable sum to charity. He was buried in St. Faith's Church, and his epitaph has been preserved by Dugdale. [History of St. Paul's, p. 122.]

DOESBORCH (JAN VAN), printer in Antwerp, appears to have succeeded about 1508 to the business of Roland van den Dorpe and his widow, and to have taken on their premises with the sign of the Iron Balance near the Cammerpoorte. In 1508, the date of his first dated book, he is entered in the books of the St. Lucas Gilde as an illuminator. He apparently kept a shop in London, for there is an entry in the Subsidy Rolls of 1523-4, under the Parish of St. Martin-in-the-Fields, "De Johanne van Dwysborow, extraneo, pro xl.s per annum, ii.s." [R. of A., p. 7.] He printed altogether about thirty-two books, and of these more than one half are in English, some being translated by Lawrence Andrewe the printer. Most are illustrated with a careless selection of woodcuts. Doesborch's device consists of a figure of

Fortune, with two attendant figures of Good and Ill Luck, which is found in several states. He also used a mutilated device which had belonged to Roland van den Dorpe. [Proctor, *Jan van Doesborch.*]

DORCASTER (NICHOLAS), printer in Wittenberg, is mentioned by Herbert [III, pp. 1576-7] as issuing three books in May, 1554, John Knox's *Admonition*, the *Confession of certain poor banished men*, and the *Doctrine of the Mass Book*. The names, both of printer and place, are probably fictitious, but the books may have been printed at Antwerp.

DORNE or THORNE (JOHN), stationer in Oxford, is perhaps identical with the Johannes Dorn who printed at Brunswick from 1506 to 1517. In 1524 he paid the alien tax at Oxford as a "Dutchman," under the name of Thorn. The day-book, containing a list of the books he sold with their prices, from January 19th to December 23rd, 1520, and two leaves of an earlier ledger, are in the library of Corpus Christi College, Oxford, and were edited for the Oxford Historical Society by F. Madan. [Madan, *Day-book of John Dorne*. Bradshaw, *Collected Papers*, pp. 421–451.] It is probable that the I. T. for whom Treveris printed an *Opus Insolubilium* was John Dorne, for the book occurs often in his accounts. He lived in the Parish of St. Mary, and the latest dated reference to him is in 1528, though there are reasons for believing that he lived some years longer.

DOTIER (MARTIN), *see* Dature (M.).

DOWGHTON (JOHN), bookbinder in Ludlow, is mentioned twice in the church accounts in 1555–56. " Paid to John Dowghton for the bendynge of a prycke songe booke, iiij s." " Paid to John Dawghton for the bendynge of iiij Processionales and for the mendynge of one Antyphonar, iij s. viij d." [*Churchwardens' accounts of the town of Ludlow*, edited by Thomas Wright. Camden Society, London, 1869, pp. 68, 71.]

DROSELER, or DRESLARE (JOHN), bookbinder in Oxford, is mentioned in the register of Magdalen College as having bound and chained books for the library in 1502–9. [Gibson, *Oxford Bindings*, p. 46.]

DUBLE (HUBERT), *see* Danvillier (H.).

DUBLIER (HUBERT), *see* Danvillier (H.).

DUMAEUS (GODOFRIDUS), *see* Haeghen (G. van der).

DU PRÉ, DE PRATO, or LARCHER (JEAN), printer in Paris, began to print in 1481. He was the first to print service books in France, and most of his work was of that class. His place of business was in the Rue St. Jacques at the sign of the Two Swans. In 1500 he printed an edition of the Sarum *Missal*, of which three copies, all slightly imperfect, are known, which was to be sold by the booksellers in St. Paul's Church-yard. He died in 1501, and was succeeded by his widow. [Renouard, *Imprimeurs*, pp. 111, 112. *Documents*, p. 80.]

DUXWELL (THOMAS), stationer in London, is mentioned in Foxe [vol. viii, p. 74.] "One W. Gie . . . bought a Bible and service book of Richard Waterson, who then dwelt with master Duixile in Paul's Church-yard." In the list in the charter of 1557 Duxwell's name is seventeenth, and he soon became an "assistant," and in 1559-60 one of the Wardens. He entered one copy of a ballad in 1561–62, and is not found mentioned in the registers after 1566.

EDMONDS (ALEXANDER), printer in Basle, is mentioned in the colophon of John Philpot's *True report of the disputation had and begun in the convocation house at London Oct 18 1553*. "Imprinted at Basil by Alexander Edmonds." [Herbert, III, 1574.] The name is probably fictitious, and the book to all appearances was printed at Antwerp. [Sayle, III, 1364.]

EGMONT (FREDERICK), stationer in London and Paris, is first found in 1493, when he published an edition of the York *Breviary*, printed at Venice by Joannes Hertzog. [Bodl.] In 1494 he entered into partnership with Gerard Barrevelt, and together they issued in that year two editions of the Sarum *Missal*, one in folio and one in octavo, and about this time three editions of the Sarum *Breviary*, known only from fragments. In 1495 they issued a Sarum *Breviary* in 16mo, and a Sarum *Horae*, known only from fragments, belongs also to about this period. In 1499 Egmont, in partnership with Peter Post Pascha, commissioned Pynson to print an edition of the *Promptorius Puerorum*. In 1502 Egmont brought an action in the University Court of Oxford to recover £10 from George Strele, a goldsmith. He appointed Eliseus Ruthyn and Antonius de Andover his procurators on November 22nd. The device used by Egmont and Barrevelt consists of a circle divided by a perpendicular line produced beyond the top of the circle, the projection being crossed by two bars. In the left-hand division of the circle are the initials and mark of Egmont, in the right those of Barrevelt. The whole is enclosed in a square frame, and the background filled with arabesque floral design. Some time after 1502 Egmont moved to Paris, where, in partnership with a certain I. B., he published some six or seven books, using in them a device very similar to his earlier one, with the initials I. B. substituted for G. B. [Brunet, ed. 1863, v. 1279.] Egmont and his partner were in business in the Rue St. Jacques. Egmont was also a bookbinder and had at least two signed panels. One has in the centre the Tudor rose, and round it are vine leaves, in an oblong compartment. The initials and mark of Egmont are in the border. The second and more important panel contains a wild man and woman standing on either side of a tree, bearing in one hand flowering boughs, while with the others they assist in supporting a shield suspending by a belt from the branches above. Upon the shield are Egmont's mark and initials and at the base his name in full. A third panel used with the last contains three rows of arabesques of foliage surrounded by a border having ribbons in the four corners inscribed with the names of the Evangelists. The last book issued by Egmont and I. B. was an edition of Maydeston's *Dormi Secure*, dated 1527, of which there is an imperfect copy in the Bibliothèque Nationale. [*The Library*, 1890, pp. 210–16. *Bibliothèque de l'Ecole des Chartes, Tome* LI, 1890, pp. 305-309.]

EMLOS (THEOPHYLL), pseudonym. This name is found in the colophon of *A treatys callyde the Lordis flayle*, by Thomas Solme. "Printyde at Basyl by me Theophyll Emlos, vndere the sygne of sente Peters kay." [*c.* 1550.] As the printer's name is merely the author's spelt backwards it may be presumed to be a pseudonym.

EMPEROUR (MARTIN), *see* Caesar (M.).

ENDHOVEN (CHRISTOPHER VAN), *see* Ruremond (C. van).

ENGLAND (NICHOLAS), stationer in London, was an original member of the Company of Stationers, although his name is not mentioned in the charter. He lived in Paternoster Row, and published books from 1558 to 1568, employing the presses of H. Sutton, J. Day, J. Kingston, R. Hall, and H. Bynneman. He published at least twelve books, and is last mentioned in the Stationers' Registers in 1568-9.

ERVE (EGIDIUS VAN DER), printer in London, is mentioned with his wife Anna in the registers of the Dutch Church in 1551 and 1550-60. [R. of A., I, 202, 212.] He was also known as Gellius Ctematius, and it is said that the name Collinus Volkwinner (*q.v.*) was a pseudonym used by him. On Mary's accession he fled with many others, to Emden. [*Ostfriesisches Monatsblatt*, VI, 11; VII, 1.] He printed several books at Emden up to about the year 1566.

EVANS (HERMAN), stationer in Oxford, was admitted a University stationer in 1554, but was pronounced "contumax" in October, 1563. [Madan, p. 274.] There are many references to him in the University Archives between the years 1538 and 1563.

F. (G.), bookbinder. He made use of a roll containing medallion heads, birds, foliage, and his initials. [Weale, *Bookbindings*, p. 147.]

FAKES (RICHARD), *see* Faques (R.).

FAQUES (RICHARD), printer in London, succeeded William Faques and began to print with his material in 1509. He was doubtless a near relation and a native of Normandy, and we may put aside as without foundation the statement of Thomas Wilson, who, in a letter to Joseph Ames, informed him that Richard Fawkes, printer, was second son of John Fawkes, of Farnley Hall, Yorkshire, and that in a pedigree he had of that family he is called printer of London. [Herbert, I, 467.] Richard Faques' first dated book was the *Salus corporis salus anime* of Gulielmus de Saliceto, issued in December, 1509, and in 1511 he joined with W. de Worde and others in the production of a Sarum *Missal*, printed for them at Paris by Raoul Cousturier. At this period the printer always spelt his name Faques, and carried on business at the sign of the Maiden's Head in St. Paul's Churchyard. An edition of the *Liber Festivalis* [Lambeth] and a curious work by W. Hendred, *A booke of the pylgrymage of man* [Queen's Coll., Oxf.], belong to the early time. His very handsome device, found in these books, consists of a large arrow from which is suspended a shield, supported by two unicorns. On the shield are the initials R. F. above a maiden's head, in reference to his sign. Below all is a ribbon with the name Richard Faques cut upon it. The next dated book is an edition of the *Horae ad usum Sarum*, printed for him at Paris by J. Bignon in 1521. [Bodl.] In it his address is given as the sign of the

A. B. C., in St. Paul's Churchyard, and his name is spelt Fakes. He had also altered his device by cutting out from the ribbon the "ques" of his name and inserting in its place "kes" in type. In 1523 he printed an edition of Skelton's *Goodly garlande*, from the colophon of which we learn that his dwelling-house and printing office were in Durham Rents, outside Temple Bar. He had now altered his name to Faukes, and this became Fawkes in the last dated book he issued, the *Myrroure of Our Lady*, printed in 1530 at the request of the Lady Abbess of the monastery of Zion. On the reverse of the titlepage of this book is a woodcut with the engraver's mark, E. G., also found on a cut of St. Katherine used by Pynson. Though there are only five dated books with Faques' name, there are about twenty undated, but the greater number of these can, either from their subject, the spelling of the printer's name, or the state of the device, be assigned to their period. After 1530 nothing is known of Richard Faques, but in the lists of denizations is a curious entry dated 1544 relating to one Amelyne Faxe, widow, aged 70 years who had lived in England 55 years "Hath the Kinge's Magestie's proteccon of his grace gyft to Richard Faxe her husband, late deceased, to remayn and dwell within this realm, but her landlorde will not suffre her to dwell in house." [Westm. Deniz. Roll, 36 Hen. VIII.] There is a possibility that this entry may refer to the printer and if so he died in 1538 and was buried in the Parish of St. Martin in the Fields.

FAQUES (WILLIAM), printer in London, and the first to hold the official position of printer to the king. He was a Norman by birth and the only year in which he issued dated books was 1504, when he printed a proclamation about the coinage, the *Statutes of An. XIX Hen. VII* and a *Psalter*. In these books he speaks of himself as working "within St. Helen's" which was just off Bishopsgate Street. He moved later to Abchurch Lane, an address mentioned in the colophons to his *Omelia Origenis* and *Vulgaria Terentii*. He printed altogether some eight books. He probably died in the year 1508, for in that year Pynson begins to call himself king's printer, and it appears to have been the custom to appoint a new one immediately on the decease of the old. His device consisted of two interlaced triangles, on the one in white letters on a black ground is the text "Melior est patiens viro forti et qui dominat." On the other in black letters on a white ground "Melius est modicum justo super divitias peccatorum multas." In the centre is the monogram G L pierced by an arrow. William Faques' material passed on his death to Richard Faques no doubt a relation.

FAWKES (MICHAEL), printer in London, was probably a relative of Richard and William Faques. His name is only found twice, once in the colophon to *A deuout treatyse called the tree and twelve frutes of the holy goost.* The first part was printed by Robert Copland alone in 1534, the second part finished in October, 1535, was printed by Copland with Myghel Fawkes. [Herbert, I, 348, 538.] The other book he printed was the *Consolatori of timorouse and fearfull consciencys* by William Bonde [B.M.] a quarto without date.

FAYREBERNE (JOHN), stationer in London, was an original member of the Company at its incorporation. He acted as beadle to the Company and the Registers are apparently in his handwriting. He took out a license to print a ballad in 1570. After 1573 his name is not found.

FERRALL (JASPER), printer in London, was an assistant to Edward Whitchurch. He was entered in the Subsidy Roll of 1549 as taxed four shillings on goods worth four pounds. [R. of A., I, 180.]

FERREBOUC (JACQUES), printer in Paris, was at work from 1492 to about 1529. As early as 1510 he went into partnership with J. Bienayse and together they issued two Sarum *Missals* and two *Breviaries*. Ferrebouc sometimes used a punning device of a man and stag.

FERROM (JOHN), printer in London, is entered in the Subsidy Roll of 1549 as an assistant to Edward Whitchurch and was taxed four shillings on goods valued at four pounds. [R. of A., I, 180.]

FILKINS (JOHN), *see* Fylkyn (J.).

FLETEMAN (HENRY), printer in London, was an assistant to John Day and is entered in St. Anne and St. Agnes Parish, Aldersgate Ward in the Subsidy Roll of 1549. [R. of A., I, 173.]

FOLLINGHAM (WILLIAM), printer in London, is mentioned by Herbert [I, 613] as having printed one book in 1544. This was *The anatomy of a hande in the manner of a dyall.* "Imprinted at Holy Well by William Follingham for Richard Bankes." Follingham was also the author of the tract.

FOSTER (RICHARD), stationer in London, is mentioned in the colophon of Bale's *Dialogue or communycacyon to be had at a table betwene two chyldren* "printed at Lond : for Rich : Foster. an. MDXLIX." [Herbert, III, p. 1834.] He was presumably a member of the Stationers' Company, for we find in their Register [Arber, I, p. 186] "Recevyd of John Foster for his Admyttinge to be freman of this Companye by his faythers Copye the xxj Daye of octobre Anno 1561. iij^s iiij^d." The father must therefore have been a freeman of the Company before 1537.

FOXE (FRANCIS), printer in Strasburg, is known as the printer of the *Psalter of David* in English in 1530 known as the *Psalter of Feline* [B.M.], the first printed English translation of the Psalms.

FOXE (JAMES), stationer in London, came to England about 1533. He took out letters of denization in 1541 "April 14 James Foxe, from the dominion of the Emperor. In England 8 years." [Deniz. Roll, 32 Hen. VIII.] In the Subsidy Rolls of 1541 and 1544 he is entered as an assistant of John Reynes, living in St. Faith's Parish. [R. of A., I, 67, 93.] In Reynes' will, proved February, 1544, he is mentioned as "Jamys my dutchman" and received a legacy of twenty shillings. [Plomer, Wills, p. 6.]

FOXE (JOHN), stationer in London, was an original member of the Stationers' Company having been made free in March, 1555. He is frequently entered in the Registers sometimes as taking apprentices, sometimes as paying fines for non-attendance on quarter-days. He was admitted to the Livery in 1564-65. He is last entered in August, 1570, when he took Humphrey Foxe as an apprentice. It would appear that he died at the end of the year, as there is an entry between November 13th, 1570, and January 5th, 1571, "Receyved of Mistres Foxe for the herse cloth xij d."

FRANCKENBERGK, or VRANKENBERGH (HENRY), stationer in London, is first mentioned in a deed in the Record Office "Demise to Henry Franckenbergh and Barnard van Stondo, merchants of printed books of an alley in St. Clement's Lane called St. Mark's Alley. May 10 . 1482." About 1486 he paid for an edition of Watton's *Speculum Christiani* which was printed for him by William de Machlinia.

FRANCKINE (JOHN), bookbinder in York, is mentioned in the *Fabric Rolls of the Minster* 1509-10 [p. 95] "Pro les bynding librorum Johanni Hurson et Johanni Franckine 15 s. 4ᵈ."

FREEMAN (CONRAD), pseudonym, is the name found in the colophon of a book by Luther *A faythfull admonycion* stated to have been printed at Greenwich in 1554. It is clear however from the type used, that the book was printed at Zurich by Christopher Froschauer.

FREEZ (FREDERICK), *see* Wandsforth (F.).

FRELLON (JEAN), printer in Lyons, issued in 1549 *The images of the Old Testament* with wood engravings by Hans Holbein. [Herbert, III, p. 1565.] A Jean Frellon was a printer at Paris in 1508, went to Lyons in 1518 and returned to Paris in 1522. [Renouard, p. 138.] This may very probably be the father of the later Lyons printer.

FRENCHE (PETER), stationer in London, was an original member of the Company on its incorporation. He is mentioned frequently in the Registers as taking apprentices, entering copies and paying fines. He is not mentioned after 1580, so that he probably died about that time. His daughter Mary married July 3rd, 1593, Robert Lewes of St. Bride's London, stationer. [*London Marriage Licenses*, p. 208.]

FRIES (AUGUSTINE), printer in Zurich and Strasburg, began to print at the former place about 1540. In 1547 he printed two books in English by John Hooper. [Heitz, p. 39.] Soon after this he moved to Strasburg and there printed among other things several works in Spanish by Franzisco de Enzinas in 1550 and 1551. [Wiffen, I, pp. 179, etc.]

FROOST (JAN), *see* Troost (J.).

FROSCHAUER (CHRISTOPHER), printer in Zurich, was born at Neuburg but became a citizen of Zurich in 1519 and started a press in that city shortly afterwards. His earliest dated books appeared in 1521 and from that time onwards up to his death in 1564 he printed a very large number of books especially noteworthy for their scholarly character. He printed a large number of English books generally without, or with a false, imprint. His most important undertaking was the first edition of the *Bible* in English which was published by James Nicholson of Southwark in 1535. It has for long been a vexed question where and by whom this Bible was printed but the matter seems now definitely settled. In 1545 Froschauer printed William Turner's *Rescuynge of the Romishe Fox* which has as a colophon "Imprynted have at Winchester 1545. 4. nonas Martii. By me Hanse hit prik" and which has occasionally been quoted as a Winchester printed book. Another of his books with a false imprint is Luther's *Faythfull admonycion of a certen trewe pastor*, with the colophon "Imprinted at Grenewych by Conrade Freeman in the month of May 1554." In 1555 he issued Gesner's *Mithridates* which contains specimens of printing in Welsh. His devices, which however do not occur in the English books contains figures of frogs, a punning allusion to his name. [Rudolphi. *Die Buchdrucker-Familie Froschauer in Zürich*, 1869. 8vo.] Mr. Sayle [Cat. III, p. 1413] attributes also to Froschauer, on account of the similarity of type, *De Christlicke Ordinancien*, of which the colophon runs "Ghedruckt buyten Londen, doer Collinus Volckwinner, anno 1554." It has also been supposed that Collinus Volckwinner was a pseudonym of Egidius van der Erve or Gillius Ctematius a refugee printer in London about that period. In any case the work of Froschauer for England was more extensive than is generally supposed. About 1552 Christopher Froschauer II, nephew of the elder Christopher, who had gone through his course at Oxford went out to Zurich and joined his uncle in the printing business to which he succeeded altogether in 1564.

FROST (FRANCIS), bookseller in Edinburgh, and William Frost were two of the four booksellers who infringed the patent granted to Walter Chapman and who were restrained by an injunction granted January 14th, 1509–10. [Dickson and Edmond, p. 84.]

FROST (WILLIAM), *see* Frost (Francis).

FRYER (ROBERT), stationer in London, is mentioned in the following entry; "1553 Item paid to Robert Fryer for two antiphons, ij grales, ij masse boks, one legend one manuell, one venite booke, iij processyons and one dirige booke x li. xvi.s. viij d." [*Transcript of the Registers of the united parishes of S. Mary Woolnoth and S. Mary Woolchurch Haw*. 8vo, 1886, p. xix.]

G

FYDLYNGE (RICHARD), stationer in London, was an original member of the Stationers' Company having been made free on December 13th, 1556. He presented apprentices in 1593 and 1598.

FYDYON, stationer in Cambridge, was "stationarius" to the University about 1481-2. He appears to have been dishonest in his work, and his goods and house were sold to make good his debts.

FYLDE (DAVID), bookbinder in London, lived in St. Anne's Parish, Aldersgate Ward, and is entered in the Subsidy Roll of 1541. [R. of A., I, 49.] As he had no goods, and simply paid the poll tax of fourpence, he was probably an assistant to someone else and not in business on his own account. He is mentioned in St. Botolph's Parish, Aldersgate, about 1544 when his goods were valued at twenty shillings and in St. Giles' Cripplegate in 1549 when his goods were worth forty shillings. [R. of A., I, 84, 174.]

FYLKYN, or FILKINS (JOHN), stationer in London, though not entered on the charter, was an original member of the Stationers' Company, having been made free April 27th, 1557. He was admitted into the livery in June, 1570. He lived in the Parish of St. Bride's Fleet Street. His will dated 1574 was proved in the Prerogative Court of Canterbury. [24, Martyn.]

G. (E.), bookbinder, made use of two panels. On one is a shield with the arms of England and France, supported by a dragon and greyhound and above these the sun and moon and two shields with St. George's Cross. Below is the Tudor rose supported by angels with two scrolls bearing the motto "Hec rosa virtutis de celo missa sereno, Eternum florens regia sceptra feret." Above the angels are the sun and moon and two shields with the binder's mark. The other panel contains a large shield with the arms of Henry VIII and Katherine of Aragon with the binder's initials on a small shield at the base. This binding was reproduced in the Burlington Club illustrated catalogue of bookbindings. [Weale, *Bookbindings*, pp. 125-6.]

G. (G.), bookbinder in London, made use of two panels. On one is a large shield with the arms of England and France supported by angels. On the other is the Tudor rose supported by angels with the motto on a ribbon

"Hec rosa virtutis de celo missa sereno: eternum florens regia sceptra feret." In the upper corners are two shields containing the cross of St. George and the arms of the City of London, and at the base a shield with the binder's initials and mark. [Weale, *Bookbindings*, p. 123.]

G. (G.), bookbinder, *see* Godfrey (Garrat).

G. (I.), bookbinder, was in partnership with W. G. They made use of a roll ornamented with a dragon, a gryphon, and flowers and their monograms. [Weale, *Bookbindings*, p. 118.] A volume in Archbishop Marsh's library, Dublin, is tooled with this roll worked in gold.

G. (I.), bookbinder, made use of a panel with a figure of St. John Baptist in the upper part, the rest being filled up with artichoke ornament and scrolls of bramble and other foliage. [Weale, *Bookbindings*, p. 136.]

G. (N.), binder in Cambridge, is mentioned by Weale [Bookbindings, I, xxxix] and Gray [*Cambridge Stationers*, p. 52]. It appears clear that the G is a badly-formed S and as the binder's mark is identical with that of Nicholas Speryng we may conclude that the latter was the binder.

G. (S.), bookbinder in England, who made use of two panel stamps. On one is St. George and the Dragon on the other a formal pattern. His initials joined by a knot are on a shield.

G. (S.), bookbinder, used two panel stamps. One divided into four parts contains figures of St. John, St. Barbara, St. Katherine and St. Nicholas. Round all is a border of birds and foliage with the binder's initials at the base. The other panel contains a column from which spring four branches terminating in flowers and fruit with a border of cresting terminating in acorns. [Weale, *Bookbindings*, pp. 134-5.] Three books printed by W. de Worde are known in this binding.

G. (T.), bookbinder, *see* Godfray (Thomas).

G. (W.), bookbinder about the end of the fifteenth century made use of a small shield-shaped die containing his initials and mark. From the lining of his bindings most of the known fragments of the *Horae ad usum Sarum* printed by William de Machlinia about 1485 have been obtained. This mark and initials as well as the initials I.G. joined by an ornamental knot are found on an early roll with fabulous animals and foliage, which may be dated about 1520.

GACHET, GASCHET or GATCHET (JOHN), stationer in York and Hereford, was a native of France. He is first mentioned in the colophon of a York *Manual* printed at London by Wynkyn de Worde in 1509 "pro Johanne gaschet et Jacobo ferrebouc sociis." Jacques Ferrebouc was a Paris stationer and there is nothing in the colophon to show whether Gachet was with him in Paris or in business in York. If he was not, he soon afterwards settled there, for in 1514 he was admitted a brother of the Corpus Christi Guild. In 1516 and 1517 he issued several service books of York use printed for him at Rouen by P. Olivier. Soon after February, 1517, Gachet seems to have left York and gone to Hereford, for he issued there in May an edition of the *Ortus Vocabulorum* printed at Rouen by J. Caillard. During the nine years after 1517 nothing more is known of Gachet nor were any books printed for York, but in 1526 he reappeared there and published a *Breviary* printed for him at Paris by F. Regnault. Between 1530 and 1533 he issued a few more service books but seems after that to have given up publishing. The last entry concerning him is in the registers of denizations. [Pat. 27 Hen. VIII, p. 1, m. 15.] "John Gatchett, alias Frencheman of the city of York, bokebynder, from the dominion of the King of France, 10 May 1535." As he was neither a denizen nor a freeman of the City during his business career, he lived in the precincts of the Cathedral, in the Parish of St. Michael le Belfry, probably in "Bookbinder's Alley" on the south side of the close, perhaps in the house vacated shortly before 1516 by Ursin Mylner on becoming a freeman. Gachet had apparently three sons, John, a soldier, sent in 1545 from York to Newcastle [Corp. Minutes, xvii, 100b] who died at Rawcliffe in 1551, George, and William, a stationer who was admitted to the freedom of the City in 1549-50.

GACHET (WILLIAM), stationer in York, was most probably a son of John Gachet. He was admitted to the freedom of the City in 1550-51. [*Freemen of York*, p. 270.]

GALTIER (THOMAS), *see* Gaultier (T.).

GAMLYN or GAMMON (ALLEN), stationer in London, was an original member of the Stationers' Company. His son Vincent was admitted a freeman by patrimony in 1582 but it is not stated in the register whether or not the father was dead.

GARNETT (RICHARD), stationer in York, was entered with his wife Isabel in the Register of the Corpus Christi Guild in 1490. [*Register of the Guild of Corpus Christi*, p. 123.] In 1492 he was one of the Chamberlains of the City. [*Freemen of York*, p. 217.] He is mentioned again in 1502 "March 10, 17 Hen. VII. Item it is agreed and graunted by the sayd presence that Ric. Garnet stacioner shall pay iiij^li and be discharged of beryng any office within this Citie for ever and therof to have sufficient wryttyng in discharge of ye same under the comon seale." [York City House Books, No. 8.]

GARRET, stationer in Oxford, was an apprentice to Garret Pilgrim who in his will dated 1536 left him six and eightpence and a new coat. [Arch. Univ. Oxon., Registrum E.E.E.]

GASCHET (JOHN), *see* Gachet (J.).

GASTUS (HENRY), printer in London, was an assistant to Rayner Wolfe and is entered in St. Faith's Parish in the Subsidy Roll of 1549. [R. of A., I, 159.]

GATCHET (JOHN), *see* Gachet (J.).

GAULTIER, GALTIER or GUALTIER (THOMAS), printer in London, was a native of France. He took out letters of denization in 1544. "Thomas Galtyer, born in France. Has been long in England and married to an English woman. 1 July, 1544." [West. Deniz. Roll, 36 Hen. VIII.] He printed only between 1550 and 1553 and was appointed King's Printer for French service books. His printing office was in the Parish of St. Martin's, Ludgate, near Fleet bridge.

GAVER (JAMES), stationer in London, was a member of the large family of Van Gavere, binders in the Low Countries. He was employed as an assistant by Wynkyn de Worde who on his death bequeathed him books to the value of twenty marks and appointed him one of the executors of his will, the other being John Byddell. On March 2nd, 1535, Gaver took out letters of denization in which he is described as "stationer from the dominion of the Emperor." [Pat. 26 Hen. VIII, p. 2, m. 42.] He appears to have continued to live with Byddell in De Worde's house, the Sun in Fleet Street and in 1539 issued from that address an edition of

Stanbridge's *Accidence* apparently identical with the edition issued by N. Bourman. In 1541 Gaver's goods were valued at five pounds and in 1544 at thirty. [R. of A., I, 94.] He died in 1545 and his will was proved on June 15th of that year. He requested to be buried in St. Bride's Church near Wynkyn de Worde and appointed as overseer to his will his son-in-law William Stewarde, a stationer. Bequests are left to his wife Joan, his daughter Mary Stewarde and his grandchildren Barbara, John and Catheryn. [*The Library*, N.S., vol. ii, p. 384.]

GEE (THOMAS), stationer in London, was an original member of the Stationers' Company having been made free May 9th, 1555. Beyond having given a subscription he is not mentioned elsewhere in the Registers.

GEMINI (THOMAS), engraver and printer in London, is best known from the plates and extremely beautiful titlepage of the *Compendiosa totius anatomiae delineatio* issued by John Hertford in 1545. This was printed again in 1552 by N. Hill and in 1559 by Gemini himself, and in both these later editions alterations have been made in the titlepage owing to the altered dedications to Edward VI and Elizabeth. In 1554 he is mentioned in the Stationers' Register "21 July. Rec. of Tho. Gemyne stranger for transgressynge the ordenaunce of this house, callynge a brother of the companye falsse knave, xij d." [Arber, I, p. 44.] He also gave the Stationers a subscription of xx^d· for the house at Brydewell. Besides the last edition of the book on anatomy, he printed in 1555 Digges' *Prognostication* [U.L.C.] and in 1562 his *Boke named Tectonicon*. [U.L.C.] The name of Gemini is not found in the list of denizations, nor in the Returns of Aliens, but as there are no returns between 1544 and 1564, he may have died or left England before the latter date. His place of business was in the Blackfriars, a part mainly inhabited by foreigners as being one of the liberties where they could not be disturbed in their trade. [D.N.B.]

GEYSON (GYSBERD), printer in London, was an assistant to John Day, and is entered in St. Anne and St. Agnes Parish, Aldersgate Ward in the Subsidy Roll of 1549. [R. of A., I, 173.] He is perhaps the same as the Gysbert Goversoen entered in the list of members of the Dutch Church 1550-60. [R. of A., I, 204.]

GIBSON (THOMAS), printer in London, was born at Morpeth, Northumberland, and perhaps educated at Cambridge. He apparently only carried on business between the years 1535 and 1539. In 1535 he printed a *Concordance to the New Testament* [B.M.] of which he appears to have been the compiler, and in 1536 a book on the Plague [Lambeth]. On the completion of *The institution of a christian man* by the bishops, Latimer endeavoured to persuade Cromwell to entrust the printing to Gibson but without success and in 1537 it was issued by Berthelet. In 1538 Gibson is mentioned in the minute book of the Court of Aldermen. " Item. That Mr. Chamberleyn shall pay unto the prynter Thomas Gibson for diverse papers and other bookes prynted by him concernynge the thamyse and ward mote enquests li.s. iiii d." [Bibl. Soc. Trans., VI, 17.] In 1539 he printed a *Herbal* and a *Paraphrase on the Psalms.* [B.M.] Herbert gives altogether five books as printed by him. The woodcut with the initials T. G., used by Gibson as a device was later on in the possession of John Day and it has been supposed that he was Gibson's apprentice, but this was not the case. Gibson seems to have ceased printing in 1539, but continued in London until Mary's reign when he fled to Geneva with his wife and daughter. In Elizabeth's reign he returned and practised medicine, dying in London in 1562. [D.N.B.]

GILES, bookbinder in Oxford, is entered in the registers of Magdalen College as having bound books for the library in 1507-10. [Gibson, *Oxford Bindings*, p. 46.]

GODDARD (GILES), *see* Godet (G.).

GODET (GILES), stationer in London, took out letters of denization April 8th, 1551 [Pat. 5 Edw. VI, p. 5, m. 28], and was admitted a brother of the Stationers' Company May 16th, 1555. In 1562 he was living in Black-friars and is mentioned in the Returns of Aliens [I, 290]. His best known work was the *Genealogie of the Kings of England*, a series of sheets containing large woodcuts, for which he obtained a license in 1562-3. He seems to have been a wood engraver and his publications consisted almost entirely of woodcuts. In 1564 and 1567 he is entered in the Returns of Aliens [I, 303, 360] as Goddard and Gubbett, and is said in the last entry to have been in England twenty years. The last entry to him in the Stationers' Registers was between July, 1567, and July, 1568.

GODFRAY (THOMAS), printer in London, issued only one dated book, the first complete edition of *Chaucer's Works* published in 1532. Of undated books he printed a large number and from internal evidence one book at least can be proved later than 1535, a date referred to in Christopher St. Germain's *Answer to a letter.* [Queen's Coll., Oxon.] In two books only does Godfray mention any address, the grammar of Stanbridge, *Sum Es Fui* was printed "in the Old Bailey," the *Exoneratorium Curatorum* "at Temple Bar." His press seems in some mysterious way to have been connected with that of Berthelet and some have gone so far as to assert that Godfray was not a printer at all and that the books with his name were printed by Berthelet. With our present knowledge this seems more than doubtful, though Berthelet certainly came into possession of Godfray's material and many undated and unsigned books are dubiously assigned to one or the other printer. Almost all Godfray's books were of a religious or controversial nature, but amongst the exceptions may be named Skelton's *Colin Clout* and Giles Dewes' *Introductorie for to lerne Frenche.* [Bodl.] In the latter book is found the woodcut border used so frequently at a later date by Berthelet and it was while this book was being printed that the block split down the centre, for it occurs in both states. In 1534 Godfray printed for William Marshall the *Gift of Constantine*, and writing about it to Cromwell Marshall states "On the book of Constantine I have laid out all the money I can make, and for lack of it cannot fetch the books from the printer's." [*Letters and papers of Henry VIII*, vol. vii, p. 178, etc.] Unfortunately Marshall does not mention the name of the printer. Over thirty works are ascribed to Godfray's press and perhaps others are his which are at present given to Berthelet. He used no device, that ascribed to him by Herbert and others is apparently a monogram on a shield composed of the letters T or F and G which is found on a panel binding in renaissance style with heads in medallions.

GODFREY (GARRAT), stationer in Cambridge, was apparently a native of Graten in Limburg. He is first mentioned as a stationer in a document of 1503. He lived in the parish of St. Mary's and from 1513 onwards was closely connected with the Church. In 1523–4 he is entered in the Subsidy Roll as "Garrard Goddefrey Ducheman" and his goods were valued at twenty pounds. In 1534 he was appointed one of the three University stationers and various entries occur in accounts relating to him up to 1539.

He died in the autumn of that year, and his will dated September 12th was proved on October 11th. In it he left bequests to Segar Nicholson the stationer his cousin, and to his brother Martin's children James, Katherine and Elizabeth. His binding material he left to his assistant Nicholas Pilgrim and the residue of his estate to his wife Agnes. He used several handsome rolls on his bindings. The largest has figures of a lion, a wivern, a gryphon and the binder's mark and initials amongst branches of foliage. A smaller roll is divided into compartments containing a rose, a pomegranate, a fleur-de-lys and castle gate-way all surmounted by a crown, and the binder's initials. Another roll has the same emblems and in addition a shield with three horse-shoes between the initials G. G. [Gray, *Cambridge Stationers*, pp. 28–43.]

GOES (HUGO), printer in York, is generally presumed to have been connected with Mathias van der Goes a printer of Antwerp, but for this there is no more evidence than the similarity of names. In 1509 he printed an edition of the York *Directorium*, the only specimen of his work now known. The type used in this book is an early one of W. de Worde's which he had used at Westminster. There is good evidence for ascribing two other books to Goes as they are described in a manuscript note written by Christopher Hildyard [July 12th, 1667] in his copy of his List of Mayors etc. of York, 1664. These are a *Donatus minor cum Remigio* and an *Accidence*, both without date but bound up with a grammar printed by W. de Worde in 1506. Ames mentions a broadside belonging in his time to Thomas Martin of Palgrave "containing a wooden cut of a man on horse-back, with a spear in his right hand and a shield of the arms of France in his left ' Emprynted at Beverley in the Hyegate by me Hewe Goes' with his mark or rebus of a great H and a goose." Ames also mentions a Latin grammar printed at London which was in the Harleian Library, and to this a note of Bagford's [Harl. MS. 5974, 95] may refer; "Donatus cum Remigio impressus Londoniis per me Hugonem Goes and Henery Watson, with the printer's device H. G." A Henry Watson was an assistant of De Worde's as early as 1509. Goes' place of business at York was in the Steengate but no sign is mentioned.

GONNELD (JAMES), stationer in London, was an original member of the Company on its incorporation. Though neither printer nor publisher he seems to have been an important member of the Company. He was

Warden on four successive occasions 1565-6, 1567-8, 1572-3, 1576-7 and
Master on three 1579-80, 1582-3, and 1585-6: he also frequently acted as
auditor.   He had a son Benjamin in holy orders.   His will dated 1594 was
proved in the Prerogative Court of Canterbury.   [85 Dixy.]   He lived in
the Parish of St. Sepulchre.

GORE (JOHN), stationer in Oxford, is mentioned in the Magdalen College
Register as having taken a lease of a house and garden in St. Mary's Parish,
next to that of Pole, a stationer, 17th May, 1551, for 20 years at an annual
rental of 36s. 8d.   He is mentioned as a bookseller in another lease in 1574.
[Madan, p. 274.]

GOUGE, or GOUGH (JOHN), see Gowghe (J.).

GOUPIL (RICHARD), printer at Rouen about 1510, lived at the sign of the
"Tuile d'Or."   He printed an edition of the *Cato cum commento* for Martin
Coffin of Exeter of which no copy is now known.   [Herbert III, p. 1531.]

GOVERSOEN (GYSBERT), see Geyson (G.).

GOWGHE, GOUGE, or GOUGH (JOHN), stationer in London, began
business on his own account in 1526 in Fleet Street.   In 1528 he was
examined on suspicion of dealing in heretical books and in his examination
stated that he had only been in business for two years and before that was
servant to another.   [*Letters and papers of Henry VIII*, vol. iv, pt. ii,
p. 1803.]   By 1532 he had moved to Cheapside at the sign of the Mermaid,
Rastell's old shop, and in that year W. de Worde printed two books for him.
In 1535 he was an overseer of De Worde's will and received a legacy of
four pounds in books, besides forgiveness of debts.   In the year following
he was a witness to John Rastell's will.   The majority of Gough's books
were printed for him by J. Nicholson or John Mayler and he seems to
have done little or no practical printing himself.   In 1540 he is described as
living "in Lombardstrete, at the sygne of the Marmayde, agaynste the
stockes market."   In 1541 he got into trouble for resorting to Thomas
Lancaster who brought over prohibited books [Foxe, vol. v, p. 448] and
on January 8th he was sent to the Fleet for printing and selling seditious
books.   [*Acts of the Privy Council*, vol. vii, p. 107.]   He died in 1543
and his will is preserved in the Prerogative Court of Canterbury.   [132

Story.] His son John was vicar of Braintree in Essex from 1554 to 1556 and of St. Peter's Cornhill from 15th November, 1560, to 1567. [*Diary of Machyn*, p. 269, and note. D.N.B.]

GOWGHE (JOHN), stationer in London, is mentioned in the list in the Stationers' Company's charter of 1557 but his name is not found again. It is improbable that he was the son of the earlier John Gowghe who died in 1543, as that John Gowghe was a clergyman, though Robert Crowley, another stationer, was in holy orders. A John Goughe, scrivener, is mentioned in 1553-5 in the accounts of the churchwardens of St. Martin-in-the-Fields.

GOWTHWAITE (JOHN), bookbinder in York, was made a freeman in 1555-6. [*Freemen of York*, p. 277.] He is mentioned in the *York Minster Fabric Rolls* [p. 114] in 1567-8 "To John Gowethwayt for the Salme bookes 3ˢ· and for a Byble to the churche bought by Mʳ— 26ˢ 8ᵈ."

GRAFTON (RICHARD), printer in London, was the son of Nicholas Grafton of Shrewsbury. In 1526 he was apprenticed to John Blage of London and became a freeman of the Grocers' Company in 1534. He early turned his attention to the printing of Bibles and in partnership with Edward Whitchurch and assisted by Anthony Marler produced several editions. In 1541 he was imprisoned for printing some ballads relating to the death of Cromwell. [*Acts of the P.C.*, Series I, vol. vii, p. 107.] He was again imprisoned along with a number of other printers in 1543 for printing unlawful books. [*Acts of the P.C.*, New Series, vol. i, pp. 107, etc.] About this time Grafton's productions consisted mainly of service books, and in 1544 he obtained together with Whitchurch an exclusive patent for printing such books. In 1547 on the accession of Edward VI Grafton was appointed printer to the King and during the reign issued a very large number of books, including the various issues of the *Prayer-book*. On the death of Edward VI Grafton printed the proclamation of Queen Jane which brought down on him the vengeance of Mary who deprived him of the office, appointing John Cawood in his place. After this Grafton printed but little. He died in 1573 having been twice married, leaving four sons and one daughter Joan who married Richard Tottel, the printer. Grafton's place of business was in the Greyfriars, and he used as a device a branch or graft issuing from a tun. [D.N.B.]

GRANDYSSHE (NICHOLAS), stationer in London, is mentioned in the list of contributions made by members of the Stationers' Company to Bridewell in 1556. [Arber, I, 47.] He may have died about this time as he is not mentioned in the charter of 1557, nor is his name found after that date in the Registers.

GRAPHAEUS (JOANNES), printer in Antwerp, was born at Alost in 1502. He was admitted as a printer in the St. Lucas Gilde in 1532. His place of business was in Broad Street at the sign of the Pen. He used four devices, two with a figure of Charity and two with a hand holding a pen. [Van Havre.] In 1534 he printed an edition of the *Rudimenta Grammatices* for the use of Wolsey's school at Ipswich and may also have printed in the same year the *Historia Evangelica* of Juvencus, which was to be sold in that town by Reginald Oliver. [*Bibliographica*, II, p. 33.]

GRAVE (NICOLAAS DE), printer in Antwerp, commenced to print about 1499 near the church of Notre Dame by the Camerpoorte. He continued to print at least as late as 1535. [Olthoff, p. 41.] He issued in 1516 an English translation of the *Prognostication* of Jasper Laet for 1517 with the colophon "Emprented by Nycolas the Grave." [B.M.]

GRENE (RICHARD), stationer in London, was an original member of the Stationers' Company on its incorporation. He appears to have taken a number of apprentices and was received into the Livery in 1570-1. In 1577-79 he was Renter and in 1587-88 was chosen a Warden but refused to serve for which he was fined £5. After this date his name is not found. He was still alive in May, 1590, when his daughter Jane was married to Lewis Winton of the Inner Temple. [*London Marriage Licenses*, p. 186.]

GRESSOP, bookbinder in Oxford, was in business about 1525. He is mentioned in a note in a manuscript in the Bodleian which was "resarcitus per Gressopum." [Madan, p. 273.]

GREY (THOMAS), printer in London, was an assistant to Thomas Petyt, and is entered in St. Faith's Parish in the Subsidy Roll of 1541. [R. of A., I, 67.]

GROWTE or GROYAT (JOHN), stationer in London, was a native of Normandy and took out letters of denization on October 1st, 1535. [Pat. 27 Hen. VIII, p. 1, m. 16.] He carried on business "within the Blackfriars, next the church door." Between 1532 and 1534 he had three editions of the Sarum *Horae* printed for him at Paris by Yolande Bonhomme, widow of Thielman Kerver, and one edition of the York *Horae* printed at Rouen by Nicholas le Roux in 1536. In 1541 he is mentioned in the Returns of Aliens as a bookbinder dwelling in the Parish of St. Anne's Ludgate and in 1544 as dwelling in Blackfriars ; in both cases he is taxed on goods valued twenty pounds. [R. of A., I, pp. 67, 94.] In 1549 he is again entered in the Parish of St. Martin's Ludgate.

GRYFFYTH (WILLIAM), printer in London, commenced to print about the year 1552 when he issued a broadside by Churchyard against Camell, and in 1553 issued Beeard's *Godly psalme of Mary Queen*. At first he printed at the sign of the Griffin in Fleet Street a little above the Conduit but in 1556 his address was "the Falcon against S. Dunstan's church" while his books were to be sold at the Griffin. At a still later date the shop with the sign of the Griffin was apparently given up, and books were to be sold "at the little shop in St. Dunstan's churchyard." Gryffyth was an original member of the Stationers' Company on its incorporation and is very frequently entered in the Registers. Considering the large number of copies he entered, his books are curiously few and scarce. Herbert mentions only seven and only about double that number are known. As a device he used a griffin seated holding a shield with his mark and with a spray of "Sweet William" in its mouth.

GRYPHIUS (JOANNES), printer in Venice, was one of the large family of printers of that name who worked also at Paris and Lyons. He began to print about 1550 and continued in business for many years. As a device he used the figure of a griffin. In 1551 he printed a work by Thomas Raynalde, *The vertues of the Oyle Imperial*. [Herbert, III, p. 1570.]

GUALTIER (THOMAS), *see* Gaultier (T.).

GUBBETT (GILES), *see* Godet (G.).

GUERIN, printer in London, was an assistant to John Rastell. He is mentioned in the account of a law-suit relating to Rastell's printing office in 1534-5. Though there called a Dutchman he was more probably a Norman. [*Bibliographica*, II, 440.]

GUERIN (PIERRE), stationer in Rouen, carried on business from 1505-17 in the Rue Ganterie at the sign of La Hache. In this last year he is said to have issued a Sarum *Missal* printed by Daubet, but its existence is doubtful. From 1520 to 1547 he lived in the Rue de L'Ecureuil in the Parish of St. Lawrence and while there issued a Sarum *Horae*, of which the only copy known [B.M.] is unfortunately imperfect at the end, so that the name of the printer cannot be ascertained. Guerin's device was a shield on which are his mark and initials hanging from an oak tree with flowers on either side, and at the base the name P. Guerin.

GYBKYN (JOHN), stationer in London, is first mentioned in the year 1541 in the Returns of Aliens, at which time he was an assistant to John Cockes another alien stationer. By the year 1547 he was apparently in business on his own account, and in 1549 had an assistant named Conrad Molyer. Strype in the *Ecclesiastical Memorials* [vol. ii, p. 317] under the year 1551 speaks of him as a Dutchman lately made free. In this same year he had a shop in St. Paul's Churchyard with the sign of the Spread Eagle and had two books, the *Summa Christianae religionis* by F. Perussellus and the *New Herbal*, printed for him by Stephen Mierdman, a refugee printer from Antwerp. Gybkyn, though a foreigner and though his name is not found in the Registers, was an original member of the Stationers' Company as we learn from the following curious entry April 11th, 1586 [Arber, II, 696], "John Gypkin sonne of John Gypkyn Cytizen and Stationer of London Deceased, Admytted a freman [per patronagium] the Day and yere abouesaid but not sworne 'quia surdus et mutus est.'"

GYBSON (THOMAS), *see* Gibson (T.).

H. (A.), bookbinder, used two panels. On one is the Annunciation with the binder's initials below, on the other the Tudor rose and angels supporting a ribbon with the motto "Hec rosa virtutis de celo missa sereno: eternum florens regia sceptra feret" and at the base the binder's initials. [Weale, *Bookbindings*, p. 126.] This binder used a kind of sheepskin and not the more usual calf.

H. (G.), one of the two persons for whom J. Higman and W. Hopyl printed an edition of the Sarum *Missal* in 1500, " I B, G H, me fieri fecerunt."

H. (I.), printer in London, was in partnership about 1496-7 with Julian Notary and Jean Barbier when they were printing in London. It seems extremely probable that the initials stand for Jean Huvin.

HACKET (JOHN), bookbinder in London, was a native of France and came to England in 1547. In 1567 he was living in the Tower Ward, but in 1571 he was entered in the Returns of Aliens in St. Faith's Parish " John Hackett, booĸebynder, borne in France, servaunte to Francis Caldock, in England 24 yeares, and in the said warde ij yeares." [R. of A., I, 411.] In 1566 he is mentioned in the Stationers' Registers " Recevyd of John Hackett for his admyttinge brother of this howse the xiij of Januarii ij.s. vj d." [Arber, I, 318.]

HACKET or HAQUET (THOMAS), bookbinder in London, appears to have come to England about 1534. In 1544 he took out letters of denization " Thomas Hackette, Frenchman : in England 10 years. Married to an English woman. 1 July 1544." [Westm. Deniz. Rolls, 36 Hen. VIII.] He lived in St. Olave's Parish, Tower Ward and occurs in the Subsidy Roll of 1547 with goods valued at £5 and taxed 3s. 4d. [R. of A., I, 136.] In 1550 with goods the same value he is taxed 5s. [R. of A., I, 185.] In 1562 and 1564 he is again mentioned but in the latter year his goods are only valued at £2 and his tax is 4s. [R. of A., I, 289, 294.] In the two full returns of 1571 he is called a bookbinder from St. Nicholas in Normandy who had lived in St. Olave's Parish twenty-four years and in London thirty years. He had a servant named Matthew, a Dutchman. [R. of A., I, 454; II, 135.] The last entry of his name is in 1582 when he was still working as a bookbinder in Tower Ward. [R. of A., II, 280.] In 1564 he had two assistants Nicholas Gillet and John de Sheron.

HACKET (THOMAS), printer in London, was an original member of the Stationers' Company though not entered in the list in the Charter of 1557. In 1560 when his first dated book was issued his shop was " in Cannynge strete over agaynste the three Cranes." In 1562 he had moved to Lombard Street while in 1568 he was in St. Paul's Churchyard at the sign of the

Key. In 1574 his shop was "the Greene Dragon in the Royall Exchange" while his final move (by 1584) was to "Lumberd streete under the signe of the Pope's head." In 1569 he came on the Livery of the Stationers' Company and in 1576 acted as Renter. In June, 1582, his son Ambrose became a freeman by patrimony. Thomas Hacket seems to have been a prolific printer and entered a very large number of copies in the Registers. He is last mentioned in 1589 and his last dated book was issued in 1590.

HAEGHEN (ANGELL VAN DER), bookseller in Antwerp and London, was perhaps the widow of Godfried van der Haeghen. She is mentioned in some Exchequer accounts of the latter part of the reign of Henry VIII "Engell Vanderhage of Antwerp, wedowe, hathe in bookes prynted in thaundes of Eheret Harkes her factor, xxli." Harkes had a shop in St. Paul's Churchyard.

HAEGHEN (GODFRIED VAN DER), or DUMAEUS (GODOFRIDUS), printer in Antwerp, was at work between the years 1527 and 1536. He was entered as a printer in 1533 in the St. Lucas Gilde but most of his printing appears to have been done for him by Martin Caesar. He issued some editions of the Grammar of Colet and the *Liellus de octo orationis partium constructione* of Lily and Erasmus and also the English *New Testament* of 1534-5. [Bradshaw, *Collected Papers*, pp. 354-70. Olthoff, p. 43.]

HAGHE (INGHELBERT), stationer in Hereford, was a native of Rouen where an edition of the Hereford *Breviary* was printed for him in 1505. On a loose sheet of paper [in the Bodleian] which once formed a flyleaf to a volume of a *Bible* in Gloucester Cathedral is the inscription "Dedi bibliopole herfordensi Ingleberto nuncupato pro isto et sex reliquis libris biblie xlvj s. iiij d. quos emi ludlowie anno domini incarnationis millesimo quingentesimo decimo circiter diem nundinarum lichefeldensium."

HALL (ROWLAND), printer in Geneva and London, appears to have been an original member of the Company of Stationers though his name is not in the Charter. At the time it was passed he was probably in Geneva where he printed until 1560. On returning to England he started a printing office in London at the sign of the Three Arrows in Golding Lane near Cripplegate, moving shortly after to the Half-Eagle and Key in Gutter Lane. Between 1560 and 1563 he printed a large number of books, mostly theological. He died in September, 1563, and was buried on the 18th at the church of St. Vedast in Foster Lane. He used as a device the Geneva arms, a half-eagle and key.

HALLYAR or **HOLLYARDE** (JASPER), bookbinder in London, came to England about 1540. In 1549 he was entered in the Subsidy Roll as an assistant to Edward Whitchurch and paid a tax of four shillings on goods valued at four pounds. [R. of A., I, 180.] In June, 1567, he took out letters of denization and is described as "from the dominion of the King of France." [Pat. 9 Eliz., p. 3, m. 40.] In the same year he is entered in the Return of Aliens as a bookbinder who had married an English wife and had been in England 25 years. [R. of A., I, 320.] In 1571 he is entered in St. Andrew's Parish Castle Baynard Ward, as a printer and householder, a Frenchman and a denizen, in England 33 years: with one daughter, Elizabeth. [R. of A., I, 478; II, 86.]

HAMILLON (RICHARD), printer in Rouen, was in business between the years 1541 and 1559. He printed a considerable number of Sarum service books in the reign of Mary for Robert and Florence Valentin.

HAMMAN (JOANNES), see Hertzog (J.).

HAMMANDE (HENRY), stationer in London, was an original member of the Stationers' Company though not mentioned in the charter, having been made free on October 1st, 1556. He is mentioned in the Registers as having presented apprentices in 1558, 1562 and 1566.

HAQUET (THOMAS), see Hacket (T.).

HARDOUYN (GERMAIN), printer in Paris, was at work from the commencement of the sixteenth century to about the year 1541. He worked at the sign of St. Margaret between the two gates of the Palace. [Renouard, pp. 175-6.] He issued several editions of the Sarum *Horae* and *Enchiridion* about 1530.

HARDY (EUSTACE), printer in Rouen, is not mentioned by Frère. He printed an edition of the Sarum *Missal* in 1518 for J. Caillard.

HARFORD (JOHN), see Hertford (J.).

H

HARKES (EHERET), bookseller in London, is mentioned in some Exchequer accounts dating towards the end of Henry VIII's reign. "Engell Vanderhage of Antwerp, wedowe, hathe in bookes prynted in thaundes of Eheret Harkes her factor, xx li." He carried on business apparently in St. Paul's Churchyard.

HARKES (GARBRAND), stationer in Oxford, was a Dutch Protestant refugee. He is first mentioned in the year 1539 when along with others he was brought under the notice of the authorities for eating meat in Lent. [*Letters and papers of Henry VIII*, vol. xiv, pt. i.] In the reign of Edward he is said to have made considerable purchases at the sales of monastic libraries. In 1551 he supplied books to Magdalen College [Bloxam, II, 273], and in 1556 his house was noted as a refuge for Protestants. In 1566 he was licensed to sell wine. [Clark, I, p. 323.] His shop was in Bulkeley Hall. He had several sons, one of whom, Richard, was a bookseller and another the intimate friend of Bishop Jewel. [D.N.B., under Garbrand.]

HARMAN (HENRY), stationer, is mentioned in 1541 as being factor and keeping shop for Arnold Byrckman in Paul's Churchyard. He had as an assistant John Rowe a bookbinder. Harman may quite probably be identical with the following.

HARMANSON (HENRY), stationer in London, is mentioned in the lists of denizations "Henry Harmanson, stationer, from Daventer, in the Diocese of the Bishop of Utrecht under the obedience of the Emperor 19. Feb. 1535." [Pat. 26 Hen. VIII, p. 2, m. 41.]

HARRINGTON (JOHN), bookseller in London, seems to have been in partnership in 1549 with Thomas Raynald at the Star in St. Paul's Churchyard in which year they published Sir T. Wyat's *Certayne psalmes.* In 1550 the widow of John Hertford printed for him W. Hunnis' *Certayne psalmes.*

HARRIS (GARRAT), printer in London, was an assistant to Katherine Hertford widow of John Hertford and is entered in St. Botolph's Parish Aldersgate Ward in the Subsidy Roll of 1549. [R. of A., I, 172.]

HARRIS (THOMAS), stationer in London, was admitted a brother of the Stationers' Company on January 13th, 1557. He was dead before June 4th, 1587, on which day his son Andrew was bound apprentice to Thomas Hacket.

HARRISON (JOHN), was a member of the Stationers' Company at the time of its incorporation though his name is not in the original list as he was not made free until August 19th, 1556. He came on the Livery in 1564 and was three times Warden and three times Master. He printed at the White Greyhound in St. Paul's Churchyard and the Greyhound in Paternoster Row. Harrison died at the beginning of 1617 and his will was proved on February 11th. [Plomer, Wills, 48-9.] To his wife Juliana [Barnes] whom he married in December, 1586, and who was apparently his second wife he left a third of his property, a third went to his son and daughters, the remainder in various legacies. His half-brother John Harrison, also a stationer, died in 1618.

HARRISON (LUKE), stationer in London, was made free of the Stationers' Company May 21st, 1556, and came on the Livery in 1568. He printed at the sign of the Crane in St. Paul's Churchyard up to the year 1577 and died shortly after, for in July, 1578, his widow sold his copies. Her name was Helen, and she was a daughter of Edward Whitchurch by his first wife. Harrison seems to have printed little for himself, most of his work being done by other printers.

HARRISON (RICHARD), printer in London, was a member of the Stationers' Company at the time of its incorporation, being forty-seventh on the list. He printed only in the years 1561 and 1562 issuing some half-dozen books. In July, 1562, he was appointed a Warden for the ensuing year but died soon after January, 1563. His device, as described by Camden, was "an hare by a sheafe of rye in the sun for Harrison" and this was used later by John Harrison who was probably his son. Richard Harrison appears to have been the ancestor of the very numerous stationers and printers of that name.

HARRY, stationer in Oxford, was a workman with Garret Pilgrim who in 1536 left him by will a doublet and a pair of hose. [Arch. Univ. Oxon., Registrum E.E.E.] He may be the same as Harry Renkens.

HARVEY (JOHN), stationer in London, lived in Lombard Street at the sign of the Lamb. He is mentioned in the colophon of Taverner's *Garden of Wisdom* printed in 1539. [Herbert, I, 406.]

HARVEY (RICHARD), printer in London, was an original member of the Stationers' Company. He is quoted by Herbert [III, p. 1312] as the printer of *A decree between Churchyarde the poet and Camell*, in which his address is given as Foster Lane. He also in 1557-8 had license to print *Devoute prayers*. He was also a bookbinder and was fined by the Company for binding great books in sheep's leather. His name is not found after 1565-66.

HATLEY (WALTER), stationer in Cambridge, was in business from about 1485 to 1504 and is entered many times in the Grace book as binding and repairing books for the University. About 1500 he became parish clerk of the church of St. Mary the Great. He appears to have died about 1504. [Gray, *Cambridge Stationers*, pp. 12–14.]

HATSOO (GODFRAY), printer in London, was apparently an assistant to Stephen Mierdman, and is mentioned in the Subsidy Roll of 1549. [R. of A., I, 161.]

HAUKYNS (JOHN), printer in London, appears to have been an assistant to Richard Pynson for he finished the printing of Palsgrave's *L'Esclarcissement de la langue Francaise* which was in the press at the time of Pynson's death. One part of the book was finished in July, 1530, and it was issued some time after September 2nd, the date of the privilege. Beyond the printing of this book nothing is known of him, nor is he mentioned in Pynson's will. Herbert suggests that he was the John Haukin or Hankyn mentioned in the *Twelve merry gestys of one called Edyth*, printed in 1525, and was the father of that "lyeng wydow" but there is no foundation for this conjecture.

HAVY (NOWELL), bookbinder in London, was a native of France and came to England in 1523. In 1535 he received a bequest from W. de Worde " To Nowell the bokebinder in shoo lane the value of xx s sterling in books." In 1541 he took out letters of denization. "Nowell Havy from France, married to an English woman. In England 18 years 14 April 1541 "

[Deniz. Roll, 36 Henry VIII], and in the same year is mentioned in the Returns of Aliens as dwelling in Shoe Lane and paying a tax of four pence. [R. of A., I, 56.] In 1544 he is again entered, his goods being valued at twenty shillings, and his tax is again four pence. In 1545 he received a legacy from Edward Ylle of three shillings and four pence. [Plomer, Wills, p. 8.] He is last mentioned in the Returns of Aliens in 1550 when he was still living in Shoe Lane. His goods were valued at five pounds and he paid a tax of five shillings. In the two wills where he is mentioned as a binder only his Christian name is given, but W. de Worde gives the address, and we find from the Lay Subsidy Rolls of 1540-41 that he was the only person in Shoe Lane with the name Nowell.

HAWLEY (EDMUND) was an apprentice to Richard Kele, who bequeathed to him in 1552, forty shillings in "ware." [Plomer, Wills, p. 10.]

HECTOR was an assistant to W. de Worde who bequeathed to him five marks sterling in books. [Plomer, Wills, p. 4.]

HEERSTRATEN (EGIDIUS VAN DER), printer in Louvain, was at work between the years 1484–5 and 1488 issuing some eighteen books. About 1486 he issued an edition of the *Regulae Grammaticales* of Nicolaus Perottus which contains a number of renderings into English and was perhaps intended for the use of English students at foreign universities.

HENRY, bookbinder in Oxford, is mentioned in the registers of Magdalen College as having bound and chained books for the library in 1530-2. [Gibson, *Oxford Bindings*, p. 47.]

HEREFORD (JOHN), *see* Hertford (J.).

HERON (JOHN), stationer in London, belonged to the Company of Haberdashers. He occupied part of John Rastell's shop near Paul's gate with the sign of the Mermaid during three years about 1523-6. [*Bibliographica*, II, 439.]

HERT (THOMAS), stationer in London, appears as one of the parties in a Chancery suit on a bond of suretyship, between 1463 and 1468. [Early Chancery Proceedings, Bundle 30, No. 66.]

HERTFORD, HARFORD, HERFORD or HEREFORD (JOHN), printer in St. Alban's and London was most probably of foreign birth. He was settled in St. Alban's by 1534, in which year he issued Lydgate's *Life of St. Alban*, and continued to print there until 1539 when the Abbey was handed over to Henry VIII. He printed in all seven books, in some of which is found his curious device containing the initials R.S., standing no doubt for his patron Richard Stevenage the Abbot. In October, 1539, the printer had apparently got into some trouble, for the Abbot in a letter to Cromwell writes, "Sent John Pryntare to London with Harry Pepwell, Bonere [Bonham] and Tabbe, of Powlles churchyard stationers, to order him at your pleasure. Never heard of the little book of detestable heresies till the stationers showed it me." [*L. and P. Hen. VIII*, xiv, pt. 2, No. 315.] The book here referred to is probably one hitherto undescribed entitled *A very declaration of the bond and free wyll of man. The obedyence of the gospell, and what the very gospell meneth* [J.R.L.]. The book has no name of printer or date, but only the name of the place. There seems nothing in any of the other books printed at St. Alban's savouring of heresy and most of them were printed under the direct supervision of either the Abbot, Robert Catton, or his immediate successor Richard Stevenage. The suppression of the abbey in 1539 prevented Hertford from returning there to print and we do not find him mentioned again until 1544, when he was printing in London in Aldersgate Street. In the Subsidy Roll of 1544 we find in Aldersgate Ward a John Hartford entered with goods worth x. li. [R. of A., I, 84] and in 1549, the year when we find Hertford's widow printing, there is entered at the same address Kateryne Harford, wydowe and Garrett Harrys her servaunt. [R. of A., I, 172.] The exact agreement of the dates make it probable that these entries refer to the printer and his widow. Hertford began his work in London with the issue of a small work of Leland's and in 1545 published the *Compendiosa totius anatomiae delineatio* with illustrations engraved by Thomas Geminie, the second book issued in England with copper-plate engravings. Hertford printed altogether in London some twenty-four books mainly for Robert Toy. He seems not to have printed for himself or to have done any retail trade and this is no doubt the reason why he had no sign to his house. As no book of his is dated later than 1548 it is probable that he died in that year.

HERTFORD (KATHERINE), printer in London, was the widow of John Hertford, and carried on business in Aldersgate Street for a short time after his death. She is entered with her servant Garret Harrys in the Subsidy Roll of 1549. [R. of A., I, 172.] She printed altogether four books, for W. Lynne, R. Stoughton and J. Harrington, two of which are dated 1550.

HERTFORD (WILLIAM), printer in London, was probably the son of John and Katherine Hertford, and continued to print at their old address in Aldersgate Street. He printed about 1555 for W. Seres a work by John Aungell and in 1559 a broadside prayer in verse by John Pyttes, but beyond these nothing of his work is known, nor was he a member of the Company of Stationers.

HERTZOG or HAMMAN (JOANNES), printer in Venice was a native of Landau. He began to print in the year 1488 and continued up to the beginning of the sixteenth century. He was specially noted for his finely printed service books and of these he produced a considerable number according to the uses of York and Sarum for Frederick Egmont and Gerard Barrevelt in the years 1493-95. His device consisted of a circle divided by a horizontal line from which springs a double armed cross. In the circle are his mark and initials. There are three varieties of this device, one very plain used up to 1493, the next more ornamented used to 1495 and a third more elaborate still. [*The Library*, 1890, pp. 305-309.]

HESTER (ANDREW), bookseller in London, was an apprentice to Robert Aylton who against the rules of the City passed him over to a "foreigner" to learn his craft. Accordingly on July 11th, 1538, it was agreed that Hester should be made free of the Stationers' Company paying for his admission six shillings and eight pence, while Aylton had to pay the fees of the Master Chamberlain. [Bibl. Soc. Trans., VI, p. 19.] He was one of those for whom the editions of Bishop Hilsey's *Primer* were printed in 1539. In 1550 he issued a *Bible* in quarto printed for him at Zurich by Chr. Froschauer, and in 1551, W. Turner's *Preservative agaynst the poyson of Palagius*, printed by Jugge. His place of business was at the sign of the White Horse in St. Paul's Churchyard. He was an original member of the Company of Stationers, but died in 1557 immediately after their incorporation. An Anne Hester widow, citizen and stationer took an apprentice in 1564. [Arber, I, 251.]

HEUEL (DAVID), bookseller (?) sold a manuscript to J. Gunthorp, Dean of
Wells in July, 1492. [James, *Sources of Archbp. Parker's MSS. at C.C.C.,
Cambridge*, p. 37.]

HEWTEE (JOHN), stationer in Oxford, is mentioned in a suit held at Oxford
in 1501 concerning the goods of Sebastian Actors, stationer deceased.
Hewtee who had married Margaret Actors claimed certain goods including
binding tools on behalf of his father-in-law Peter Actors. [Univ. Archives,
Registrum ℂ ff., 91-2.]

HIGMAN (JEAN), printer in Paris, was a German by birth and began to
print at Paris in 1484. In 1494 he became a partner with Hopyl and
continued printing with him until his death in 1500. [Renouard, pp. 181-2.]
Bradshaw ascribed to his press the first edition of the Sarum *Legenda*, known
only from fragments, but it was more probably printed by Maynyal. Higman
and Hopyl printed a Sarum *Missal* in 1500 [Bodl.] for I. B. and G. H.

HIGMAN (NICHOLAS), printer in Paris, worked from about 1495 to about
1535. [Renouard, p. 182.] He printed a Sarum *Missal* in 1519 for Regnault
and Birckman and three editions of the Sarum *Horae* about the same time.

HILL (JOHN), stationer in London, was an original member of the Company
of Stationers. He is not the same person as John a Hill, with whom he is
always confused, as we find both names occurring in single lists. John
Hill was a more senior member being forty-fifth in the charter. He does
not appear to have practised much as a stationer and at the beginning of
1568 paid seven pounds to the Company on being set over to the Vintners.
[Arber, I, 365.]

HILL (JOHN a), stationer in London, was made free August 19th, 1556, but
does not appear in the original charter list of 1557. He is entered in the
Registers as taking apprentices in 1559 and 1560 and was fined in 1562 for
not appearing on Quarter Day. Beyond this nothing is known of him.

HILL, MONTANUS or VAN DE BERGHE (NICHOLAS), printer in
London, was a native of the Low Countries who came to England in 1519.
In 1544 he took out letters of denization "Nicholas Hilles, printer, born in
the dominion of the Emperor. In England 25 years 1. July 1544." [Westm.
Deniz. Roll, 36 Hen. VIII.] In the same year he is entered in the Subsidy

Roll as paying four pence tax on twenty shillings' worth of goods and living in St. John's Street. In 1546 the earliest book with his name in it as a printer was issued, and between this date and 1553 he printed twenty-three books, mostly for other people. He appears to have done no retail trade as a bookseller, which may account for his house having no sign or at least none ever mentioned. In 1549 in the Subsidy Roll his goods were valued at forty shillings and his tax was two shillings, and an assistant of his is mentioned called Urban Lynyng, perhaps the Urban van Cuelen described as a printer shortly afterwards. [R. of A., I, 157.] In 1550 and 1551 he is again on the Subsidy Rolls, but the value of his goods had sunk to twenty shillings and his tax to one. [R. of A., I, pp. 200, 215.] In the list of members of the Dutch Church made in 1551 he is entered as Nicolais vand Berghe, met Elizabeth, and in a fuller list compiled between 1550 and 1560 he is " Nicolais van de Berghe, met Elizabeth, impressor " but the entry has been struck out, no doubt at the time of his death, about 1553. [R. of A., I, 208-9.] His books are dated up to that year, but he is not entered in the assessment of aliens in St. John Street in 1553. In a list of widows belonging to the Dutch Church written in 1560 is entered " Vidua Nicolai Bergensis, calcographi, cum suis orphanis."

HILL (RICHARD), stationer in London. There were apparently two stationers of this name as one occurs thirty-second on the charter list and must therefore have been a fairly senior member, whereas the other was not made free until August 19th, 1556, too late to be placed on the list. The only entry about this Richard is a note of his being fined twelve pence for fighting with an apprentice.

HILL (WILLIAM), printer in London, lived at the sign of the Green Hill in St. Paul's Churchyard. He apparently printed only during the years 1548 and 1549 when he produced about sixteen books, some in partnership with W. Seres others with T. Raynalde. In the list of stationers in the charter of 1557 he was fortieth. He is entered several times in the Registers as taking apprentices, and once is fined for binding Primers in parchment, so that he appears to have been in business as a bookbinder. He was still alive in 1586 when his son William was admitted a freeman " per patronagium." In the Prerogative Court of Canterbury is the will dated 1564 [another grant September 10th, 1580] of " William Hyll, stacioner, Sainte Gregories, City of London." [25, Stevenson.]

HILLENIUS or HILLEN (MICHEL), printer in Antwerp, son of John Hillenius and Catherine Dibbouts, was born at Hoochstraeten. He came to Antwerp and was entered as a citizen in 1508. In 1518 he purchased a house in the Cammerstraet with the sign of the Turnip (in de Rape). Here he printed continuously up till 1546 when, after the death of his son John, he handed over his printing establishment to his son-in-law John Steelsius, who had married his daughter Margaret. Michael Hillenius died July 22nd, 1558, and was buried in the convent of St. Francis. He used a number of devices, all containing a figure of Time. [Van Havre, pp. 213-4.] He printed several books for the English market, the *Enchiridion locorum communium adversus Lutheranos* of Eckius for Henry Pepwell, and an edition of the Sarum *Hymns and Sequences*.

HITPRIK (HANS), pseudonym, is found in the colophons of two books, Wraghton's *The Rescuynge of the Romishe Fox* whose imprint runs "Imprinted have at Winchester Anno Domini 1545 4 nonas Martii. By me Hanse hit prik," and *the Dysclosing of the Canon of the popysh Masse* 1549 with the imprint "Imprinted have at all Papists By me Hans hitprycke." The "imprinted have at Winchester" means not that it was printed there, but that the book was an attack on Stephen Gardiner, Bishop of Winchester. From the type it is clear that it was printed by Christopher Froschauer. The printer of the second book has not been identified.

HOCHSTRATEN (JOHN), printer at Lübeck, issued according to Panzer two books in 1531 and 1532. In 1533 *The richt way to hevin* by John Gau was published, which had the following colophon "Prentit in Malmw Be me Jhone Hochstraten the xvi day of October. Anno M.D. xxxiii." If this imprint is correct, which is very doubtful, Hochstraten must have moved to Malmoe. [*Bannatyne Miscellany*, vol. iii.]

HOFFE (UBRIGHT), printer in Leipzig, is known only as printing one book, Melanchthon's *Godly Defense, defending the marriage of Priests* translated by Lewes Beuchame issued in 1541. [Maittaire, *Index*, I, 134. Herbert, III, p. 1833.] The name is no doubt fictitious and the type in which the book is printed is that of John Oswen of Ipswich. [Sayle, III, 1418.]

HOLDER (ROBERT), stationer in London, was originally an assistant to John Reynes, who on his death in 1544 left him a legacy of ten pounds in books. Reynes also desired him to stay with Lucy Reynes the widow for two years to help her to get in the debts and dispose of the stock. Afterwards he was to have the option, along with Edward Sutton, of purchasing the trade material. On the expiration of the two years he seems to have left Lucy Reynes, or she had herself given up business, for in her will, dated April, 1548, she leaves twenty shillings to "Robert Holder, late my servant." [Plomer, Wills, pp. 6, 7, 9.] In 1549 he was settled in Paul's Churchyard, with a foreign assistant Garret Williams. [R. of A., I, p. 159.] He appears to have prospered in business and soon after the incorporation of the Stationers' Company in 1557 became one of the assistants. He interested himself largely in the affairs of the Company and his name is frequently found up to the year 1566, when he took a John Hoder as an apprentice.

HOLLINDER (JOHN), printer in London, was an assistant to John Day and is entered in St. Anne and St. Agnes Parish, Aldersgate Ward in the Subsidy Roll of 1549. [R. of A., I, 173.] Another John Hollinder appears in 1559 and 1571 but he was a leather dresser. In 1561-62 the printer was fined by the Stationers' Company for leaving his master without leave [Arber, I, p. 183], and in 1564-5 he was paid two shillings "in Rewarde for his departure the Realme." [Arber, I, 282.]

HOLLYARDE (JASPER), see Hallyar (J.).

HOLLYBUSH (JOHN), see Ruremond (H. van).

HOLWARDE (THOMAS), printer in London, was an apprentice to John Reynes who in his will dated April, 1542, left him "a hundredth shillings in bokes" as soon as he should have finished his apprenticeship. [Plomer, Wills, p. 6.]

HOLYLAND (JAMES), stationer in London, was an original member of the Stationers' Company in 1557. He must have been an old man as he was eighth on the charter list and one of the assistants. The only entries relating to him in the Registers, beyond notes of subscriptions, are fines for being disobedient, and the last entry 1558-59 runs as follows: "James Holylande for his Dysobedyennce to the Master and Wardyns and for mysbehavynge hym selfe ys Dessemyssed from the assententes tyll suche tyme he Reconsyle hym selfe and also ys fyned." [Arber, I, 94.]

HOLYLAND (JOHN), stationer in London, is mentioned in the Archives of the City of London. He apparently lived in St. Paul's Churchyard and at one time had a quarrel with Reginald Wolfe which was settled by the arbitration of Thomas Petit and Robert Toye. [Bibl. Soc. Trans., VI, p. 24.] He was doubtless some relative of James Holyland, an original member of the Stationers' Company.

HOPYL (WOLFGANG), printer in Paris, was a native of Utrecht and worked from 1489 to 1521. In 1489 he lived at the sign of St. Barbara in the Rue St. Jacques and in the following year moved to the house next door with the sign of St. George. From 1494 to 1500 he was in partnership with Jean Higman and in 1502-3 with Henri Estienne. He printed very largely for foreign stationers. [Renouard, pp. 183-4.] Hopyl began to print for the English market in 1494, issuing an edition of the *Liber synonymorum* for Nicolas Lecomte and he followed this in the following year with a *Liber Festivalis* printed for the same stationer. In 1496 and 1497 he had in his employment a certain David Lauxius, a native of Edinburgh who was afterwards a schoolmaster at Arras and a friend of Badius Ascensius. In the *Festival* of 1495 Hopyl used his earliest device, a stork pecking at a tree and the initials A. T. W., round all the motto, partly derived from Tibullus, "Munere vivit amor, celat sua furta Venus." From 1500 to 1519 Hopyl issued many Sarum service books, all after 1512 being printed for F. Birckman. From 1505 to 1512 he printed many books for the stationers at the sign of the Trinity. A favourite device used at this time consists of two circles joined by chains and supported by birds behind each bird being a fruit tree. In most of his books is found his motto "Fortuna opes aufferre: non animum potest."

HORSPATH (JOHN), bookbinder in Oxford, is mentioned in the University Registers [Reg. Aaa] under the year 1457, July 27th, "John Horspath Bokebynder famulus quondam Johannis Dolle convictus est de perturbacione pacis."

HOSTINGUE (LAWRENCE), printer in Rouen, was in partnership about 1505 with Jamet Loys and lived near the Marché-Neuf. In 1508 he left Rouen and settled in Caen. The two partners printed at Rouen an edition of Stanbridge's *Vocabula*, without date, for Martin Coffin of Exeter, but no copy is now known. [Herbert III, p. 1530.] The edition of the Sarum *Sequences* and the *Garlandia*, printed for Andrew Myllar in 1505-6 have been ascribed to this press, but were really printed by P. Violette.

HOTHERSALL (JOHN), stationer in London, is mentioned in 1486. "Exemption to John Hothersall, notary public and citizen and stationer of London, from being compelled to serve in any office under the Crown, and from all penalties which he may incur from refusing so to serve. 5 Aug." [*Materials, Hen. VII*, pp. 536-7.]

HOUDOUIN (HENRY), printer in Geneva, is mentioned by Herbert [III, p. 1595] as printing with J. Poulain Gilbie's *Treatise of Election* in 1556.

HOWBERGHE (WILLIAM), stationer in Oxford, is mentioned in November, 1507, when three members of the University became surety in £20 for his good behaviour. [Univ. Arch., Reg. F., fol. 36.] He is mentioned also in 1507-8 as binding books for the library of Magdalen College. By 1524 he was appointed a University stationer, but resigned his post on October 11th, 1532. He died in 1537 and his will was proved on June 11th of that year. [Gibson, *Early Oxford Bindings*, p. 46.]

HOWE (WILLIAM), printer in London, was admitted a freeman November 29th, 1556. He had entered copies of ballads as early as 1565. In 1566 he took over the printing office of Abraham Veale for whom he continued to print for many years. He married in 1569 Alice Farrare. [*London Marriage Licenses*, p. 43.] In 1573-4 he came upon the Livery and in 1582 was Renter to the Stationers' Company. He continued to print up to about 1590 but only owned one press. His son was apprenticed in 1597 and the last mention of him in the Registers is in 1603. He lived in Fleet Street and used a device which had belonged to R. Hall, a boy with wings and a weight.

HUBY (EDWARD), stationer in York, is twice mentioned in the *Fabric Rolls of the Minster* between the years 1525 and 1528 [pp. 101, 103]. "Domino Edward Huby pro xvij antiphonariis de les v partis 20 . s." "Edwardo Huby pro xiij libris de les priksong, 40.s."

HUCKE (GILES), *see* Huke (G.).

HUGUELIN (JEAN), *see* Kerbriant (J.).

HUKE or HUCKE (GILES), stationer in London, was an original member of the Stationers' Company in 1557. He is mentioned in the Registers as taking an apprentice in 1565 but he appears to have fallen into poverty and became porter to the Company. The last entry relating to him occurs in 1580–81. "Item paide to Giles Huke the porter towarde the buriall of his wife, v.s." [Arber, I, 490.]

HULTON (JOHN), stationer in London, died in 1475 and was buried in the church of St. Michael-le-Quern. [Stow, I, p. 681.]

HUNSWORTHE (JOHN), stationer in London, was made free April 31st, 1556, though he is not mentioned in the charter of 1557. In 1569-70 he took out a license for a small religious work, but does not appear to have printed. He is entered several times in the Stationers' Registers up to April, 1589, as taking apprentices. He died before 1604 when his widow Winifred presented an apprentice.

HUNTE (THOMAS), stationer in Oxford, is first mentioned in the year 1473. He was then a University stationer and is mentioned in a note in a MS. Latin *Bible* in the British Museum. In 1483 he is mentioned in a list of books which he agreed to sell for two stationers Peter Actors and Johannes de Aquisgrano. Soon after he appears to have gone into partnership with Theodoric Rood the printer, and both their names are to be found in the colophon of the *Phalaridis Epistolae* of 1485. They apparently also produced the *Festial* of 1486, but after this period nothing is known of Hunte.

HURSON (JOHN), bookbinder in York, is mentioned in the *Fabric Rolls of the Minster* 1509-10 [p. 95] "Pro les bynding librorum Johanni Hurson et Johanni Franckine, 15.s. 4d."

HUVIN (JEAN), stationer in Rouen, carried on business as a publisher and bookbinder from 1490 to 1522, occupying two shops at the "Portail des libraires." His device contains a shield with his initials supported by a youth and an old man. Behind the shield stands Death pointing an arrow at both. This device is also found stamped upon his bindings. He issued a Sarum *Breviary* in 1501 and *Missals* in 1506 and 1508. There is some reason for believing that either he or another Rouen stationer Jacques Huvin was for a time in England and was in partnership about 1496-7 with Jean Barbier and Julian Notary. [*Library*, vol. i, pp. 102-5.]

I. (H.), bookbinder, *see* Jacobi (H.).

IRELAND (ROGER), stationer in London, was an original member of the Stationers' Company in 1557 being twenty-eighth on the list. In 1550 a Roger Ireland married Johanna Maptide. [*London Marriage Licenses*, p. 12.] By 1562 he was one of the assistants, in 1563-64, 1568-69 a Warden. He had licenses for printing an *Almanack* and a book called *Beware the Cat*. He seems to have got into debt to the Company and the final entry relating to him, under the year 1575-76 runs "Paide to Roger Irelande of benevolence by Comon consent at one tyme v.s. and at an other tyme iij s. iiij.d."

JACOB, printer in London, was an assistant to Richard Grafton. Two assistants of this name are entered in the Subsidy Roll of 1549, but the surnames have been obliterated. [R. of A., I, 159.] One was no doubt J. Wolferte.

JACOBI (HENRY), stationer in London and Oxford, was most probably a Frenchman and his name first occurs in an entry in a manuscript [Add. MS. 7099, fol. 93] in the British Museum which speaks of him as a bookseller in 1505, when Henry VII bought from him books to the value of forty-six pounds ten shillings to present to the monastery at Richmond. In 1506 in partnership with another bookseller Joyce Pelgrim, and assisted by a wealthy London merchant William Bretton, he issued three books, a *Psalterium cum hymnis*, a *Horae ad usum Sarum*, and the *Constitutiones* of Lyndewode and Athon. In 1507 and 1508 three grammatical books were printed for them at Antwerp, probably by Thierry Martens. In 1509 Jacobi was at work by himself and commissioned a part of an edition of the *Ortus Vocabulorum* printed by Pynson. While some copies were to be sold by the printer, others have an imprint stating that they were to be sold by Jacobi at his shop in St. Paul's Churchyard at the sign of the Trinity. In 1510 Bretton again paid for the printing of two books, the *Pupilla Oculi* of J. de Burgo and the *Speculum Spiritualium* of Richard Rolle of Hampole. These books were printed at Paris by W. Hopyl and certain copies have his imprint on the titlepage in place of that of Jacobi. Between September, 1510, and the end of May, 1511, four small works of Savonarola were printed at Paris by Badius Ascensius, all of which were to be sold by Jean Petit, Henry Jacobi and Ascensius. It is probable that Jacobi was in Paris at this time but he was back again in London in 1512, when he published an edition of the Sarum *Diurnale* printed for him at Paris by W. Hopyl. This little book also contains on the last leaf the device of Francis Byrckman, who may have joined with Jacobi in its production. Soon after this Jacobi moved to Oxford and opened a shop there with his old London sign of the Trinity, and issued an edition of the *Formalitates* of Antonius Sirectus, printed for him at London by Wynkyn de Worde. On December 11th, 1514, administration of the effects of Henricus Jacobi, deceased, was granted to William Bretton through his agent Joyce Pelgrim. [Oxf. Univ. Archives.] Jacobi's shop in London was the sign of the Trinity in St. Paul's Churchyard. It was at the east side at the new schools built by Colet. He used two devices; the first, used when he was in partnership with Pelgrim, consisted of a blank shield with a ribbon behind it on which was printed "Nosce teipsum" with his mark and initials on one side and Pelgrim's on the other. His second device, found only in the book issued at Oxford, contains a representation of the Trinity with a king and knight in armour on either side and his name and mark below. This device was used afterwards by Henry Pepwell with the name Jacobi cut out. Jacobi was also a bookbinder and used three pairs of panels containing the arms of France and England crowned supported by the dragon and greyhound, and the Tudor rose surrounded by a ribbon with a motto and supported by two angels. These have also his initials and mark. Another pair contain pictures of an Image of Pity and of Our Lady of Pity round which runs the legend beginning "Salve mater misericordiae" and ending with the initials H. I. joined by a knot. An example in the Bodleian containing some tracts of Savonarola, including some printed for Jacobi, has an inscription showing that it was executed in 1510. Besides these he also made use of a large square die with the figure of a dragon which had belonged to Caxton. [*Bibliographica*, I, pp. 92-113, 189-191.]

JACOBSON (OLIVER), printer in Zurich, issued in 1543 *Yet a course at the Romish Fox* by John Harryson. [Herbert, III, 1554.] He is not known to have printed any other book and the name is probably a fictitious one.

JAQUES (JOHN), stationer in London, was one of the oldest members at the time of the incorporation of the Company, being thirteenth on the list. He is entered in the Registers as subscribing freely and giving several gifts to the Company and served as one of the Wardens in 1558-9. His name is not found after 1560. It is just possible that he may be identical with the person mentioned in the Denization Rolls "John Jaques born in the dominion of the Emperor. In England six years, 1 July, 1544." [Westm. Deniz. Roll, 36 Hen. VIII.]

JEHANNOT (JEAN), printer in Paris, commenced to print about 1488 and died in 1522. Neither Hain nor Renouard mention him as a fifteenth century printer, but in 1498 he printed an edition of the *Horae ad usum Sarum* for Nicholas Lecomte. He carried on business at the sign of St. John Baptist in the Rue neuve Nostre Dame. [Renouard, p. 193.]

JENYNS, bookbinder in Oxford, is mentioned in 1539 as having been summoned for eating meat in Lent. [*Letters and papers of Henry VIII*, vol. xiv, pt. i, p. 339.]

JOHANNES DE AQUISGRANO, stationer in England, appears to have travelled about to supply books in partnership with Peter Actors. In 1483 they were at Oxford and supplied a number of books to Thomas Hunte the bookseller on sale or return. [Madan, *Day-book of John Dorne*, p. 142.]

JONES (THOMAS), printer in London. Known only from an inscription at the end of a manuscript in the Cambridge University Library. [MS. Add. 3137, f.] "Here endeth the prologe and mirror of life compiled by me Thomas Jonys of London prenter the thirde day of Novembre in the xxiij yere of the reigne of K. Henry the viii." [1531].

JOY (GEORGE), reformer and author, is mentioned by Herbert [I, 567] as a printer on the strength of the colophon to a book entitled "*A Contrarye (to a certayne manis) Consultacion*" which runs "Prynted at London by George Joye." Though Joy had been connected with the press at Antwerp, correcting for the press two editions of the *New Testament* printed by the widow of Christopher van Ruremond [both in B.M.], there is no evidence beyond the colophon mentioned above for believing that he ever practised printing on his own account. [D.N.B.]

JUDSON (JOHN), printer in London, was a senior member of the Stationers' Company on its incorporation, being fifteenth on the list. He was a Warden of the Company in 1560-61, 1562-3 and 1570-71 and Master in

I

1587-88. He is frequently mentioned in the Registers as taking apprentices and entering copies. He died in 1589 and his will dated 4th May, 1588, was proved on March 18th following. [Plomer, Wills, p. 28.] He left a widow Alice and two sons Richard and Thomas, the latter having been made free of the Stationers by patrimony in January, 1581.

JUGGE (RICHARD), printer in London, is supposed to have been born at Waterbeach in Cambridgeshire and to have been educated at Eton, whence he passed in 1531 to King's College. On October 4th, 1541, he was admitted a freeman of the Stationers' Company, and about 1547 began to print in St. Paul's Churchyard at the sign of the Bible. He had license to print the *New Testament*, the prices of which were fixed by the Privy Council in June, 1552. After the incorporation of the Stationers' Company he occupied an important position in it, being a Warden in 1560, 1563, and 1566, and Master four times between 1568 and 1574. On the accession of Queen Elizabeth he became royal printer conjointly with Cawood. He printed in 1568 the first edition of the *Bishops' Bible*, remarkable for the beautiful copperplate portraits in it. Jugge's device was the figure of a pelican feeding her young. He resided first in St. Paul's Churchyard, but about 1573 moved to Newgate Market. He died in 1577 and his will was proved October 23rd of that year. [Plomer, Wills, p. 24.] He left to Joan his widow a third part of his goods, another third to his children, not mentioned by name, but one, Katherine, married Richard Watkins May 3rd, 1569. [*London Marriage Licenses*, p. 42]. Other daughters were Elizabeth and Anne and there was a son John also a member of the Stationers' Company. John Wight and William Norton were appointed overseers. [D.N.B.]

K. (L.), bookbinder, made use of a roll containing the initials K L joined by a knot, a fleur de lys, lion and pomegranate, the initials L K, a rose, a lion and a portcullis. The binder who used this roll had come into possession of Julian Notary's stamps and they are found together upon one book. [Weale, *Bookbindings*, p. 134.]

KAETZ (PETER), stationer in London, was a native of Antwerp and appears to have come to England to act as agent for Christopher van Ruremond. From 1523 to the beginning of 1525 he issued seven Sarum service books, two *Manuals*, two *Processionals*, a *Horae*, a *Psalter* and a *Hymni cum notis*, all printed by C. van Ruremond. Early in 1525 Kaetz returned to Antwerp and carried on business in a shop which had belonged to Hendrik Eckert van Homborch with the sign of the House of Delft in the Cammerstraete. From this address he published the edition of the *Bible* in Dutch printed by Hans van Ruremond. After this time his name is not found though we know he was a young man. He is known to have had some business with Siberch the first printer in Cambridge, for a business letter from him to Siberch was discovered in the binding of a book in Westminster Abbey Library. [*Cambridge Ant. Soc. Proc.*, VII, p. 186.] His device consisted of two lions supporting a shield emblazoned with three roses suspended from a tree; below, on a ribbon are his name and mark. His place of business in London was in St. Paul's Churchyard.

KELE (JOHN), stationer in London, was a younger brother of Richard Kele and still an apprentice in 1552. He had been freed before the passing of the Stationers' Company's charter and is entered in the list. He is mentioned in the Registers as taking apprentices up to the year 1571.

KELE (RICHARD), printer in London, began to print in 1542, when he issued an edition of the *Prymer in Englysh*. On April 8th, 1543, Kele along with several other printers was summoned before the Privy Council for printing unlawful books and sent to the Fleet. He was freed on April 23rd, but was compelled to pay a fine and also send in a return of what books and ballads he had bought and sold in the space of three years. Up to 1546 Kele printed " at the long shop in the Poultry under St. Mildred's Church " issuing from there some of Skelton's works, the *Mirror or glasse of helthe* and one or two other books. By 1547 he had moved to the Eagle in Lombard Street and there he continued until 1552. He printed little for himself and most of his work was done by W. Copland, W. Seres or R. Wyer. Kele died in 1552 and his will dated September 10th was proved on October 19th. He was apparently a young man and his three children were under age. His brother John to whom he left the lease of the Long Shop and twenty pounds in books was still an apprentice. Amongst other legatees were Richard Kele an uncle, Richard Lant, Mark Norton, John Allde and four other apprentices, and considerable sums were given to charities. [Plomer, Wills, pp. 9-10.] The will of a Richard Kele stationer of London dated 1564 is amongst the wills proved in the Prerogative Court of Canterbury.

KELE (THOMAS), stationer in London, occupied for a year about 1526 part of the shop named the Mermaid as under tenant to John Rastell. [*Bibliographica*, II, 439.] He was probably the father of Richard and John Kele.

KEMMYSE (LEWIS), bookbinder in London, came to England about 1535. He took out letters of denization in 1544 "July 1, Lewes Kemmyse, bookbinder, born in Rone. Married to a French woman. In England 9 years." [Westm. Deniz. Roll, 36 Hen. VIII.] In 1564 his goods were valued at twenty shillings. In 1567-68 he was fined twelve pence by the Stationers' Company for keeping another man's servant. [Arber, I, 367.] In 1571 he is entered in St. Andrew's Parish, Holborn "Lewesse Kemysse, Frenchman, in England xxxviii yere, denyzon, and Ellyn his wyfe, Douchwoman, and hathe bene in England xvj yere, dwellinge in the parishe of St. Androwes xxvj yere, booke bynder. Stephan Keamysse his man." [R. of A., I, 425.] There were also two sons Thomas and Lewes. In 1576 "Lewes Comes" was still living in St. Andrew's Holborn, but by 1582 he was dead and "Ellin Comes, widowe" is entered instead. A fine early binding roll with the initials L. K. may perhaps have belonged to this binder. The house in which he lived belonged to Berthelet, and he may have been in his employment as a bookbinder.

KEMPE (ADRIAEN), stationer in Antwerp, was a native of Bouckhout. He used as a device a figure of St. Paul with a stone in the foreground on which are his mark and initials. This is found in the *Storys and prophesis out of the holy scriptur* printed by Simon Cowke in 1536 and in an English *New Testament* of the same year without printer's name. In 1537 a book was printed for him by Matthew Crom.

KEMPEN (GOTTFRIED VON), *see* Kempen (Johann von).

KEMPEN (JOHANN VON), printer in Cologne with his brother Gottfried apparently printed two works by Bale, *the First* [*and lattre*] *examinacyon of Anne Askewe* said in the colophons to have been printed at "Marpurg in the land of Hessen" in 1546 and 1547. The first contains the device of the printers with monogram and the motto Amor vincit omnia. [Heitz, p. xxviii. Tafel xliii.] In the same type is printed *A godly medytacyon of the christen sowle* by Margaret d'Angoulême, 1548. [Herbert, III, p. 1564.]

KEMPEN (ZACHARIAS), bookbinder in London, was an assistant to H. Singleton. He is entered in the register of the Dutch Church 1550-60 as living by the "Staelhof in griet Alderheleghen," that is the Steelyard in Thames Street, where Singleton lived at the Double Hood. [R. of A., I, 211.]

KERBRIANT or HUGUELIN (JEAN), printer in Paris, was at work from 1516 to 1550. He was probably a native of Brittany. At first he was in partnership with Jean Adam. He printed a very large number of service books for provincial churches. [Renouard, p. 197.] In 1516 he printed a Sarum *Missal* in partnership with Jean Adam, Jean Petit and Jean Bienayse.

KERVER (THIELMAN), printer in Paris, was born at Coblentz and carried on business between 1497 and 1522. In 1497 he commissioned J. Philippe to print a Sarum *Horae* for J. Richard, but soon began to print on his own account, first at the sign of the Unicorn on the Pont St. Michel, and afterwards at the Harrow in the Rue St. Jacques. In 1520 he gave up this house to his son and moved to the Unicorn in the Rue St. Jacques. He died in 1522 and was succeeded by his widow Yolande Bonhomme. Kerver and his widow printed a large number of Sarum service books, mostly for F. Byrckman. His device consists of his mark on a shield supported by two unicorns. [Renouard, pp. 198-199.]

KERVER (THIELMAN), widow of, *see* Bonhomme (Y.).

KEVALL (JOHN), stationer in London, was an original member of the Stationers' Company on its incorporation in 1557. Save as subscribing towards a benevolence in 1559 he is not mentioned in the Registers. He was still alive in 1562, when his son Stephen was baptised. [Registers of S. Mary Woolnoth.]

KEVALL (RICHARD), stationer in London, was made free May 9th, 1555, and is entered in the list in the charter of 1557, but after the incorporation of the Company his name is not again mentioned in the Registers. From the name being entered Richard Kevell, junior, it would appear that there was an older Richard, a member of the Company, but no such person is known. The Richard senior mentioned in the index to Arber [V, p. 246] is a mistake for Stephen.

KEVALL (STEPHEN), stationer in London, was born at Calais and was made free of the Company of Stationers November 23rd, 1535. [Bibl. Soc. Proc., VI, p. 18.] On the incorporation of the Company in 1557 Kevall was ninth on the list and was one of the Masters. In 1560 and 1565 he was Warden. There are very numerous entries relating to him in the Registers but almost all are connected with his official work, and two refer to his taking apprentices. He died on April 13th, 1571, and his will was proved on April 20th. He divided his property between the Stationers' Company and the poor of the Parish of St. Mary-at-Hill with a life interest to his wife Jane, who died in 1573. [Plomer, Wills, p. 18.] He was brother of John Kevall.

KEYSERE (MARTIN DE), see Caesar (M.).

KING (JOHN), printer in London, was an original member of the Company of Stationers on its incorporation. In 1556 he was settled in Paul's Churchyard, and we learn from the will of R. Toy that his shop was next door to, and under the same roof as J. Cawood's. He printed from 1555 to 1561 and apparently died in the latter year. One undated book, *Certaine bokes compyled by mayster Skelton*, was printed by John Kynge and Thomas Marshe in Creede Lane.

KING (WILLIAM), bookbinder, probably in Oxford, is mentioned in 1491. [Gibson, *Oxford Bindings*, p. 46.]

KINGSTON (ANTHONY), see Kitson (A.).

KINGSTON (JOHN), printer in London, was from 1553 to 1557 in partnership with Henry Sutton in St. Paul's Churchyard and together they issued a considerable number of Sarum service books. Kingston by himself was at the west door of St. Paul's and he printed mainly for others. He appears to have continued in business up to the year 1584. Kingston was not a member of the Stationers' Company, but apparently of the Grocers'.

KITSON (ANTHONY), bookseller in London, was a member of the Drapers' Company. He was several times in trouble with the Stationers' Company who fined him for offences against their rules. He issued only a few books which were printed for him by others. His first wife Margaret, by whom he had eleven children, died in 1567 and was buried in St. Faith's; he married again Mary, by whom he had a son John. He died in 1578 and his will was proved on July 12th. [Plomer, Wills, p. 25.] He was apparently a wealthy man and left considerable legacies to his children.

KNIGHT (THOMAS), bookseller, is known from a letter written by him from Venice on January 23rd, 1547, to Henry Bullinger, in which he signs himself Thomas Knight, Anglus, Bookseller. This letter is preserved in the town archives of Zurich. In 1551 John Burcher mentions him in a letter to Bullinger " as my friend Thomas Knight writes me word from England."

KYRFOTH (CHARLES), printer in Oxford, seems to have succeeded John Scolar, as he carried on business at the same address, St. John's Street near Merton College. He issued only one book, the *Compotus manualis ad usum Oxoniensium*, dated February 5th, 1519 [U.L.C.]. He had probably left the city before 1524, as he does not occur in the lists of those paying taxes. [Madan, p. 263.]

L. (P.), bookbinder, made use of a roll of renaissance ornament in compartments with his initials. [Weale, *Bookbindings*, p. 145.]

L. (R.), bookbinder, used two panels. On one is a shield with the arms of England and France, supported by a dragon and greyhound, and the binder's initials below. On the other is the Tudor rose supported by angels and surrounded by a ribbon with the motto " Hec rosa virtutis de celo missa sereno : eternum florens regia sceptra feret." In the upper corners are a fleur-de-lys and a shield with the cross of St. George and at the base the binder's initials and mark. [Weale, *Bookbindings*, pp. 123-4.] The use of the fleur-de-lys in place of the arms of London would seem to denote that the binder was a Frenchman working in England and not a citizen. A book is known having a panel of this binder on the one cover and a panel of R.O. on the other.

L. (T.), bookbinder in London, made use of two panels, one having a shield with the arms of England and France and below this a sheaf of arrows, Queen Katherine's badge, the binder's initials, and a shield with the arms of the City of London. On the other are the rose, pomegranate, castle and fleur-de-lys and in the centre a shield with the binder's initials. [U.L.C. St. John's Coll., Oxf.] [Weale, *Bookbindings*, p. 137.]

LACY (ALEXANDER), printer in London, was made free of the Stationers' Company April 31st, 1556. In 1559-60 he took the shilling to serve the Queen but this does not seem to have disturbed his business for we find him taking out licenses for printing in the following year and these continue without a break until 1571. Most of his work consisted of ballads, the majority of which have now perished, and the few books which he printed are rare. Herbert mentions only two and to these may be added the unique *Dives Pragmaticus* of 1563. [J.R.L.] Lacy does not seem to have printed or published after 1571, but he lived to a considerably later period, for in October, 1581, he presented his son John Lacy who took his freedom " per patronagium."

LANT (RICHARD), printer in London, was made a freeman of the Stationers on the 6th September, 1537, and paid forty-four shillings for the privilege. About 1542 he printed W. Tolwyn's *The manne of synne*, which was re-issued at Zurich by Bale in 1543. For this or some other book now unknown he was brought, along with several other printers, before the Privy Council for printing unlawful books contrary to the proclamation, and on April 8th committed to prison. On April 23rd he was fined and released from the Fleet, but bound to bring in a true declaration of what books and ballads he had bought or sold within the last three years and to give the names of any merchants that he knew to have brought in prohibited books. [*Acts of the P.C.*, vol. i, N.S., pp. 107, 117.] Between 1542 and 1547 Herbert quotes five books and a sixth a *Prognostication* for 1544 is known. [B.M.] After this time Lant seems to have printed nothing of importance but confined his attention mainly to ballads and other broadsides. He issued several about 1552 dealing with the controversy between Churchyard and Camell, and in 1558 a number were printed by him which had been licensed to W. Riddell. On March 16th, 1556, he was brought before the Privy Council and bound over to deliver to Cawood all the copies which he had printed of Cranmer's *Recantation* to be burnt. [*Acts of the P.C.*, vol. v, N.S., p. 249.] When he started printing he was living in the Old Bailey in St. Sepulchre's Parish, and at the end of his career "in Smithfield in the Parish of St. Barthelmewe's Hospital " and between these periods he lived first in Aldersgate Street where he published some ballads, and then in Paternoster Row. Books from his press are remarkably rare, there are but two in the British Museum and none in the Cambridge University Library. He was an original member of the Stationers' Company, and in 1552 received a bequest of forty shillings under the will of Richard Kele. [Plomer, Wills, p. 10.]

LARCHER (JEAN), *see* Dupré (J.).

LAROUGE (FRANCOISE), *see* Caesar (M.).

LATHUM (ROGER), printer in London, is mentioned by Herbert [I, 500] as follows "Dwelt in the Old Bailey. The only piece Mr Ames saw of his printing is intitled A grammer of the Latin tounge, 4°. 1535, among the late Earl of Oxford's books. I do not find it in the Bibl. Harleiana." There is however a small undated tract in the Bodleian entitled *Parvulorum institutio ex Stanbrigiana collectione* with the colophon "Imprynted at London in the olde Bayly. By me Roger Lathum" and this may very well be the piece to which Ames refers. Nothing else of this printer is known.

LAURET (GILES), bookbinder in London, is mentioned in the Subsidy Rolls of 1541 as dwelling in Shoe Lane with goods valued at £4 and taxed 4s. [R. of A., I, 56.] In 1544 the value of his goods was given as £3. [R. of A., I, 95.] In 1545 he is mentioned in the will of Edward Ylle, stationer "Gyles Lauret, bynder iii s. iiij d." He is last mentioned in the Subsidy Roll of 1549 when his goods were worth £12, and he paid a tax of twenty-four shillings. [R. of A., I, 181.] He may perhaps be identical with "Giles Lawrence, born in Croofelde in Normandy, aged 43 years. Married to an English woman and has 5 children English born. In England 34 years. 1 July, 1544." [Westm. Deniz. Roll, 36 Hen. VIII.]

LAUXIUS (DAVID), *see* Hopyl (W.).

LAWE (THOMAS), stationer in London, died in the year 1548. His existence is only known from his will, dated in that year. [Comm. of London, 211, Story.]

LAWND (WILLIAM), stationer in London, died in the year 1517 in which year his will was proved. [Comm. of London, 29, Bennet.] Nothing else is known of him.

LE BLANC (JEAN), printer in Paris, succeeded Jean Amazeur at the sign of the Golden Sun in the Rue du Paon in 1555 and continued to print up to about 1600. [Renouard, pp. 219-20.] He printed some editions of the Sarum *Breviary* in 1556 and 1557.

LEBLONDE (NICHOLAS), bookbinder in London, came to England about 1553 and took out letters of denization in 1564. "Nicholas le Blonde from the dominion of the King of France 19 Aug. 1564." [Pat. 6 Eliz., p. 11, m. 19.] In 1567 he is entered in the Subsidy Roll as Nicholas Blone [R. of A., I, 329] and in 1571 there is a more full entry "Nicholas Leblowne, denizen and bookebinder and his wife, of the French nation hath byn here xviij yeares." [R. of A., I, 436.] He lived in Aldersgate Ward.

LECOMTE (NICHOLAS), stationer in London, was a Frenchman and a member of the University of Paris. Madden [*Lettres d'un Bibliographe, V,* p. 252] gives 1493 as the first date at which his name is found in a book, but this is most probably incorrect and should rather be 1494 in which year on November 23rd he issued an edition of the *Synonyma* of Garlandia printed for him at Paris by Wolfgang Hopyl. His next book, dated February 26th, 1495, was an edition of Mirk's *Liber Festivalis* also printed by Hopyl. The third and last book was an edition of the Sarum *Horae*, printed at Paris in 1498 by Jean Jehannot. In the colophon Lecomte is spoken of as a member of the University of Paris and a merchant of books living for the time in England. The colophon of the *Synonyma* gives his address in St. Paul's Churchyard at the sign of St. Nicholas. Lecomte's device which occurs in all three books represents St. Nicholas restoring to life the three children in a tub and has also a shield containing his initials and mark. Round the whole runs the legend In domino confido . M. Nicholas Leconte. Beyond his appearance in England from 1494 to 1498 nothing is known of him. He was also apparently a bookbinder for the initials N.C. and a mark almost exactly identical with that found on his device occurs on a panel stamp [U.L.C.] ornamented with animals and flowers enclosed within the curves of a branch, while round all is a border of foliage.

LEEU (GERARD), printer in Gouda and Antwerp issued his first dated book at the former place in 1477. In 1484 he removed to Antwerp and while there printed at least seven books for the English market. The first an edition of the *Vulgaria Terentii* was issued in 1486 and this was followed by a Sarum *Directorium Sacerdotum* in 1488 and a little later by a Sarum *Horae*. In 1492 and 1493 he printed four books of more general interest. Three were reprints of books already printed by Caxton, the *Life of Jason*, the *History of Paris and Vienne* and the *Chronicles of England*. The fourth book was the *Dialogue or Communing between the Wise King Salomon and Marcolphus*, not otherwise known in English. While the edition of the *Chronicles* was being printed Leeu was struck on the head by one of his workmen and killed.

LEGRAUNDE (PETER), bookbinder in London, came to England in 1538 and took out letters of denization in 1544. "Peter Legraunde, bookbinder, French born. In England 6 years. 11 July 1544." [Deniz. Roll, 36 Hen. VIII.] He lived in the Parish of St. Andrew, Holborn in a house belonging to Berthelet, and was probably one of the bookbinders in his employment.

LEMPEREUR (MARTIN), *see* Caesar (M.).

LENDON (MICHAEL VAN), printer, is mentioned in the Subsidy Roll of 1549 as an assistant to John Day, working in Aldersgate Ward. [R. of A., I, 173.]

LEONARD of Christ's College, bookbinder in Cambridge, is mentioned in 1527-8 in the accounts of Trinity Parish as having mended and bound books. [Gray, *Cambridge Stationers*, p. 65.]

LE PREST (JEAN), printer in Rouen, was in business between the years 1544 and 1556. He printed in 1554 and 1555 some editions of the Sarum *Horae* for Robert and Florence Valentin.

LE ROUX or ROWSE (JEAN), printer in London, was a native of Normandy, and probably one of the large family of printers of that name settled there. He is first mentioned in December, 1536, when he gave evidence in a case relating to an attack on a certain Frenchman and he is there called "John de Rowsse of Normandy, printer, dwelling in the parish of St. Brigide." [*Letters and papers of Henry VIII*, vol. xi, p. 537.] He lived with his wife Marion in Shoe Lane, his next three neighbours being all bookbinders and is entered thrice in the Subsidy Rolls in 1541, 1544 and 1549. In this last year his goods were valued at ten pounds. [R. of A., I, pp. 56, 94, 181.] He is perhaps identical with "John Rowse, aged 70 years, born in Normandy : in England 52 years" who took out letters of denization July 1st, 1544. [Westm. Deniz. Roll, 36 Henry VIII.]

LE ROUX (NICHOLAS), printer in Rouen from 1530 to 1557, lived in the Rue de Ruissel in the Parish of St. Vivian. From 1533 onwards he printed a large number of Sarum service books. His device depicts St. Romain with a chained dragon on one side and a kneeling prisoner on the other. [Frère, *Livres de liturgie*, p. 37.]

LESQUIER (WILLIAM), stationer in Oxford, died at the beginning of 1501 and a record of a grant of administration after his decease, dated February 1st, 1501, is preserved in the University Archives. [Reg. ℭℓ., p. 122.] He died very heavily in debt, his principal creditor being a certain John Richard, probably the Rouen stationer of that name who had extensive dealings with England. Cyprian Relia was another creditor and the deceased's goods were divided *pro ratâ*.

LE TALLEUR (GUILLAUME), printer in Rouen, was at work from 1487 to 1490, in which period he printed about seven books. His printing office was in the Rue Saint-Lô. About 1490 he printed two law books for Richard Pynson who had probably been his assistant ; these were Statham's *Abridgement* and Litilton's *Tenures*. Le Talleur's device resembles that of Pynson, being simply his monogram in white upon a black ground.

LETTOU (JOHN), printer in London, was the first to introduce the art into that city where he began to print in 1480. It is probable from his name he was originally from Lithuania, but he appears to have learnt to print in Rome, for the type with which he started to print in London was used just previously in Rome by a certain John Bull of Bremen. Lettou's first production was an *Indulgence* and this was followed by an edition of *Antonius Andreae super XII libros metaphisice Aristotelis*. In 1481 he printed an edition of *Thomas Wallensis super Psalterium* which like the earlier book was printed at the expense of a certain William Wilcock, either a stationer or a patron. About 1482 Lettou joined in partnership with William de Machlinia, and together they printed a few legal works. Their place of business was by the church of All Saints. After this time Lettou's name is not found. [Duff, *Early Printed Books*, pp. 160, 161. *Printers of London and Westminster*, pp. 34–9. D.N.B.]

LEVET (PIERRE), printer in Paris, was at work between the years 1485 and 1502. At first he carried on business at the Silver Balance in the Rue St. Jacques and in 1494 was at the sign of the Golden Cross at St. Germain-des-Prés. In 1499 he was in partnership with Raoul Cousturier and Jean Hardouyn and in 1502 with Jean Barbier and François Foucher, [Renouard, pp. 244-5.] In 1494 he printed an edition of the Sarum *Breviary*.

LEWIS (PATRICK), *see* Lowes (P.).

LISLEY (ANDREW), stationer in Winchester, is mentioned as early as 1502 in the Oxford University Registers. In 1520-21 he was at Eton and was employed for 199 days in binding and repairing books in the College library. His materials were supplied to him and he received fourpence a day in wages, and one shilling a day in commons. [Weale, p. xxxix.]

LOBLEY, LOBBLE or LOBEL (MICHAEL), stationer in London, is first mentioned in 1531 amongst the persons who abjured. [Foxe, IV, pp. 585-6.] He is described as an assistant to Pepwell and the articles against him were that he, being at Antwerp, bought certain books inhibited as the *Revelation of Antichrist*, the *Obedience of a Christian Man*, the *Wicked mammon*, Frith against Purgatory; also for speaking against images and purgatory. A little later his wife was in trouble on religious matters, and he himself, according to Bonner was much vexed and troubled by Bishop Stokeslaye. [Foxe, V, p. 412.] In 1539 he was one of the booksellers who sold Hilsey's *Primer*, and by that time he was settled in St. Paul's Churchyard at the sign of St. Michael. Herbert quotes an *Almanack*, probably of 1545 as printed by him, but he does not appear to have practised printing himself, and his other books were printed by John Wayland, H. Sutton, R. Hall and Owen Rogers. His name occurs in the list of members of the Stationers' Company. Herbert says of him [p. 569] "He appears to have been a very orderly member of his company, subscribing x. s. towards the necessary expences at their first establishment; and was fined only twice, once for his late appearance on a court-day, and another time for his non-attendance on the Lord Mayor on Christmas-day, being thereunto warned, vi. d. In Feb. 1557-8 he made William Lobble his apprentice free. He was upper warden of the company 1 Eliz. when she confirmed their charter, and again in the year 1562. In Aug. 1560, soon after his first wardenship expired, he was, with Mr Judson, the new under warden, in the counter, by command of the Lord Mayor; on what account does not appear in the company's book; however they paid them their charges. In the latter part of his life he is found to be so poor as not to be able fully to discharge his note for 7£. which he owed the company; but paying 3£ the rest was forgiven him by the whole table." He died in 1567, and his will is preserved in the Registers of the Commissary of London at Somerset House.

LOKSMYTH (ROBERT), bookbinder in York, is mentioned in the *Fabric Rolls of the Minster* in 1530-31 [p. 105] "Roberto Loksmyth emendanti velum quadrigesimale. 12ᵈ."

LONGE (JOHN), stationer in London, was made a brother of the Stationers' Company before their incorporation in 1557. His name is found among other brethren who subscribed towards Bridewell in 1556 as giving twelve pence. [Arber, I, 48.] Being a brother he was no doubt a foreigner and may be identical with the person entered in the Lists of Denizations "John Longe, born in the Isle of Bille. In England 32 years. Married to an English woman and has by her 4 children. 1 July, 1544." [West. Deniz. Roll, 36 Hen. VIII.]

LORRAINE (JEAN DE), printer in Rouen, was in partnership from 1500 to 1506 with Pierre Olivier in the Rue Damiette near the church of St. Maclou. In 1500 they issued an edition of the Sarum *Manual* and in 1501 a Sarum *Missal.* [Frère, *Livres de Liturgie*, p. 28.] It is quite possible that Jean de Lorraine is identical with Jean Mauditier.

LOUIS (JAMET), *see* Loys (J.).

LOW (HANS), stationer in London, was a brother of the Stationers' Company before their incorporation. In 1565 he was fined thirteen shillings and four pence for arrears in his quarterage. [Arber, I, 315.] There is a chance that he may be identical with John Loye.

LOWES or LEWIS (PATRICK), bookbinder in Edinburgh, is known from the binding of a manuscript in Scottish which was written shortly after 1456. The binding is elaborately tooled with a variety of dies including figures of the apostles and evangelists. His name is stamped on the binding Patricius Lowes me ligavit. He is perhaps identical with a Patrick de Lowes who lived in the High Street Edinburgh and died before 1466. [*The Scottish Antiquary*, vol. xvi, pp. 133-9.]

LOYE (JOHN), stationer in London, is mentioned in the Subsidy Roll of 1547 as living in St. Paul's Churchyard with Th. Purflytte [Purfoot] and having goods valued at ten pounds. [R. of A., I, 134.] In 1549 he is returned as living in St. Paul's Churchyard with Andrew Hester. [R. of A., I, 159.]

LOYS or LOUIS (JAMET), printer in Rouen, lived near the New Market. He was in partnership about 1505 with Laurent Hostingue and together they printed an edition of Stanbridge's *Vocabula* for Martin Coffin of Exeter. In 1508 he printed a Sarum *Missal* for J. Huvin.

LUFFT (HANS), printer in Wittenberg, was at work from 1523 to 1572 and produced an enormous number of Luther tracts. There are however a number of English books which bear his name, but which can only doubtfully be assigned to him. These were issued between 1528 and 1535 and consist of controversial works by Tindale and Frith such as *The Parable of the Wicked Mammon, The obedience of a Christian Man, The Revelation of Antichrist, The Practise of Prelates* and two editions of the *Pentateuch.* All these profess to be printed by Hans Lufft "at Marlborowe in the land of Hesse" by which name Marburg is meant. But for every year between 1523 and 1546 we have numbers of books printed by Lufft at Wittenberg. Where the English books were printed it is difficult to suggest. Sayle [Catalogue iii, p. 1406] suggests perhaps Cologne, while putting one book under Antwerp. He also puts *A declaration of the Mass, 1547* "Wyttenberge by Hans Luft" under printers unknown. It is perhaps safe to assume that if the earlier English books were printed at Marburg they were not printed by Lufft or if printed by Lufft were not produced at Marburg, and most probably neither.

LYGHTES (OLIVER), is mentioned in the Subsidy Roll of 1549 as an assistant to Thomas Hacket the bookbinder.

LYNNE (WALTER), bookseller in London, was a native of the Low Countries and had settled in England before 1540. In 1541 and 1544 he is mentioned in the Subsidy Rolls as living in Billingsgate Ward and his goods were valued at twenty shillings. [R. of A., I, 61, 85.] In 1547 he is again mentioned and his goods had increased to eight pounds in value. [R. of A., I, 134.] In this same year he began to issue books, all of a theological character and by 1550 had published some two dozen books printed for him principally by N. Hill, R. Jugge, J. Hertford and John Day. He does not appear to have been a printer himself but busied himself as a translator, " being one that spendeth all hys time in the settynge forth of bokes in the Englysshe tounge " as he says in the preface to *Carion's Chronicles*. In 1549 he was taxed twenty shillings on goods worth ten pounds, and his servant Adrian Turner [or De Tolna] was taxed eight pence. Lynne's dwelling-house was on Sommers Key, Billingsgate, but he had also a shop in St. Paul's Churchyard, next the great school, at the sign of the Spread Eagle, and used as a device in his books a ram and a goat with the initials W. L. He appears to have issued no books after 1550 but he is mentioned in the Registers of the Dutch Church in 1551 "Wauter Lint, met Anna." In 1551 the shop in St. Paul's Churchyard with the sign of the Spread Eagle was in the occupation of John Gybkyn. In 1567 "Walter Lyn, and his wyf" are mentioned in the account of strangers and he is spoken of as not a denizen and having resided for thirty years. [R. of A., I, 331.] In the two returns of 1571 we find Annys Lin or Lyne, widow, of the Dutch nation, born in Zeland, hath been in England and in this Ward [Billingsgate] thirty years. [R. of A., I, 443 ; II, 70. D.N.B.]

LYNNELL (RICHARD), stationer in London, is first mentioned in 1563 when he presented an apprentice before the Stationers' Company. His name does not occur in the charter, but as it is not found in the lists of those made free after its passing he must have been a freeman before, many who were freemen at the time having been omitted.

LYNYNG (URBAN), printer in London, was an assistant to Nicholas Hill and is entered in St. John Street in the Subsidy Roll of 1549. [R. of A., I, 157.] It is just possible that he is identical with the printer named Urban van Cuelen [*q.v.*]. In 1561 he appears in the Registers of the Dutch Church as Luninck or Lininck. [R. of A., I, 277, 283.]

LYVEDALE (DERICK), stationer in London, came to England about 1547. He lived in St. Paul's Churchyard and is entered in 1571 in St. Faith's Parish "Derick Lyvedalle, stacioner, born in Flanders, in England 24 yeares, in the said warde 7 yeres." [R. of A., I, 411.]

MAAS (ROBERT), was an assistant to Wynkyn de Worde who left him in his will two pounds in printed books. [Plomer, Wills, p. 4.]

MACÉ (RICHARD), stationer in Rouen, was in business from 1502 to about 1525. He was also a bookbinder and used panels containing pictures of the Annunciation and Coronation of the Virgin, the latter containing his name in full. He commissioned some copies of the Sarum *Breviary* of 1515 printed by J. Ferrebouc and J. Bienayse, for the copy in Caius College Cambridge, unlike that at Oscott, has an extra line after the imprint "Impensis honesti viri Richardi mace."

MACHLINIA (WILLIAM DE), printer in London, joined partnership about 1482 with John Lettou the first printer in London. Machlinia, from his name was doubtless a native of Mechlin in Belgium. In partnership the two printers issued five books all of a legal character, printed in a very cramped gothic letter and abounding with contractions. About 1483 Machlinia was at work by himself in a printing office near Flete-bridge the office "near the church of All Saints" which the partners had occupied having been given up. At Flete-bridge Machlinia printed eight books and then moved to Holborn where he printed fourteen. One of the books printed here, the *Speculum Christiani*, was printed for a bookseller, Henry Frankenbergk living in St. Clement's Lane. Machlinia certainly printed as late as 1486 for he issued a *Bull* of Innocent VIII confirming the marriage of Henry VII and Elizabeth of York which is dated March 27th, 1486. Machlinia's work was of the most careless description, and he made no use of any ornament, either initial letters or illustrations, with the exception of a rude border in his edition of the Sarum *Horae*. His books are with or without signatures for no apparent reasons, very few have a colophon, not one has a date, and it is impossible to arrange them in any definite order. [D.N.B. Duff, *Printers of London and Westminster*, pp. 36-46.]

MADELEY (ROGER), printer in London, is known only as the printer of one ballad, *An invective against treason*. In the imprint he is stated to have carried on business at the sign of the Star in St. Paul's Churchyard, where at an earlier date we find Thomas Raynald.

MAHEU (DESIDERIUS), printer in Paris, was born in 1474 and carried on business from 1510 to 1542. He lived at the sign of St. Nicholas in the Rue St. Jacques. In 1526 he printed a *Manuale ad usum Sarum*. [Renouard, p. 253.]

MANNYNG (THOMAS), printer in London, was an assistant some time before 1540 to Thomas Raynald who was then living at Hallywell. [Bibl. Soc. Trans., VI, 20.]

MANSION (COLARD), printer in Bruges, was for many years a writer and illuminator of manuscripts, being entered under that head from 1454 to 1473 in the books of the Guild of St. John. When Caxton was in search of someone to assist him in printing, he joined with Mansion as a partner and together they set up the first press at Bruges about 1474-5. In partnership they printed three books *The Recuyell of the Histories of Troye*, the first book printed in English, *The Game and Playe of the Chesse* and *Les quatre derrennieres choses*. In 1476 Caxton returned to England and in that year Mansion's first dated book appeared. He printed steadily up to May, 1484, issuing some twenty-five books. Soon after this date he fled from Bruges and his printing office over the porch of the church of St. Donatus was let to a bookbinder named Jean Gossin. [Duff, *Early printed books*, pp. 105-6.]

MANSTENER (JEAN), *see* Philippe (J.).

MARCANT (NICHOLAS), printer, is known only from the colophon of an edition of the little grammar called *Parvula* [J.R.L.] which runs " Here endeth a treatise called parvula, for the instruction of children. Emprentyd by me Nicole Marcant." There is no clue to the place of printing or date, apparently about 1500. The printer was probably one of the numerous family of Marchand or Mercator.

MARCHANT (JEAN), stationer in Rouen about 1536-42 lived opposite the church of St. Maclou at the sign of the Two Unicorns. In 1536 an edition of the York *Horae* was printed for him and John Growte of London by Nicholas le Roux at Rouen. In 1537 another *Horae* of Sarum use printed by Le Roux for J. Cousin was issued which contains Marchant's device. In this book many woodcuts are signed I.M. which Frère [*Livres de Liturgie*, pp. 46-7] conjectures may mean that they are Marchant's work. He used two devices, one of which contains his initials on a shield hanging from an oak and supported by two unicorns; above all are two clasped hands emerging from clouds. The second is a shield containing his initials, surrounded by a wreath of laurel.

MARDELEY (JOHN), yeoman, has been sometimes erroneously mentioned as a printer, perhaps on account of an order of the Privy Council forbidding him to publish or print, any book, ballad, or other print not licensed. August 13th, 1549. [*Acts of the P. C.*, vol. ii, N.S., pp. 311-12.] He was a clerk in the King's mint at Suffolk House, and the writer of a considerable number of controversial pamphlets about this time. [D.N.B.]

MARE (JOHN), *see* More (J.).

MARESCALUS (HENRICUS), *see* Marshall (H.).

MARLER (ANTHONY), of London, was a wealthy member of the Haberdashers' Company who assisted Grafton and Whitchurch with money to print Bibles. In 1540 he presented a copy on vellum of the April edition to Henry VIII. [B.M.] Cromwell, who favoured the printers Grafton and Whitchurch, had the sole right of giving permission to print the Bible, and on his death Marler applied for an exclusive privilege which was granted him in 1541 to run for four years. In April, 1541, the Privy Council settled the price of the Bibles at ten shillings unbound and twelve bound, and in May, in answer to Marler's petition who represented that he should be ruined unless his Bibles were sold, issued a proclamation to compel all churches to provide themselves at once with a Bible. [*Acts of the P. C.*, O.S., vol. vii, pp. 181, 185.]

MARSHALL, MARESCALUS (HENRY), stationer in Rouen about 1539, is not mentioned by any writer on the Rouen Press. He is only known from the colophon to an edition of the Sarum *Horae* "Venundantur Rothomagi apud Henricum Marescalum bibliopolam commorantem in via magna horologii." [Hoskins, p. 53, No. 145.]

MARSHALL (WILLIAM), publisher in London, was strongly interested in the Reformation and caused several books to be printed for him to further the movement. Among them are the *Gift of Constantine* printed by Godfray, *Erasmus on the Creed* by Redman, *De vetere et novo Deo* by Byddell and the *Defence of Peace* by Wyer. His zeal seems often to have outrun his discretion and funds were not always available to pay for what he had commissioned. Some interesting letters concerning his books written to Cromwell will be found in the *Letters and Papers of Henry VIII.* [Vol. vii, pp. 178, etc.] He was also the author of several treatises and translations, two of which, *Pictures and Ymages* and *The chrysten Bysshop and counterfayte Bysshop* were apparently printed by John Gowghe, though Herbert states that the colophon of the latter runs "Emprynted by Wyllyam Marshall." The reformed *Prymer* of 1535 was also printed for him. He used a large woodcut of his coat-of-arms as a device. [D.N.B.]

MARSHE (THOMAS), printer in London, began to work in 1554 at the sign of the Prince's Arms in Fleet Street or, as it was also called, the King's Arms. He was an original member of the new Stationers' Company, was taken into the Livery in 1562 and was a Warden in 1575 and 1581. He printed continuously up till 1587, issuing a very large number of books. He had also a privilege to print grammars. He used as devices a monogram and also more rarely a figure of Fortune.

MARTENS (THIERRY), printer in Alost and Louvain, introduced printing into the former town in partnership with John de Westphalia in 1473. He continued on alone at Alost from 1487 to 1493 when he moved to Antwerp, moving on again in 1498 to Louvain. In or about 1502 he returned to Antwerp, but settled again in Louvain in 1512 up to the end of his career in 1529. He left Louvain in this latter year and returning to Alost died on May 28th, 1534, aged about eighty-five. His device was a four-fluked anchor. [Van der Meersch, pp. 70-83.] Martens printed two books for the English market, an edition of the *Liber synonymorum* with the commentary of Galfridus Anglicus at Antwerp in 1493 and a Sarum *Breviary* at Louvain in 1499. [Duff, *Printers of London and Westminster*. p. 66.]

MARTYNE (WILLIAM), printer in London, is first mentioned in 1552. "June 7. William Marten, printer, being brought before the Lordes for printing a seditious ballet set forth by one John Lawton, was this day bounde in recognisaunce of one hundreth poundes to appere every weeke once before theyr Lordshippes untill they shall take farther ordre with hym, and in the meane tyme to bring in as many of the same ballates as he may cume by." [*Acts of the Privy Council*, N.S., vol. iv, p. 69.] Martyne was an original member of the Stationers' Company. Between November, 1560, and March, 1561, he had a license to print *The hurte of herynge of masse* and this was printed for him by W. Copland. In it he gives his address "joyninge to the mydle North dore of Paules, at the syne of the blacke boye." In 1562-63 he was fined with many others for selling *Nostradamus* and apparently died soon after, as his widow Joan took an apprentice in December, 1564.

MARTYNSON (SIMON), stationer in London, was a native of Haarlem, and took out letters of denization February 26th, 1535. [Pat. 26 Hen. VIII, p. 2, m. 42.] As he is the only person named Simon connected with the book trade that I can trace, he may be the person mentioned by De Worde in his will "Simon my servant the value of xx.s in books." In the Records at the Guildhall is an entry dated September 17th, 1538, "Item the Kyngs most gracious letters written in favor of a denisyn called Symond Martinson, stacyoner to be fre of London." [Repertory, 10.]

MASKALL (THOMAS), stationer in London, was an original member of the Stationers' Company in 1557. Beyond the entry of his name in the charter and some subscription lists nothing is known of him.

MASSELLIN (ROBERT), printer in Paris from 1550 to 1553. He lived first " Aux trois trenchoirs rouges devant saincte Geneviefve du Mont" a shop occupied shortly after by his brother Marin, and in 1552-53 "Près le collège Montaigu à l'enseigne de la Palme." In 1554 he went to Rouen, and in 1556 and 1557 is found as a printer at Thiers in Auvergne. In 1553 he printed an edition of the *Rudimenta artis grammaticae* of John Vaus, a professor in the University of Aberdeen.

MATHER (JOHN), *see* Moptid (David).

MAUDITIER (JEAN), printer in Rouen, was in partnership in 1502 with P. Olivier in the Rue Ancrière near the church of St. Pierre, when they issued an edition of the Hereford *Missal*. Mauditier printed afterwards by himself up to 1517, living near the church of St. Laurent. [Frère, *Livres de Liturgie*, p. 63, *L'Imprimerie à Rouen*, pp. 33, 34.] There are very strong grounds for believing that Jean Mauditier was the same as Jean de Lorraine who printed with Olivier in 1500 and 1501 a Sarum *Manual* and *Missal;* these two books as well as the Hereford *Missal* were all produced for J. Richard.

MAYHEWE (WILLIAM), printer in London, was born about 1514 and in 1531 became an apprentice with John Rastell. He occurs as one of the witnesses in the trial concerning Rastell's printing house in 1534-5. [*Bibliographica*, II, 439-40.]

MAYLER (JOHN), printer in London, was a member of the Grocers' Company. He began to print in 1539, producing some editions of Hilsey's *Primer* for J. Wayland, Andrew Hester and Michael Lobley. In 1540 he printed an edition of the *New Testament* in Latin and in the following year was in trouble on account of the Six Articles, being accused as a railer against the Mass. [Foxe, V, 445.] In 1541 he began to print for John Gowghe for whom all his books were printed until the latter's death in 1543. The books issued in that period were almost all works by Thomas Becon, and one to which he wrote a preface, Coverdale's translation of Bullinger's *Christian state of matrimony*, was certainly a prohibited book. On April 8th, 1543, Mayler with seven other printers was brought before the Privy Council " for printing off suche bokes as wer thowght to be unlawfull, contrary to the proclamation made on that behalff " and was committed to prison. On April 23rd he was delivered from the Fleet prison, but fined and bound to send in a true declaration what number of books and ballads he had bought within three years, what he had sold, and what merchants he knew to have brought in prohibited books. [*Acts of the Privy Council*, N.S., vol. i, pp. 107–117.] After Gowghe's death in 1543 Mayler appears to have done little. In 1544 and 1545 he printed a *Prognosticon* of J. Mussemius and some works of Leland, but after 1545 nothing further is known of him. He lived in Billingsgate Ward, in Botolph Lane at the sign of the White Bear.

MAYNMOUR or MYNDMER (ROMAYN), printer in London, was born at Rouen in Normandy, but came to England about 1553. He was for a considerable time an assistant to John Day at Aldersgate. He is mentioned in the full Return of Aliens in 1571 [R. of A., I, 421], " Romyn Maynmour, printer, Frenche man borne, and Frauncis, his wyfe, beinge a denizon, hathe bene in this realme xviij yeres, and in this ward [Grenes Rentes, Farringdon Without] vii yeres." He is mentioned in 1576 with a son Josias, and again in 1582. [R. of A., II, 171, 249.] In 1591 though his name occurs in the Subsidy Roll, he is marked as " Not to be founde." [R. of A., II, 439.] Though he is spoken of as a denizen, his name is not found in the lists of denizations. He apparently was never in business on his own account, for throughout his career he is never entered as possessing any goods, but simply pays the poll-tax of four pence which was levied on all foreign workmen assistants.

MAYNYAL (WILLIAM), printer in Paris from 1487 to 1490, was probably a relation of the better-known printer George Maynyal, and both are conjectured by M. Claudin on somewhat slight grounds to have been of English birth.   In 1487 William printed for Caxton an edition of the Sarum *Missal*, of which one imperfect copy survives [Lord Newton], and about the same time, probably also for Caxton, an edition of the Sarum *Legenda*, only known from fragments.   Besides these two books he only printed two others, a *Manuale* and the *Statutes* of the church of Chartres, dated 1489 and 1490.

MEGUISSHER or MEGUSSHER (JOHN), printer in London, came to England about 1541.   He is entered in the Returns of Aliens [I, p. 421] in 1571, "John Megussher and Margaret his wyfe, French, howsholder, a denizon, of occupacion a printer hathe bene in this realme xxx yeares, and in this ward [Farringdon Without] x yeares."

MELTYNBE (JOHN), bookbinder in York, was made a freeman by patrimony in 1536–37: he is entered as "Johannes Meltynbe, bokebynder, fil. Willelmi Meltynbe, sadler."   [*Freemen of York*, p. 256.]

MEN (HORMAN), bookbinder in Oxford, was summoned with many others in April, 1539, for eating meat in Lent.   [*Letters and papers of Hen. VIII*, vol. xiv, pt. i, p. 339.]

MERLIN (GUILLAUME), printer in Paris, was in business between the years 1538 and 1572.   He lived on the Pont aux Changes at the sign of L'homme Sauvage and used as his device a swan carrying a cross with the somewhat profane punning motto "In hoc cygno vinces," for which he got into trouble.   He published several editions of the Sarum *Breviary* and *Missal* in 1555–57.   He was also a bookbinder and several bindings are known stamped with his device.

MERYSON (GEORGE), stationer in London, was apparently a member of the Stationers' Company who had died shortly before their incorporation. On October 4th, 1557, a certain Richard Cowper was made free who had been an apprentice to Meryson but had been turned over to Randal Tyrer. [Arber, I, 69.]

MESLIER (HUGO), printer (?), was associated with R. Pynson in printing the *Principia* of Peregrinus de Lugo for G. Chastelain the Oxford bookseller. The colophon runs "Impressa ... Londini per Richardum pynson cum solerti cura ac diligentia honestissimi iuuenis ac prudentissimi Hugonis Meslier." [Herbert, I, 252.] The name appears to be French and a Denis Meslier carried on business as a stationer in Paris at the close of the fifteenth century. [Renouard, p. 267.]

MESSYNGHAM (JOHN), bookbinder in York, is mentioned in the *York Minster Fabric Rolls* [p. 82] as binding a book in 1473 "Johanni Messyngham pro ligatura i libri vocati antiphonarii, emendacione defectuum ejusdem, coopertura ejusdem, custodibus et correo rubeo."

MESSYNGHAM (THOMAS), bookbinder in York, was made free in 1450–51. In 1485 he is mentioned in the *York Minster Fabric Rolls* [p. 88] as binding a book. "Thomas Messyngham pro ligatura unius gradalis pro choro ecclie. Cath: custodibus, bosses, clavis et duabus pellibus pro eodem gradali, et uno libro de novo facto empto pro choristis, 23s. 1½d."

METEREN (JAMES VAN), *see* Cornelii (J.).

MICHAEL of Antwerp, printer in London, is mentioned in the Subsidy Roll of 1541 as an assistant to Walter Prynter in St. Olave's Parish Southwark. [R. of A., I, 35.]

MIDDLETON (WILLIAM), printer in London, succeeded Robert Redman at the sign of the George in Fleet Street after Redman's widow was married to Ralph Cholmondeley, and was admitted a freeman on July 5th, 1541. In the same year he issued his first dated book and, like his predecessors in the same house, issued numerous law books. In April, 1543, along with several other printers, he was brought before the Privy Council "for printing off suche bokes as wer thowght to be unlawfull, contrary to the proclamation" and was committed to the Fleet, but liberated after a fortnight's imprisonment. He was however compelled to pay a fine and send in a list of all books and ballads which he had printed and sold within three years. He printed a very large number of books up to 1547, in June of which year he died, and his will dated June 4th was proved on the 17th of the same month. He left his property to his wife Elizabeth who testified her sorrow by marrying, within two months, another printer William Powell. Middleton used two devices, the smaller consists of two half-length winged figures supporting a shield on which is a tun inscribed with an M, a W below and his mark above. The other contains a similar shield hanging from a fruit tree and supported by two figures ending with the legs of goats and tails of dragons, with the name in full below on a ribbon Wyllyam Myddylton.

MIDILTON (GODFREY), stationer in London, is mentioned in a Chancery suit brought between 1475 and 1485 by Robert Skarlet, barber, for recovery of debt. Midilton's wife was Joan, widow of Nicholas Vagode, plumber. [Early Chancery Proceedings, Bundle 64, No. 983.]

MIERDMAN (STEPHEN), printer in Antwerp, London and Emden, first appears in 1543 when he issued the first edition of the *New Testament* translated into Spanish by Franzisco de Enzinas. The book is beautifully printed in Roman letter with good woodcut illustrations, but little else is known of the printer's work at Antwerp. A very full account of the printing of this book with some curious details will be found in a work written by Enzinas himself, *Histoire de l'estat du Pais Bas, et de la religion d'Espagne*, 1558 [p. 66, *et seqq.*]. By 1549 Mierdman had come over and settled in England along with many other foreign refugees and is entered in that year in the Returns of Aliens as living in St. Mary-at-Hill Parish, Billingsgate Ward. [R. of A., I, 161.] In 1550 he took out letters of denization dated October 29th [Pat. 4 Edw. VI, p. 4, m. 2] and is also entered along with his wife Elizabeth in the lists of members of the Dutch Church. He seems to have set up printing on quite a large scale and employed a number of foreign journeymen, no doubt fellow-refugees. Between 1550 and 1552 he issued a considerable number of books, at least twelve being known, the majority being tracts in Latin, Dutch or French either relating to, or written by members of the reformed Dutch Church settled in London under John A Lasco. The two English books which he printed are *The market or fayre of usurers*, and Turner's *New herball, with the names of herbes in Greek Latin English Dutch Frenche*. Many of his books were to be sold by John Gybkyn, a foreign stationer in St. Paul's Churchyard. No dated book of Mierdman's is known printed in London after 1552 and on the accession of Mary, along with many others he fled again to the Continent settling after some wandering at Emden, where he took the oath of citizenship April 26th, 1554, and is entered in the Bürgerbuch as "Stheven Mermann uth Brabant." At Emden he printed several books.

MIGHEN (PETER), bookseller in London, is mentioned in the Privy Purse expenses of Henry VIII under January, 1530, "Item the xv daye paid to Sr John Russell for so moche money by him paied to one Peter Mighen for divers books, iii li." [Nicholas, *Privy Purse expenses of Henry VIII*, p. 18.] Several London booksellers named Meighen occur at a later date.

MOCKYLL (JOHN), stationer in London, supplied books to the church of St. Martin-in-the-Fields in 1553. [*Accounts of the churchwardens, 1525–1605, transcribed and edited by J. V. Kitto*, 1901, p. 136.]

MOLYAR or MYLLAR (CONRAD), printer in London, is mentioned in the Subsidy Roll of 1549 as an assistant to J. Gybkyn in St. Faith's Parish. [R. of A., I, 159.] He was admitted a brother of the Stationers' Company some time before their incorporation and in 1556–7 was fined eighteen pence for "mysnamynge" another brother. He subscribed eight pence to the collection for Bridewell and in December, 1557, paid the Company twelve pence for the use of their hearse cloth at his wife's funeral. [Arber, I, 45, 48, 70.] In 1563–4 Nicholas Cleston was fined for calling Conrad Myller a drunkard. An interesting memorandum addressed to the Lord Treasurer by Sir W. Cecil dated 21st April, 1564, refers to a large consignment of books about to be imported by Arnold Birckman and Conrad Mollar of Cologne, merchants, from the Frankfort fair. [Arber, II, 63.] On January 27th, 1567, he was admitted a University bookseller at Oxford [Clark, I, p. 321], was licensed to sell ale in St. Mary's Parish September 16th, 1572; and was still alive in 1588. [Clark, I, p. 325. Madan, p. 274.]

MONTANUS (NICOLAUS), *see* Hill (N.).

MOPTID (DAVID), printer in London, in partnership with John Mather is mentioned in the British Museum catalogue as printing a book by Anthony Gilby in 1547. The book is really about thirty years later, and Moptid was not bound apprentice to Thomas East until 1566.

MORE or MARE (JOHN), stationer in Oxford, is mentioned in the Magdalen College Register [vol. ii, p. 213] as having sold a manuscript on October 21st, 1457, to T. Wyche. His name occurs as a stationer in the University Archives [Register Aaa] between the years 1443 and 1470.

MOREUX (PETER), bookbinder in York, was made free by patrimony in 1493-94. He is entered as "Pet. Morewx, texwritter et boukbynder, fil. Thomae Moreux, walker." [*Freemen of York*, p. 219.]

MORIN (MARTIN), printer in Rouen from 1490 until about 1517, is celebrated for the number and beautiful workmanship of the liturgical works he produced. At least eighteen service books are known to have been printed by him for the English market between 1492 and 1517. He lived in the Rue St. Lô at the sign of St. Eustace. His mark is a circle divided horizontally by a line from which rises above the circle a double barred cross. In the upper part of the circle are the initials M.M., in the lower a Moor's head. [Frère, *L'Imprimerie à Rouen. Livres de Liturgie.*]

MORIN (MICHAEL), stationer in London, is first mentioned in 1497 [1498] when Pierre Levet printed at Paris an edition of the *Destructorium Vitiorum* of Alexander Anglus "expensis Joh. Cobelens, Petri Levet, et Michaelis Morin." [H. C., 653. Pellechet, 437. Proctor, 8,069.] In 1504 he was settled in London and in that year Badius Ascensius printed at Paris an edition of *Terence* to be sold in London "in edibus W. de Worde, Michael Morin et Johannis Brachii." In 1506 an edition of the Sarum *Breviary* was printed by Kerver "ere et impensis honestorum virorum Wynkyn de Worde et Michaelis Morin mercatorum bene meritorum Londoniis moram trahentium." He was probably a relation of the Norman family of stationers named Morin.

MORRES (NEWELL), stationer in York, was made a freeman in 1519-20. [*Freemen of York*, p. 242.]

MYCHELL (JOHN), printer in London and Canterbury, printed first in London at "the long shop in the Poultry" probably after Kele left that address in 1546 and before Alde began there. In London he printed at least two books, the *Life of St. Margaret* and the *Life of St. Gregorie's mother*. In 1549 he was settled in St. Paul's Parish, Canterbury, where he printed up to the year 1556. Herbert gives some eleven books printed within this period, but besides those in his list are editions of Stanbridge's *Accidence*, *The Chorle and the Birde* and Saltwood's *Comparison bytwene four byrdes*, all undated. Herbert also fails to notice the three different editions of the

Breviat Cronicle. The last book issued by Mychell was Cardinal Pole's *Articles to be enquyred in the ordinary visitacion of the Dioces of Cantorbury, 1556.* [*Bibliographica,* II, pp. 41-45.]

MYDDYLTON (WILLIAM), *see* Middleton (W.).

MYLES (THOMAS), printer in London, was apparently at one time an apprentice to Richard Kele who in his will dated 1552 wrote "I wyll that Mr. Toye shall make free Thomas Myles his yeres being exspired."

MYLLAR (ANDREW), printer in Edinburgh, was the first, in partnership with Walter Chepman, to introduce the art of printing into Scotland. He is first mentioned in 1503 as a bookseller when he was paid by the Lord High Treasurer ten pounds for certain printed books. Soon after this date Chepman, anxious to set up a press on his own account, sent Myllar abroad to learn the art and obtain material. He went apparently to Rouen and while there had two books printed for him, a *Liber equivocorum* in 1505 and a Sarum *Expositio Sequentiarum* (with which doubtless went an *Expositio Hymnorum* now lost) in 1506. From the type and woodcuts it is clear that these books were printed by Pierre Violette. By 1507 Myllar had returned and in that year obtained a privilege from James IV in which it was stated that he had brought over "ane prent, with all stuff belangand tharto, and expert men to use the samyne." In the spring of 1508 Chepman and Myllar issued a series of nine poetical pamphlets only known from unique copies [Advocates' Lib., Edinburgh] the earliest with a date being *The Maying and disport of Chaucer,* of April 4th. In some of these and in the *Expositio Sequentiarum* occurs Myllar's device, probably cut in Rouen, containing the figure of a windmill to which a man ascends by a ladder. Below the mill is a shield with his mark and his name in full and in the upper corners are shields with the arms of France. It is probable that Myllar died soon after 1508 as his name does not occur in the colophon to the Aberdeen *Breviary* of 1510, and as he had been joined with Chepman in the patent for printing it his name would almost certainly have been found there had he been alive. [Dickson and Edmond, *Annals.* D.N.B. Duff, *Early Printed Books,* pp. 174-6.]

MYLLAR (CONRAD), *see* Molyar (C.).

MYLNER (URSYN), printer and stationer in York, was born in 1481. In 1511 he appeared as a witness in the law-suit between Frederick Wandsforth and Ralph Pulleyn, at which time he was living in the Parish of St. Michael le Belfry. About 1513 he printed two small service books, one the *Festum visitationis Beate Marie Virginis*, and the other a supplement to the Sanctorale of the *Breviary* containing anthems, responds, etc. for St. Thomas and St. Edmund of Canterbury. The colophons of these two books speak of him as living in the Minster churchyard, and his shop was most probably in the passage which formed the South entrance to the Minster close beside the church of St. Michael le Belfry which was formerly known as Bookbinders' Alley. At a little later date he moved to Blake Street in St. Helen's Parish, and in 1515–16 his name occurs on the roll of freemen. On December 20th, 1516, he issued Whittinton's *Editio de concinitate grammatices et constructione*. At the end is his device consisting of a shield hanging on a tree supported by a bear and an ass, the bear being an allusion to his name Ursyn. On the shield are a sun and a windmill, the latter referring to his name Mylner. Below this device is an oblong cut containing his name in full on a ribbon, with his trade mark in the centre. Mylner was also a bookbinder, for we find in the account of expenses of York Minster under the year 1516 an entry of 49 shillings and 4 pence paid to him for binding books in the choir and for painting the red alms-box which stood below the statue of the blessed Virgin. After the year 1516 nothing is known of him. [*Fabric Rolls of York Minster*, p. 97.]

MYLWARD (HENRY), stationer in Oxford, is mentioned as early as 1549. In 1579 he was living in St. Mary's Parish and in 1583 had a lease of Beef Hall. On April 11th, 1597, he retired from old age. [Madan, 273.] He is last mentioned in the University Archives under the year 1599.

MYNDMER (ROMAYN), *see* Maynmour (R.).

MYNE (WILLIAM), stationer of York, was made a freeman by patrimony in 1512–13. He is entered as "Willelmus Myne, staconer, fil. Johannis Myne, fisshemonger." [*Freemen of York*, p. 236.]

N. (H.), bookbinder, used two panels. On one is a shield with the arms of England and France supported by a dragon and greyhound and below this the binder's initials. On the other is the Tudor rose supported by angels and surrounded by scrolls with the motto "Hec rosa virtutis de celo missa sereno: eternum florens regia sceptra feret." At the base the binder's initials and mark. [Weale, *Bookbindings*, p. 119.]

N. (I.), binder, *see* Notary (J.).

NELE (RICHARD), stationer in London, is mentioned in 1525 as being transferred from the Stationers to the Company of Ironmongers. [Arber, I, xxi.]

NEWELL or NEVILL (THOMAS), bookbinder in York, is mentioned in the *York Minster Fabric Rolls* [p. 113] "1556 To Thomas Newell for mending and bindinge of bookes 7s."

NICHOLAS of Bamberg, printer, is only known as issuing Bale's *Comedy concernynge thre lawes of Nature, Moses and Christ*, 1538. [Herbert, III, p. 1548.]

NICHOLAS, bookseller in London, is mentioned in a letter dated February 24th, 1528, from Dr. London to the Bishop of Lincoln [*Letters and papers of Hen. VIII*, vol. iv, pt. ii, p. 1762] as being a bookseller in Paul's Churchyard from whom Anthony Dalaber bought a copy of the *Farragines Lamberti*, a prohibited book. The only stationer of that name known to have had a shop in Paul's Churchyard at that date was Nicholas Sutton.

NICHOLAS, bookbinder in Oxford, is mentioned in 1484 in the accounts of the Chantry of St. Thomas.

NICHOLL (THOMAS), stationer in London, was party between 1475 and 1485 to a suit in Chancery concerning trespass. [Early Chancery Proceedings, Bundle 64, No. 248.]

NICHOLSON (HENRY), printer at Wesel, is mentioned in the colophon to the second issue of William Roy's *Rede me and be not wrothe* "Prynted at Wesell in the yeare of oure Lorde, 1546, in the last of June by Henry Nycolson." [Herbert, III, 1560.] This was really printed by R. Jugge.

NICHOLSON or NICOLAI (JAMES), printer in Southwark, was a native of the Low Countries. He was a strong friend to the reformed religion and began his career by publishing in 1535 the first edition of the English *Bible*, printed at Zurich by Christopher Froschauer but for which he printed titles and prefatory matter. In 1536 he began printing on his own account issuing *A mirror or glasse for them that be syke* [U.L.C.] and a work of Tindale's. Most of Nicholson's ordinary work appears to have been done for John Gowghe. In 1537 he printed two more editions of the *Bible* in folio and quarto, the latter calling forth strong complaints from Grafton who had just expended £500 on his edition. In 1538 Nicholson issued two editions of the *New Testament*, one edited by John Hollybush, a refugee stationer most probably identical with Jan van Ruremond, but these editions professing to be Coverdale's versions were severely censured by him because of their incorrectness. After 1538 Nicholson appears to have given up printing, though he was alive at a considerably later date and an elder of the foreign church in London. His printing office was in St. Thomas' Hospital and after the cessation of his business some of his material appears to have passed into the hands of John Mayler and Edward Whitchurch.

NICHOLSON (JOHN), stationer in London, lived apparently in the Parish of St. Alphege Cripplegate, in which church he desired to be buried. His will dated October 5th, 1466, was proved October 6th, 1468. He left considerable property, and bequests to his father John, his wife Emma, his children, then under age, John and Margaret, his four sisters and his brother-in-law Richard Frampton. [*Calendar of Wills in the Court of Husting*, part ii, pp. 560–61.]

NICHOLSON (SEGAR), stationer in Cambridge, was born at Maestricht in 1500, and was educated at Gonville and Caius College, being a pensioner in 1520–23. In 1530 he is mentioned in the accounts of Queens' College as supplying two blank books. He appears to have been a strong partisan of the reformers, and in 1531 got into trouble for his heretical opinions and the possession of prohibited books. He was imprisoned for some time, and according to Foxe was very cruelly used. In spite of this he was elected in 1534 one of the three official University stationers. In 1539 his cousin Garret Godfrey bequeathed him fifteen pounds. How long he continued in business is not known, but in 1564 in his sixty-fourth year he was ordained deacon and priest by the Bishop of London. In 1557 a Francis Nycholson *alias* Seager was made free of the Stationers' Company, and in 1565 a Benjamin Nicholas *alias* Seager of Cambridge was bound apprentice for eight years. This according to the ordinary computation would make the first born about 1533, the second about 1549, so that they might quite probably be sons of Segar Nicholson. [Gray, *Cambridge Stationers*, pp. 62–64.]

NICODEMUS, is mentioned in the Subsidy Roll of 1541 as an assistant to John Byddell in Fleet Street. [R. of A., I, 56.]

NICOLAI (JACOBUS), *see* Nicholson (J.).

NOKE (RICHARD), stationer in Cambridge, was appointed by the University in 1540. He paid rent in 1545–6 for a tenement in St. Sepulchre's Parish, and as late as 1557 occurs as a witness to the will of Lawrence Moptid. [Gray, *Cambridge Stationers*, p. 66.]

NORTON (HENRY), stationer in London, was a fairly senior member of the Company on its incorporation in 1557. He is entered once or twice in the Registers as paying fines and as giving small amounts to subscriptions. He apparently held some official position in the Company for the last entry relating to him runs [1567–68] "Payd to Henry Norton for half a yere, iiij s."

NORTON (WILLIAM), stationer in London, was born in 1527. He was an original member of the Stationers' Company on its incorporation in 1557 and rapidly rose to a high position. He was Collector in 1563 and 1564, Under-Warden in 1569–70, Upper-Warden in 1573 and 1577 and Master in 1580, 1586 and 1593. He did not print himself but had a very large number of books printed for him by others. His address was the King's, afterwards Queen's, Arms in St. Paul's Churchyard and he used as a device a tun having the letters Nor upon it and a sprig of "Sweet William." He married Joan daughter of William Bonham the stationer and had one son Bonham Norton. He died in 1593 aged 66 and his will was proved January 1st, 1594. He left a large fortune in real and personal estate and made considerable bequests to charity. He was buried in the church of St. Faith and his epitaph has been preserved by Dugdale. [Plomer, Wills, pp. 30–33. D.N.B.]

NOTARY (JULIAN), printer and stationer in Westminster and London, appears to have begun to print about 1496. Many writers have suggested that he was a notary who had taken up printing, but the form of his name in his earliest books and device, Julianus Notarii, show that he was the son of one. The assertion that he was a Frenchman rests on the slight grounds of his being associated for a year or two with Jean Barbier and spelling his name Notaire in the colophon of the *Missal* of 1498. About 1496 an edition of the *Questiones Alberti de modis significandi* was printed at London by St. Thomas Apostle Church. No printers' names are given but there is a device, used later by Notary alone, containing the initials I.N., I.B., and I.H. This same device is found in a Sarum *Horae* printed April 3rd, 1497, at the same address for Wynkyn de Worde. The first two sets of initials stand doubtless for Julian Notary and Jean Barbier, but the last cannot be settled with any certainty. The most probable suggestion is that I.H. is Jean Huvin, a printer or stationer of Rouen, who was connected about this time with the production of Sarum service books. In 1498 Notary and Barbier printed a Sarum *Missal* for W. de Worde. They were then settled in Westminster and used the same device, from which the initials I.H. had been cut out. On January 2nd, 1500, was issued the *Liber Festivalis*. It is dated 1499 in the colophon, but Notary began his year on the 25th of March. It is an exact copy of the edition issued six months before by Pynson, and contains the old device with all the initials cut out and the name Julianus Notarii inserted in type. A very small sized edition of the *Horae* was printed in April of the same year, and about this time an edition of Chaucer's *Love and complaints between Mars and Venus* also appeared. At the end of 1500 W. de Worde left Westminster and very soon after Notary followed his example settling in a shop just outside Temple Bar which was probably the one lately vacated by Pynson. It had apparently had no sign previous to his occupation and he attached to it the sign of the Three Kings. The first book issued from this new address was probably a Sarum *Horae* assigned to 1503 though not dated, and this was followed in February, 1504, by an edition of the *Golden Legend*. The date in the colophon of this book is February 16th, 1503, in the 19th year of Henry VII, which shows that Notary did not begin his year until March 25th. In 1510 appeared an edition of the *Sermones de tempore et sanctis* which has an interesting imprint on the titlepage, which may be translated "They are to be sold (where they have been printed) at London in the suburb of Temple Bar near the porch of St. Clement's in the house of Julian Notary printer and bookseller carrying on business under the sign of the Three

Kings. And they will also be found for sale in Sᵗ Paul's churchyard in the same man's little shop [cellula] from which also hangs the same sign of the Three Kings." After this Notary apparently gave up his house by Temple Bar, and when he next appears, in 1515, he was living in St. Paul's Churchyard beside the west door and beside the Bishop of London's palace. *The Chronicle of England* printed this year mentions no sign, but two grammars issued in the year following mention the sign of St. Mark and this in 1518 was changed back to the old one of the Three Kings. Nothing is known of Notary after 1520. He printed in all about forty-eight books and used three devices. The first, mentioned earlier, is simply his mark, the second is a smaller variety of the mark alone with his initials and the last contains his mark on a shield with a helmet above and mantling: this fitted inside and is sometimes used with, an engraved border of birds, flowers, trees and fabulous animals. Besides being a printer Notary was also a binder and used two panel stamps. On one is a shield bearing the arms of France and England, ensigned with a crown and supported by the dragon and greyhound, on the other the Tudor rose between two scrolls inscribed with a motto and supported by angels. Beneath the rose are Notary's initials and mark. He used two different varieties of these panels which differ very slightly in minute detail, one point being that the initial N inside the mark has in one case the middle stroke running the wrong way. [D.N.B.]

NOVIMAGIO (RAYNALDUS DE), printer in Venice, was a native of Nimeguen. He commenced to work in 1479 and his last dated book was issued in 1496. During this period he produced over thirty books. In 1483 he printed an edition of the *Breviarium ad usum Sarum* of which the only known copy, printed on vellum, was stolen from the University Library, Cambridge, and is now in the Bibliothèque Nationale.

NOWELL, bookbinder, *see* Havy (N.).

NOWSELEY (JOHN), was apparently a bookbinder in London. He is mentioned in the will of Edward Ylle who bequeathed to him "my whole harnyse" by which is probably meant his binding appliances. [Plomer, Wills, p. 8.] He lived in Lombard Street.

O. (R.), bookbinder, made use of two panels. One contains a shield with the arms of France and England, and a Tudor rose, both in a circular medallion. In the upper corners are two shields, one with the cross of St. George, the other with the binder's initials and mark. On the other panel is the B. Virgin sitting with the dead Christ surmounted by an arch. [Weale. *Bookbindings*, pp. 128–9.]

OLIVER (GEORGE), stationer in London, is mentioned in the Stationers' Registers as having been fined September 30th, 1559, for late appearance on the quarter day. [Arber, I, 124.] Since his name is not found amongst those made free since the passing of the charter, he must have been a freeman before that date.

OLIVER (REGINALD), stationer of Ipswich, is mentioned, according to the Heber Catalogue [part i, No. 3809] in the colophon of an edition of the *Historia Evangelica* of Juvencus printed in 1534. This is very probably the edition of that year printed at Antwerp by Joannes Graphaeus and to a certain number of copies Oliver's name may have been added, for it does not occur in the Bodleian copy. The printer Graphaeus at any rate seems to have had some connexion with Ipswich for he printed, also in 1534, an edition of the *Rudimenta grammatices* which Wolsey had ordered to be used in the school which he had founded there. [*Bibliographica*, vol. ii, p. 33.] In the lists of denizations occurs "Reginald Oliver, from Phrisia. 15 Mar. 1535." [Pat. 26 Hen. VIII, p. 2, m. 43.]

OLIVIER (PIERRE), printer in Rouen, appears to have begun printing in 1500 in partnership with Jean de Lorraine. In that year they printed a Sarum *Manual* and in 1501 a Sarum *Missal*, both for Jean Richard. Their printing office was in the Rue Damiette near the church of St. Maclou. In 1502 Olivier was in partnership with Jean Mauditier near the church of St. Peter, when they printed a very fine edition of the Hereford *Missal*. At a little later date he went to a house near the church of St. Vivian and printed there alone. Apart from the many other books that he issued, Olivier printed at least a dozen service books, one for Hereford use, mentioned above, four for the use of York and the rest for Sarum. At first he printed for J. Richard, but later for Gachet, Bernard and Cousin. At what date he ceased printing is not exactly known, but the date given by Frère, 1521, may be taken as probable. Some later books, such as the York *Missal* of 1530, have been ascribed to him because of the use of the large initial M with his name Holivier engraved upon it, but by that time no doubt it, with other printing material, was being used by his successor.

L 2

ORYNS (JOHN), printer in London, was an assistant in 1549 to John Waley in Foster Lane, St. Leonard's Parish, Aldersgate Ward. [R. of A., I, 169.] He is not entered in any Returns of Aliens before or after this date.

OSWEN (JOHN), printer in Ipswich and Worcester, commenced to print at the former place in 1548 and in that year issued nine books all of a religious or theological nature. At the end of the year he removed to Worcester and on January 6th, 1549, received a privilege from Edward VI to print service books and books of instruction "for our subjects of the Principality of Wales and marches thereunto belonging" for the space of seven years. At Worcester Oswen printed over twenty different books among them being one edition at least of the *New Testament* and three of the *Book of Common Prayer*. Almost all Oswen's books were of a religious nature, but the last book he printed was the *Statutes An. 7 Ed. VI.* of 1553. Besides his establishment in the High Street Worcester he had an agent at Shrewsbury, for in the colophons of some of his books we find "They be also to sell at Shrewsbury." [D.N.B. *Bibliographica*, II, pp. 35–41.]

OVERTON (JOHN), printer in Ipswich, is known only as the publisher of Bale's *Illustrium majoris Britanniae scriptorum summarium* in 1548. The body of the work was printed abroad at "Wesel" by "Theodoricus Plateanus" the final sheets being added by Overton.

P. (G.), bookbinder, made use of four panel stamps. One contains an Image of Pity with the binder's initials and his mark, two crossed keys. Weale [*Bookbindings*, p. 188] describes this panel but assigns it to the Netherlands. A second panel has a picture of the Crucifixion. The remaining two contain medallion heads with Renaissance ornament almost identical with two used by Reynes. All four contain the binder's initials and mark.

P. (P.), bookbinder, made use of two rolls, one with quatrefoil diaper within lozenges, the other of curved branches with foliage and flowers. Both rolls have the binder's initials P. P. [Weale, *Bookbindings*, p. 115.]

P. (T.), bookbinder, used two panels containing two heads in medallions surrounded by a Renaissance border and with his initials in the centre. He also used a roll with Renaissance ornament and his initials. [Weale, *Bookbindings*, p. 142.]

PAFFROED (RICHARD), printer in Deventer, was at work from 1477 until well on in the sixteenth century. During the fifteenth century he printed two books for the English market, an edition of the *Compendium totius grammatice* by John Anwykyll in 1489 and the *Liber equivocorum* without date.

PAGET (RICHARD), stationer in London, was an original member of the Stationers' Company. He appears to have been an important man, as he gave the large subscription of two shillings to the house of Bridewell and presented a window to the Company's Hall. After the incorporation however his name is not met with in the Registers.

PARKER (THOMAS), stationer in London, occurs in the original list of members of the Stationers' Company and among the subscribers to the house of Bridewell, but nothing more is known of him.

PATTINSON (THOMAS), stationer in London, is mentioned in the original lists of the Company of Stationers, but nothing more is known about him.

PAULE (MICHAEL DE), stationer in London, is mentioned in the colophon of a Sarum *Missal* quoted by Herbert [I, p. 223] "Venale habes missale in domibus magistrorum vvynandi de vvorde, necnon Michaelis de Paule, London commorantibus."

PAYNE (WILLIAM), stationer in London, is mentioned in a Chancery suit between 1467-72 in connexion with William Harre, a Skinner. [Early Chancery Proceedings, Bundle 41, No. 316.]

PELGRIM (JOYCE), stationer in London, was probably a native of the Low Countries. In 1504 an edition of the *Ortus Vocabulorum* was printed for him at Paris by Jean Barbier. Soon afterwards he joined in business with Henry Jacobi and in 1506 they issued a *Psalterium cum hymnis*, a Sarum *Horae* and the *Constitutiones* of Lyndewode and Athon, the cost of all three being borne by William Bretton a London merchant. In 1507 they issued the *Liber synonymorum* of Garlandia and in 1508 the *Theodulus*, both being printed at Antwerp, probably by Thierry Martens. Bagford in a note [Harl. MS., 5904, p. 5] mentions a third book "a dialogue in Latin and English" also printed by Martens at Antwerp without date, but no copy is at present known.   After 1508 we do not find Pelgrim connected with the publication of any books, but he is mentioned in 1511 and 1512 by Erasmus in several of his letters as "Judocus the bookseller."   In 1510 he was connected with the Oxford book trade, for in that year he brought an action in the University Court against John Walker the University carrier concerning the carriage of some books.   [Univ. Archives, Reg. F., f. 123ʳ.] In 1514 he went to Oxford as agent for William Bretton to administer the effects of Henry Jacobi who had died there.   Pelgrim carried on business at the sign of St. Anne during 1506, but his address after this is not mentioned.   His shop was most probably on the east side of St. Paul's Churchyard and may have been one of the "lowe houses of boke-bynders" mentioned in the *Monumenta Franciscana* [vol. ii, p. 185] as having been cleared away in 1510–12 to make room for St. Paul's School.   Pelgrim seems to have had no device of his own but used one in partnership with Jacobi consisting of a blank shield with a ribbon behind it on which are the words "Nosce teipsum," on one side are the initials and mark of Jacobi, on the other those of Pelgrim.   [*Bibliographica*, I, pp. 93–113, 499.   D.N.B.]

PENNOWE (JOHN), bookbinder in London, was a native of France and came to England about 1540.   He lived in St. Sepulchre's Parish and occurs in the Subsidy Roll of 1564 when he pays a tax of two shillings on goods valued at twenty.   [R. of A., I, 299.]   In the return of 1571 he is entered as "John Pennowe, bookbynder, denizen, borne in Fraunce, came into this realme to worke of his occupacion about xxx yeares past."   [R. of A., II, 8.]   In the other return of 1571 he is given as dwelling in George Alley.   [R. of A., I, 423.]   Although he is spoken of as a denizen, I can find no entry of him in the lists of denizations unless by any chance he could be identical with the binder following.

PENNYS (JOHN), bookbinder in London, was a native of Normandy and came to England in 1522 when six years old.   He took out letters of denization July 1st, 1544.   "John Pennys, born in Normandy, aged 28 years.   In England 22 years and is a book-binder."   [Westm. Deniz. Roll, 36 Hen. VIII.]

PEPWELL (ARTHUR), stationer in London, was admitted a freeman on either August 19th, 1556, or March 8th, 1557.   For the first few years almost all the entries in the Registers relating to him refer to fines for various misdemeanours. In 1562 he was received into the Livery. In 1565–66 he had a license for printing a ballad by Churchyard and a copy of this ballad printed for him by A. Lacy is in the library at Britwell. At this time he was one of the Renters of the Company. Pepwell died at the end of 1568 and his will was proved on January 15th, 1569. He left a widow and two sons Henry and Humphry, both under age who were to receive two-thirds of his property. Various other bequests were left to relatives and to charities. Pepwell seems to have been twice married, first to Rose Toy daughter of Robert Toy the stationer and secondly to Joan Chambers. [Plomer, Wills, pp. 16, 17.]

PEPWELL (HENRY), printer and stationer in London, was born at Birmingham. In 1518 he began to print at the sign of the Trinity in St. Paul's Churchyard, a shop occupied from 1506 to 1512 by H. Jacobi. He printed there up to the beginning of 1524, issuing eight books of a popular character, but after that date he appears to have confined himself to his business as a stationer. In 1525–26 he was Warden of the Company of Stationers along with Lewis Sutton. In 1531 he published an edition of the *Enchiridion locorum communium adversus Lutheranos* of Eckius printed at Antwerp of which "John Harrison" [John Bale] writes in his *Yet a course at the Romish Fox* [Zurich, 1543, 8vo, p. 55] "No lesse myght harrye pepwell in Paules church yearde have out of Michael Hillenius' howse at Antwerp at one tyme than a whole complete prynte at the holye request of Stokyslaye." Bagford in one of his note books [Sloane MS., 893] enters "Paules Accidence printed att Antwarpe 1533 for pepwill" and this very likely refers to an edition, wanting the colophon, in the Pepys collection, bound up with another edition of 1534 and two later grammars printed by Pepwell. In 1535 he received a legacy of £4 in printed books from W. de Worde. In 1538 he stood bail for Bishop Stokeslaye for 500 marks. In 1539 he printed two small grammars for the use of St. Paul's School, which in spite of the definite statement of the colophon as to their having been printed in London, have every appearance of being the work of an Antwerp printer. In September of the same year he made his will, which was proved on February 8th, 1541. He divided his estate into three parts, two to go to his wife Ursula, and the third to his children who are not mentioned by name. William Bonham the stationer was appointed

a supervisor for which he received 6s. 8d.   One of the children no doubt
was the Arthur Pepwell mentioned later on in the Stationers' Registers.
Roger Shedmore who was an assistant to Pepwell is not mentioned in
the will.   Pepwell used four devices (1) the cut of the Trinity which had
been used by Jacobi, with the name cut out.   (2) A larger cut of the Trinity
having at the foot the name Henry Pepwell and on the left of the name his
mark.   (3) An oblong block containing a ribbon with the name Henry
Pepwell above which are the initials H. P. with the trade mark in the
centre.   (4) A border-piece with his mark on a shield.   [*Bibliographica*, I,
pp. 175–193.   D.N.B.]

PETIT (JEAN), stationer in Paris, carried on business from 1492 up to about
1530.   His first address was at the Golden Fleur-de-Lys in the Rue St.
Jacques and in 1496 he was at the Silver Lion in the same street.   He
printed a good deal for the Norman booksellers and had branch shops at
Lyons and Clermont.   He used five devices, the earliest having a shield with
his initials suspended from a tree and supported by a lion and leopard.
[*Renouard*, pp. 291–3.]   Between 1516 and 1530 Petit published three
editions of the *Missal* and two of the *Breviary* according to the Sarum use,
and in 1510 and 1511 issued in partnership with Henry Jacobi some tracts of
Savonarola.   There are some grounds for believing that Petit was in some
way distantly connected with Petyt the English printer.

PETRUS TURONENSIS, *see* Turonensis (P.).

PETYT (THOMAS), printer in London, began to print in 1536 issuing in that
year an edition of the *Rutter of the Sea*.   In 1543 he was imprisoned for a
short time in the Poultry Compter for printing unlawful books.   [*Acts of
the Privy Council*, N.S., vol. i, pp. 107, 117.]   He printed on until 1554
and was apparently still alive in 1556.   His place of business was at the
Maiden's Head in St. Paul's Churchyard next door to Robert Toy at the
Bell.   It has been suggested by Herbert and others that Petyt was a relation
of Jean Petit of Paris.   It is clear from the Subsidy Rolls of 1541 that Petyt
was English by birth, but some probability that there was a connexion
between the English and French families is found in an entry in the
Exchequer receipts "John Petytt of Parrys hath in thaundes of Thomas
Petytt in bookes prynted the sum of xx^{li}."

PHILIPPE, PHILIPPI or MANSTENER (JEAN), printer in Paris, was born at Kreuznach near Cologne and carried on printing between the years 1494 and 1519. In 1494 he was associated with George Wolff and printed at the sign of St. Barbara in the Rue St. Jacques, moving shortly to the Rue St. Marcel at the sign of the Trinity. [Renouard, pp. 296-7.] In 1497 he printed an edition of the Sarum *Horae* for Th. Kerver and J. Richard [H. C., 8862, Proctor, 8242] and another edition about the same time without date. In 1501 he printed a *Breviary* of Sarum use for J. Huvin. [St. Mary's Coll., Oscott.] His device contains the initials I . P surmounted by his mark, and below the words Scte Trinitatis.

PHILOPONOS (JOANNES), pseudonym, is mentioned in the colophon to *Certeine prayers and godly meditacyons* [B.M.] as the printer at Marlborow in 1538.

PICKERING (ELIZABETH), printer in London, was the widow of Robert Redman, and after his death in October, 1540, she issued a few books. The earliest, published in November, 1540, was Standish's *Little treatise against Robert Barnes*, and another work on ecclesiastical ordinances was issued in 1541. Besides these she issued a few undated books. She married Ralph Cholmondeley.

PICKERING (WILLIAM), printer in London, was an original member of the Stationers' Company at the time of the incorporation, being eightieth on the list. His first production was a broadside of the dying speech of Lord Sturton, March, 1557, which mentions him as dwelling on London Bridge his address afterwards being at St. Magnus corner under St. Magnus Church. Most of Pickering's books were of an ephemeral character and many were printed for him. No trace of him is found after 1571, the period when there is a hiatus in the books of the Stationers' Company. [Bibl. Soc. Trans., IV, pp. 57-102.]

PICORY (JAMES), stationer in Oxford, is mentioned in 1501-2 in the Oxford University Archives.

PIETER (JACOB), printer in London, was a native of Antwerp. He is entered in the list of members of the Dutch Church 1550-60 as "Jacob Pieter, prenter, met Jan Dey, van Antwerpen." [R. of A., I, 205.]

PIETERSZ or PETERSON (JAN), printer in Amsterdam, was the son of Pieter Jansz. Tyebaut, and began printing in 1546. He issued only one book, *An heavenly acte concernynge how man shal lyue* with the colophon "Printed at Amstredam be Jan Peterson." [Moes., p. 201, 202.]

PIGOUCHET (PHILIPPE), printer in Paris, was in business between the years 1488 and 1526. He lived in the Rue de la Herpe and later in the Hôtel Beauregard in the Rue Clopin. [Renouard, p. 299.] His device consisted of his monogram on a shield suspended from a tree and supported by a wild man and woman. Between the years 1495 and 1502 he printed at least six editions of the *Horae ad usum Sarum.*

PILGRIM (GERARD), stationer in Oxford, was a native of Antwerp. In 1524 he paid alien tax. In 1535 letters of denization were granted to "Gerard Pilgrome of the town of Oxford stationer born in Antwerp under the obedience of the Emperor." Pilgrim died in December, 1536, and his will was proved in the following February. [Arch. Univ. Oxon., Registrum E.E.E., f. 328.] He requested to be buried in St. Mary's and left money to the church at Lincoln. His property was left to his two young children Robert and Elizabeth, to his wife Margaret, to his brothers John and Matthew, and to Elizabeth, Matthew's daughter. There were also legacies to friends and servants. John was apparently also in business as a book-binder as he was left "of every instrument oon to work withall."

PILGRIM (NICHOLAS), stationer in Cambridge, was an assistant to Garret Godfray and is first mentioned in the Subsidy Roll of 1523–4 as "Nicholas Ducheman" with wages at twenty shillings. Godfray on his death in 1539 left him a substantial legacy, as well as a furred gown, three presses and a cutting knife, and on October 16th, 1539, Pilgrim was appointed a University stationer. He lived in the Parish of St. Mary and continued in business to 1545–6 when he died, and administration of his effects was granted to William Spyrynck John Gybbyn [? Gybkyn] and John Mere. [Gray, *Cambridge Stationers*, pp. 65, 66.]

PLATEANUS (THEODORICUS), printer at Wesel in 1548, printed the greater part of Bale's *Illustrium majoris Britanniae scriptorum summarium* which was published at Ipswich by John Overton. Nothing more is known of Plateanus.

PLOMIER (ALARD), merchant in Paris, is mentioned only in the colophon of one book, a Sarum *Enchiridion* printed at his expense by the widow of Thielman Kerver in 1528. [Hoskins, No. 83.] He is described as "probus vir Alard Plomier mercator fidelissimus." Among a series of letters scheduled in the *Letters and papers of Henry VIII* [vol. xii, pt. 1] is one from Jehan Lange to "Allart Ploumyer, Marchant demourant sus le Pont Notre Dame a l'ymage Sainct Gorge a Paris. Jan 8. 1537." There is nothing to show whether he was a stationer and he is not mentioned by Rénouard. A certain Alard Plumier is mentioned in 1543 in the *Letters and papers of Henry VIII* [vol. xvii, p. 99] as the King's jeweller.

POITEVIN (JEAN), stationer in Paris, was in business between the years 1498 and 1518. He lived in the Rue Neuve Nostre Dame. About 1498 he published an edition of the *Horae ad usum Sarum*. [Trin. Coll., Dublin.]

POLE (JOHN), bookbinder in Oxford, is mentioned August 8th, 1464, when sureties were found for Thomas Hichecock to prevent him citing John Pole in courts outside the Chancellor's. [University Archives, Reg. Aaa.]

POLLARD (JOHN), bookbinder in London, is mentioned with some others in January, 1527, as being granted pardon. [*Letters and papers of Henry VIII*, vol. iv, pt. ii, p. 1270.] He was not an Englishman as he is taxed as an alien. He lived in Shoe Lane next to Nowell Havy, another binder. In 1541 both paid a tax of four pence and again in 1544, while in 1549 they were each valued at five pounds and taxed five shillings. [R. of A., I, 56, 94, 181.]

POST PASCHA (PETER), stationer in London, is mentioned in the colophon of the *Promptorius puerorum* printed May 15th, 1499, by Richard Pynson at the costs of Frederick Egmont and Peter Post Pascha. What the real name of this stationer was has never been ascertained.

POULAIN (JACQUES), printer in Geneva, was apparently at work in Paris in 1551. [Renouard, p. 303.] In 1556 in partnership with Henry Houdouin he printed at Geneva, Anthony Gilbie's *Treatise of election and reprobation*. [Herbert, III, p. 1595.]

POWELL or POLE, stationer in Oxford, occupied in 1551 a shop in St. Mary's Parish. [Magdalen College Register E, 29.] In 1553 he is mentioned as stationarius in the University Archives.

POWELL (HUMPHREY), printer in London and Dublin, carried on business in the former city in the year 1548 when he printed some eight books at his shop "above Holborn Conduit." Whether his business was not a success or from some other cause he migrated to Ireland and there is an entry in the Acts of the Privy Council under the date July 18th, 1550, "A warrant to— to deliver xx^{li} unto Powell the printer given him by the King's Majestie towardes his setting up in Irelande." [Acts, vol. iii, p. 84.] Powell, who styled himself King's Printer set up in business "in the great toure by the Crane" and issued in 1551 an edition of the *Book of Common Prayer.* Probably much of Powell's work consisted of broadsides now lost, for nothing is known of his work for ten years. In 1561 he printed a broadside against Shane O'Neill and in 1564 another against the O'Connors. In 1566 he issued his last book a tract of eight leaves [T.C.D.] called *A Brefe Declaration of certein Principall Articles of Religion,* and his address is given as St. Nicholas Street. He was an original member of the Stationers' Company and most probably a near relation of Thomas Powell, Berthelet's nephew, as he came into possession of, and used, some founts of type which had belonged to Berthelet. [Dix, *The Earliest Dublin Printing.* D.N.B.]

POWELL (JOHN), stationer in London, was a member of the Company of Stationers some time before the passing of their charter. He is entered as subscribing several times and as presenting an apprentice in April, 1557, but his name is not entered in the original list of stationers, nor does it afterwards occur in the Registers.

POWELL (THOMAS), printer in London, was nephew of Thomas Berthelet to whom also he was for some time an assistant. Berthelet died in September, 1555, and his widow remarried at the beginning of the following year. Thomas Powell then took on the printing office and became a freeman of the Stationers' Company on July 21st, 1556. He printed very few books and his name is not found after 1563. Before he moved to Berthelet's house he lived in Snow Hill next Holborn Cross in the Parish of St. Sepulchre.

POWELL (WILLIAM), printer in London, succeeded Middleton at the sign of the George in Fleet Street, having married his widow soon after his death in 1547. Middleton's will was proved June 17th and the new marriage license granted July 26th. Having thus succeeded to a good business, Powell printed continuously between 1547 and 1567, issuing in that period over fifty books. In the list in the Stationers' Company's charter Powell was nineteenth, so that he probably became a freeman between 1535 and 1540. He is entered many times in the Registers as taking apprentices and entering copies up to the year 1566. He is last mentioned in 1568 when his son Abraham was put apprentice to H. Bynneman. On retiring from business he married a second time, " Aug. 10 1569 William Powell, of St Dunstan in the West, stationer and Jone alias Jane Starkie alias Evans, widow, of City of London." [*London Marriage Licenses*, p. 43.]

PRATT (DAVID), stationer in Oxford, came from Cambridge and was in Oxford from March 10th to October, 1536. [Boase, Reg. Oxon. p. 171.]

PRÉ (JEAN DU), *see* Du Pré (J.).

PREST (JEAN LE), *see* Le Prest (J.).

PREVOST (NICHOLAS), printer in Paris, was the son of William Prevost and carried on printing between the years 1524 and 1532 in the Rue St. Jacques at the sign of St. George. Prevost married Marie daughter of Wolfgang Hopyl and succeeded to the latter's printing office. He also made use of Hopyl's device. [Renouard, p. 305.] In 1527 Prevost printed a *Missal, Horae* and *Gradual* of Sarum use; the first two for Birckman, the last for W. de Worde, John Reynes, and Lewis Suethon. In 1530 he printed a Sarum *Processional* for Francis Birckman the younger, and in 1532 a Sarum *Gradual* for Regnault.

PURFOOT (THOMAS), printer in London, was born in 1518, so that he would probably become free of the Stationers' Company about 1542. In the list in the charter he occurs twenty-third. Although no book is given under his name by Herbert before 1564, a book was printed for him in 1546 by Richard Lant, where he is spoken of as dwelling " in Poules Churchyard at the sygne of Lucrece." He dwelt at the sign of Lucretia in St. Nicholas shambles within the new rentes, and also " without Newgate over against

St. Sepulchre's Church." He is said to have gone on printing until 1615: in which case he must have been at least ninety-seven when he died. There were however at least three printers of the name and they may have been confused.

PURSSET (THOMAS), stationer in London, is mentioned in the accounts of the churchwardens of the Parish of St. Michael, Cornhill [p. 66], under the year 1548. " Payd to Thomas Pursset for vj songes bokes for the Churche. vjs."

PYNSON (RICHARD), printer in London, was a Norman by birth, and appears to have been educated at the University of Paris, for his name is found in a list of students in 1464. He appears to have learnt to print at Rouen with Guillaume le Talleur who printed two books for him after he had come to England. Machlinia, who monopolised the printing of law books in England, ceased to print some time after 1486 and Pynson apparently came over to succeed him in a position for which his knowledge of Norman-French peculiarly fitted him. Coming over between 1486 and 1490 Pynson set to work to start his press, and in the meantime commissioned Le Talleur to print for him Littleton's *Tenures* and Statham's *Abridgement*. Pynson's earliest dated book was finished in November, 1492, but at least five books were issued earlier and one of these an edition of Chaucer's *Canterbury Tales* almost certainly before the death of Caxton in 1491. The first dated book issued by Pynson was the *Doctrinale* of Alexander Grammaticus finished on the 13th of November, 1492, in the Parish of St. Clement Danes outside Temple Bar. In 1495 Pynson issued an edition of the *Hecyra* of Terence probably intended for use at Eton. In 1499 he printed a *Promptorius puerorum* for Frederick Egmont and Peter Post Pascha. During the fifteenth century Pynson printed about eighty-four books, using in them seven distinct founts of type and three devices. In 1500 Pynson and some others brought an action in the Star Chamber against Henry Squire and his companions for assault. It appears to have been one of the usual attacks by natives on foreign workmen then so common, but Pynson stated that his servants were so terrorised that they had left him and his work was consequently at a standstill. [Leadam, *Select cases*, pp. 114–118.] The evident outcome of this case was the removal by Pynson in 1500 of his printing office from St. Clement's Parish, which was outside the City, to a house within Temple Bar at the corner of Chancery

Lane and Fleet Street next to St. Dunstan's Church, which had belonged to the College of St. Stephen in Westminster and to which he gave the sign of the George or St. George. Here he continued for the rest of his life. In 1506 Pynson, apparently assisted by a certain Hugo Meslier, printed an edition of the *Principia* of Peregrinus de Lugo for George Chastelain an Oxford bookseller. In 1508, some time after May, on the death of William Faques, Pynson succeeded him as Printer to the King. At first he received an annuity of two pounds and in 1515 the sum was raised to four pounds. This position carried with it the title of Esquire and the right to bear arms which Pynson immediately assumed and which are found the following year in his edition of the *Ship of Fools*. In 1508 he printed two books in Roman type, the first used in England. In 1521 Pynson printed the *Assertio septem sacramentorum* and as King's printer continued to issue political and controversial books concerned with the Reformation. No book of Pynson's is known issued after June 18th, 1528, and we have no information concerning the last eighteen months of his life. During his whole career he is known to have printed at least three hundred and seventy-one books, and he made use of seven devices. [Bibl. Soc. Handlist.] Pynson was also a binder and used two panels. One contains his monogram on a shield surrounded with a broad border and almost identical in design with his device No. 3. [Duff, *Early Printed Books*, p. 193, illust.] The other has in the centre the Tudor rose with a border of foliage and flowers and vine leaves in the corners. Pynson died at the beginning of 1530 and his will dated November 15th, 1529, was proved the following 18th February. He left considerable property in Chancery Lane and Tottenham. He left bequests to his apprentices John Snowe and Richard Withers. He had only one child alive, a daughter Margaret who had married first a William Campion, probably a stationer, by whom she had two children Amye and Joane, and secondly a man named Warde. Pynson's son Richard is described as recently deceased, leaving a daughter Joan, who married in 1537. It is clearly this Richard Pynson the son who took out letters of denization in 1513, for Pynson the elder could not have risen to be King's printer and have the right to bear arms without being a denizen. Indeed he was presumably naturalised, but the son who from his age must have been born abroad would require letters of denization also. [D.N.B. Bibl. Soc. Handlist. Duff, *Early Printed Books*, pp. 165–170.]

QUENTELL (HENRY), printer in Cologne, commenced to print in the year 1479 and continued into the first years of the sixteenth century. He issued about 1492 an edition of the *Compendium totius grammatice* of John Anwykyll, with the English sentences. [Roy. Lib., Munich.]

QUENTELL (PETER), printer in Cologne, was at work in that city from 1520 onwards. It was at his press that the first edition of Tindale's *Testament* was printed in 1525. When the work had got as far as sheet K the printer was ordered to cease work and Tindale fled with the finished sheets to Worms.

R. (A.), bookbinder in London, made use of at least five fine panels. One with St. Roche, another with the baptism of Christ, a third with the Annunciation, a fourth with St. John preaching and small side panels with David and Bathsheba and St. James, and last the Salutation of St. Elizabeth. At the corners of this last panel are four shields with the arms of the City of London, the cross of St. George, the cross keys and the cross swords, the last two perhaps representing St. Paul's Cathedral and Westminster Abbey [St. Peter's]. On most of the panels are the binder's initials and mark.

R. (G.), bookbinder in London, used four panels. One contains a shield with the arms of England and France supported by a dragon and greyhound. In the upper corners are shields with the cross of St. George and the arms of the City of London. On the sides of the shield are the binder's initials. Round all runs a border inscribed "Confitemini domino quoniam bonus quoniam in seculum misericordia eius. deus meus in te sper." A second panel is almost exactly the same but larger and the border has the inscription "Laudate dominum de terra dracones et omnes abyssi. G.R." The third panel, the same size as the first contains four saints, St. Barbara, St. Katherine, St. John Evangelist and an archbishop. In the background of the lowest figure are the binder's initials. The last panel is the same size as the second and contains four saints St. George, St. Barbara, St. Michael, and St. Katherine and round the outside is a border with the motto "Quidquit agas prudenter agas et respice finem. O mater dei memento mei." [Weale, *Bookbindings*, pp. 124-5.] It is worth noting that two copies of the Sarum Martyloge printed by W. de Worde 1526 [Lambeth, Archbp. Marsh's Lib., Dublin] are in bindings stamped with panels two and four.

R. (1.), binder, *see* Reynes (John).

RAIMUND (JOHN), *see* Ruremond (H. van).

RANULF, stationer in London, is mentioned in the Returns of Aliens in St. Faith's Parish in 1541 when his goods were valued at 100 marks. [R. of A., I, 67.] There is just a chance that the entry may be a mistake for Rayner, standing for Rayner Wolfe who occurs in the same place three years later.

RASTELL (JOHN), printer in London, was born in London, educated at Oxford and afterwards entered Lincoln's Inn. He married Elizabeth the sister of Sir Thomas More. He issued some time before 1516 an edition of the *Liber Assisarum* in which he referred to a proposed edition of Fitzherbert's *Great Abridgement* which was printed in that year. About 1520 he moved his printing establishment to a house next St. Paul's gate to which he gave his sign of the Mermaid, but from a lawsuit held about 1534 in connexion with this house we learn that he did not do much printing there himself but kept assistants and sublet portions to tenants such as William Bonham, John Heron, Thomas Kele and John Gough. [*Bibliographica*, II, pp. 437–451.] Up to 1526 Rastell had published but four books all connected with the law; but in the next year or two he issued some works of a popular character, *The Hundred Merry Tales*, *The merry jests of the Widow Edith* and the *Pastime of People*. He printed also several interludes and is known to have been fond of giving performances of plays, for the records of a lawsuit are still preserved between himself and a theatrical costumier. In 1530 he became involved in the religious controversies of the time and, becoming converted to the reformed religion, lost friends and position and sank into comparative poverty. In 1536 he attacked the paying of tythes and about the same time was thrown into prison where he shortly afterwards died. His will was proved on October 12th. [Plomer, Wills, pp. 5–6.] He left forty shillings to his son William and a small annuity to his son John. He left other small sums to the Lord Chancellor and Cromwell, and named Henry VIII one of his executors. He used two devices, the larger having figures of a merman and mermaid holding a shield with his monogram; above is a half-length figure of the Almighty and in the upper corners are shields with the arms of England and the Prince of

M

Wales' feathers. The smaller device contains a shield with his monogram on a ribbon with the motto Justicia Regat. [D.N.B. *Handlists of English Printers*, II. Plomer, *English Printing*, pp. 51–54.]

RASTELL (WILLIAM), printer in London, eldest son of John Rastell, was born about 1508 and went to Oxford in 1525 where he studied but took no degree. He began to print about 1530 while his father was still alive, issuing a Latin and English edition of Caesar's *Commentaries*. While still a printer he worked at the law, having been admitted a student in 1532 and called to the bar in 1539 where he practised with considerable success. He printed only between 1530 and 1534 at a house in St. Bride's Churchyard, Fleet Street, but issued more than thirty books including several plays and interludes as well as controversial works by his uncle Sir Thomas More. Unlike his father he remained a Catholic and on the accession of Edward retired abroad with his wife Winifred. In February, 1550, his house was seized as we learn from Wriothesley Chronicle [part ii, p. 34] "Feb 7. house seized of Rastall which maryed Doctor Clementes daughter." He lived in Louvain until Mary succeeded, when he returned to London and resumed practice, and was a judge in the Queen's Bench from 1558 to 1563. During this period he compiled and edited several important law books and prepared a complete edition of *More's Works* which was published in 1557. Towards the close of his life he returned to Louvain, where he died August 27th, 1565. [D.N.B.] A curious and rather confusing account of his flight will be found in the *Inquisitiones Post Mortem for London*, Index Library [pp. 108–110].

RAVYNELL (JAMES), printer in Rouen, is known only from one book. This is an edition of Mirk's *Liber festivalis et quattuor sermones* which was finished on February 4th, 1495, and is exactly copied from W. de Worde's edition of 1493–4. At the end of each part occurs a fine printer's device which contains the initials P.R on a shield suspended by a belt from a tree and supported by two muzzled bears, while two birds hold up a wreath beneath the shield. Round the whole runs the legend "Junior fui etenim senui et non vidi justum derelictum nec semen ejus querens panem." This device is unknown to bibliographers, and the initials look as though it had been made for some other member of the family.

RAYNALD (THOMAS), printer and physician in London, must have begun to work some time before 1540 though nothing printed by him before that date is known. In the Archives of the City of London is a deposition dated August 20th, 1540, made by Thomas Mannyng, John Borrell and John Day, late servants to Thomas Reynoldes printer late dwelling at "Hallywell nere unto London," relative to some property belonging to the printer. [Bibl. Soc. Trans., VI, 20–22.] In 1540 appeared a book entitled *The birthe of mankynde* printed by T.R and in 1545 was issued a new edition, "newly set furth by Thomas Raynold phisition." In 1548 he was definitely settled as a printer in St. Andrew's Parish, in the Wardrobe, and besides printing alone joined sometimes with Anthony Kitson or William Hill. In 1549 he moved to the sign of the Star in St. Paul's Churchyard where he printed on steadily to 1552 when he issued his last edition of *The birth of mankind*. In 1555 an edition of the Sarum *Processionale* was printed with the initials T.R which is ascribed to him, but it is worth noticing that in 1553 the Star in St. Paul's Churchyard was occupied by Roger Madeley. Raynald printed altogether about thirty books and most probably died before the incorporation of the Stationers' Company as his name is not found in their charter. [D.N.B.]

REDBORNE (ROBERT), printer in London, was an original member of the Stationers' Company. He is mentioned in the Registers up to the year 1566, but seems to have done little in the way of business. One book only is known printed by him, an edition of *Arthur of little Britain*, a folio with poor woodcuts. It is without date and the address of the printer is given as the Sign of the Cock in Paul's Churchyard.

REDMAN (JOHN), printer in Southwark and London, is first mentioned in the report of a law suit tried about 1530 between John Rastell the printer and Henry Walton on a matter relating to theatrical dresses. He is there described as a stationer of London aged 22 years. [Bibl. Soc. Trans., IV, p. 176.] Later on he was living in Southwark and there printed for his namesake Robert Redman an edition of the *Paradoxa* of M. T. Cicero translated by Whitinton. This would be before 1540 and about that year he moved to a shop in Pater Noster Row with the sign of Our Lady of Pity, perhaps the one which had been earlier occupied by W. de Worde. Here he printed two broadside ballads, one for Richard Bankes, an *Almanack*, and an edition of the *Epistles and Gospels* all without date but about 1540, and an edition of the *Imitatio Christi* is also ascribed to him on the authority of the Harleian catalogue. In 1542 he issued an edition of the *Genealogye of Heresye*, and after this date nothing is known of him. It is generally suggested that he was a relation of Robert Redman but there is no proof of this, and he is not mentioned in the latter's will.

REDMAN (ROBERT), printer in London, issued his first dated book in 1523. In his next dated book, the *Magna Charta* of 1525, he gives his full address, the sign of St. George in St. Clement's Parish, that is just outside Temple Bar, and this was perhaps the house previously occupied by Pynson and Julyan Notary. At this time Pynson was at work close by, at the other side of Temple Bar, his house being also called the George, and when Redman not only adopted his sign but began to issue editions of the books he was accustomed to print Pynson became indignant and abused Redman in several strongly-worded "addresses to the reader." Of these Redman apparently took no notice. Herbert and others have asserted that Redman removed to Fleet Street before April 18th, 1527, and there is an edition of the *Modus tenendi unum hundredum* of that date with a distinct colophon stating the book was printed at the George in St. Dunstan's Parish. But this date must be misprinted, for not only in two books of the beginning of 1528 is he still spoken of as in St. Clement's Parish, but he could hardly have printed an odd book in Pynson's house when Pynson was still alive. It is curious to note that in no book printed between the beginning of 1528 and the beginning of 1530 does Redman mention any address in his colophons. Immediately on Pynson's death early in 1530 Redman moved to his old house, the George in Fleet Street and issued his first book from the new address on March 23rd. The book has the printed date 1529 but Redman did not begin his year until March 25th. In 1533 he was bound over in 500 marks not to sell the book called *The division of the Spiritualty and Temporalty*, nor any other book privileged by the King. [*Letters and papers of Hen. VIII*, vol. iv, p. 215.] The greater part of Redman's work was confined to law-books and reprints, he does not appear to have ventured much on new publications. He died in 1540 some time between October 21st the date of his will and November 4th when it was proved. His property was divided into three parts, the first for legacies and funeral expenses, the second for his wife and the third for his children. One of his executors was his son-in-law Henry Smith, a printer of law-books who lived at the sign of the Trinity in St. Clement's Parish without Temple Bar, perhaps his father-in-law's old house. Elizabeth Pickering, Redman's widow, continued to print for a short time, but gave up on her re-marriage to Ralph Cholmondeley when the printing office passed to William Middleton. At the beginning of his career Redman had no definite device, but made use of three woodcuts, one of St. George in reference to his sign, one of the Trinity and one of the infant Christ seated. On succeeding to Pynson's business he obtained three of the older printer's devices which he afterwards always made use of. One, the original black grounded block with white monogram with which Pynson had first started, secondly a small metal device, rarely used by Pynson which has a pierced ribbon at the bottom in which the name of the printer could be inserted in type, and lastly Pynson's late large wood-block. [D.N.B.]

REDMAN (ROBERT), widow of, *see* Pickering (E.).

REGNAULT (FRANCOIS), printer and bookseller in London and Paris, was the most important among the foreign producers of books for the English market. He was the son of Francis Regnault the Paris bookseller who died about 1516. As a young man, about the end of the fifteenth century he was a bookseller in London and though he afterwards returned to Paris he never gave up his London business. Some time after 1516 and before 1520 he succeeded to his father's business, and well aware of the demand in England for foreign printed service books, set himself to export them. He began in 1519 with a *Breviary, Horae*, and two *Missals* of Sarum use, but for the next year or two issued little. In 1524 his large output began and continued unbroken until 1535 when two serious checks to his work occurred, the suppression of many of the service books, and the act regulating the importation of foreign books. In 1536, finding his business seriously interfered with he wrote a letter to Cromwell. [*Letters and papers of Henry VIII*, XI, No. 1488.] In this interesting document he sets out that he lived in London forty years ago, and since returned to Paris and continued his trade as bookseller in London, and likewise printed missals, breviaries, and hours of the use of Sarum, and other books. Has entertained at his house in Paris honourable people of London and other towns of England. Understands that the English booksellers wish to prevent him printing such books, and to confiscate what he has already printed, though he has never been forbidden to do so, but his books well received. Asks permission to continue to sell the said "usaiges" and other books in London and the environs, and asks Cromwell to speak to the King, the Chancellor and others. If any faults have been found in his books will correct them. Apparently Regnault received little satisfaction, for on September 12th, 1538, Coverdale and Grafton, who were then with him in Paris, wrote another letter on his behalf to Cromwell saying that he had a large stock of service books on his hands "as Prymers in Englishe, Missoles with other soche like, wherof now (by ye company of ye Booksellers in London) he is utterly forbydden to make sale, to the utter undoying of the man." They beg that he may have license to sell those already printed "so that hereafter he prynte no moo in the english tong, onlesse he have an english man that is lerned to be his corrector." [*Letters and papers of Henry VIII*, Vol. 13, pt. 2, p. 123.] Coverdale, Grafton and Whitchurch were at this time overseeing a new edition of the *Bible* which Regnault was printing. In November an edition of the *New Testament* was put out in opposition to an incorrect version printed by Nicholson in Southwark. The printing of the great Bible was proceeding slowly when in December a raid was made upon the printing office, and all that had already been printed was seized and publicly burned in the Place Maubert, Paris. Regnault printed, up to May, 1523, at the sign of St. Claude in the Rue St. Jacques, and after September of the same year, in the same street at the sign of the Elephant, though he had used an elephant as device before moving to that sign. He died at Rouen some time between November 23rd, 1540, and June 21st, 1541, and his business was carried on by his widow Madeleine Boursette. [Renouard, pp. 313, 314. *Documents*, pp. 229-234.]

REGNAULT (FRANÇOIS), widow of, *see* Boursette (M.).

REMBOLT (BERTHOLD), printer in Paris, was a native of Strasburg. He began to print in 1494 and worked for a while with Gering, the two living at the Soleil d'Or in the Rue Sorbonne. About 1510 he was alone at the Soleil d'Or in the Rue St. Jacques. [Renouard, p. 317]. In or before 1498 he issued an edition of the Sarum *Manual* and in 1513 a Sarum *Missal*. According to Renouard Rembolt died in 1518 but there is a Sarum *Missal* of 1523 containing his name. His wife Charlotte Guillard married as her second husband Claude Chevallon who thus succeeded to Rembolt's business.

RÉMONDE (CHRISTOPHER AND HANS VAN), *see* Ruremond (C. and H. van).

RENKENS (HARRY), stationer in Oxford, is mentioned as a Dutchman in the list of aliens taxed in 1524. [Madan, p. 273.] He may perhaps have been an assistant to Garret Pilgrim, and be the "Harry my servant" to whom he bequeathed a doublet and pair of hose.

REVEL (TRISTRAM), pseudonym? This name is found in the colophon of Francis Lambert's *Summe of Christianitie*, "translatyd and put in to prynte in Englyshe by Tristram Revel, the yere of our lorde 1536." [Herbert, III, p. 1547.]

REYNES (JOHN), stationer in London, obtained letters of denization on June 7th, 1510, in which he is described as a native of Wagenyng in Gueldres. The first mention of him as a stationer is in the Returns of Aliens for 1523 where he is spoken of as "stacyoner and denysen," his goods being valued at £40 3s. 4d. In the following year he appears in another capacity as supplying cloth and cotton at the funeral of Sir Thomas Lovell. In 1527 a very fine edition of the *Polycronycon* was printed for him by Peter Treveris at Southwark with Reynes' mark in red on the titlepage. He was then carrying on business in St. Paul's Churchyard at the sign of St. George. In the same year he shared with W. de Worde and L. Suethon the cost of an edition of the Sarum *Graduale* which was printed for them at Paris by Nicolas Prevost. In 1530 a Sarum and York *Psalterium cum hymnis* was printed for him abroad. About 1540 Nicholas Bourman printed for him *An introductorie for to lerne to rede...Frenche* by Giles Duwes some time librarian to Henry VIII and teacher of French to him and his daughter the Princess Mary. In 1541 and 1544 Reynes again occurs in the Returns of Aliens, his valuation having risen to £100. An apprentice or assistant of his named James Foxe is also mentioned. In 1542 Reynes appears to have joined with some other stationers in publishing editions of *Fabyan's Chronicles* and *Chaucer's Works* in folio. These editions have variant colophons containing the names of the different stationers for whom they were printed, but it is clear that Reynes must have borne a leading part in the expense as his initials are cut in the capitals. In 1544 a *Processionale ad usum Sarum*, the last book in which his name occurs, was printed for him at Antwerp by the widow of Christopher van Ruremund. Reynes is however better known as a bookbinder, and his work is the best known and commonest of all early English stamped work. His most important panel, inscribed "Redemptoris Mundi Arma," contains the symbols of the Passion treated heraldically upon a shield supported by unicorns, while in the upper corners are two small shields with Reynes' mark and initials. The companion panel, divided into two parts, contains the arms of England supported by the dragon and greyhound, and the Tudor rose supported by angels. Another pair of panels have pictures of the Baptism of Christ and the fight of St. George with the dragon within an enclosure round which run huntsmen and animals. A third pair have medallions of warriors' heads in a later renaissance style. In the centre between the medallions is the binder's mark. Reynes also used a broad roll containing his mark and figures of a hound, a falcon and a bee with sprays of flowers and foliage. Reynes died in 1544 and his will dated April 8th, 1542, was proved on February 26th, 1544. His two apprentices Thomas Holwarde and Edward Sutton were to receive one hundred shillings' worth of books valued according to the rate fixed by Arnold and John Birckman. Edward Wright and Robert Holder, his assistants were left ten pounds in books on condition they assisted the widow to realise the stock. [Plomer, Wills, pp. 6-7, 8-9.] His widow Lucy Reynes did not long survive, for her will dated April 28th, 1548, was proved October 25th, 1549. She was buried, like her husband, in the Pardon churchyard by St. Paul's Cathedral. [D.N.B.]

RICHARD, bookbinder in Canterbury, is mentioned in 1508 as binding books for the library of Christ Church. [James, *Ancient libraries of Canterbury and Dover*, p. 163.]

RICHARD (JEAN), stationer of Rouên, was in business from about 1490 to 1517. From 1496 onwards he issued books for the English market, beginning with a magnificent folio Sarum *Breviary* printed by Morin. He issued *Missals* in 1497, 1501, 1506, two in 1508 and 1510, *Breviaries* in 1496 and 1508, a *Horae* in 1497, a *Manuale* in 1500 and 1509, a *Liber Festivalis* in 1499, and the Hereford *Missal* of 1502, and all his books are remarkable for the beauty of their execution. Richard seems to have paid visits to England and was a party to a lawsuit at Oxford in 1501-2. His device consisted of his shield with initials and mark suspended from a tree and supported by a female figure and a unicorn.

RICHARDSON (JOHN), bookbinder in London, was at work about 1520. He was a native of the Low Countries. The panel stamp ascribed to him by Weale [*Catalogue of Bindings*, Introduction, p. xl] really belonged to and was used by John Reynes, for it is found used in conjunction with Reynes' signed roll.

RICHARDSON (RICHARD), stationer in London, was an original member of the Company of Stationers and from his position on the charter would appear to have become a freeman about 1540. In 1545 he was mentioned in the will of Edward Ylle and received a legacy of six shillings and eight pence. [Plomer, Wills, p. 8.] He was evidently an important stationer, giving liberal subscriptions to the Company's collections and presenting no less than four apprentices in October, 1556. By 1558–9 he was dead, for in that year two of his apprentices were set over to James Gonnell his executor. [Arber, I, 98.]

RICHARDSON (THOMAS), stationer in York, was admitted a freeman in 1532–33. [*Freemen of York*, p. 252.] In 1545 he is mentioned in a "lease by Dennes Heckelton, clerk, sub-chanter in the metropolitan church of St. Peter in York, with consent of his brethren the vicars-choral to Thomas Richardson, bookbinder of the said city, of a house in Petergate, now held by the said Thomas. Term xvj years. Rent xxxiij. iiij d." [*Historical MSS. Commission*, Sir George Wombwell, 1903, p. 61.] He is mentioned twice in the *York Cathedral Fabric Rolls* [p. 113, 118], "1559 Richardson for mendinge of bookes 2 s." "1580 Thomas Richardson for 11 Geneva Psalters 2. 4."

RICHARDSON (WILLIAM), printer in London, was an apprentice to Richard Kele who left him by his will in 1552 "fourtie shillings in ware." [Plomer, Wills, p. 10.]

RIDDELL (WILLIAM), printer in London, issued his first certain dated book in 1552, for it is doubtful whether the date 1548 on his edition of some *Sermons of Ochino* refers to the translation or printing. In 1554 he issued a ballad relating to Queen Mary, in which he gives his address as the Eagle in Lombard Street; in the *Ochino* it is given as the George in St. Paul's Churchyard. On March 12th, 1556, he was brought before the Privy

Council and bound over to deliver to Cawood all the copies which he had printed of Cranmer's *Recantation* to be burnt. [*Acts of P.C.*, vol. v., N.S., pp., 247–8.] He was an original member of the Stationers' Company and appears in the Registers up to the year 1560. He issued so far as is known only five books, the main part of his productions being ballads.

RIVERY (JEAN), printer in Geneva, commenced business with his brother Adam by printing a French *Bible* in 1553. [Maittaire, III, 619.] He died before 1597, in which year his widow Nicole Lionette married Antoine Desmarquetz a Paris bookseller. [Renouard, p. 323.] In 1556 Rivery printed Beza's *Brief declaration of the chief points of Christian religion.* [Herbert, III, 1595.]

RODDON (NICHOLAS), stationer in London, was made free between January and April, 1556, but he is not entered on the original list of 1557, nor is he again mentioned in the Registers. [Arber, I, 35.]

ROEDIUS (SIBERTUS), printer in London, produced only one book, an edition of Erasmus *De duplici copia verborum et rerum* which ends "London. excudebat Sibertus Roedius anno 1556." It contains his initials and mark on a shield in the base of the ornamental border round the title.

ROGERS (JOHN), stationer in London, is mentioned as early as 1539 in the Records in the Guildhall [Journal 14, f. 162] for on October 18th he acted as arbitrator in a suit between William Bonham and Thomas Gibson. His name occurs twenty-fourth in the Stationers' charter of 1557, but he apparently died about that time as his name never occurs again in their Records.

ROGERS or AP-ROGERS (OWEN), printer in London, was made free October 8th, 1555. He soon got into trouble, for on March 12th, 1556-7, he was bound over to deliver to Cawood all copies of Cranmer's *Recantation* which he had printed, to be burnt. [*Acts of the P.C.*, vol. v, N.S., p. 249.] It seems to have been a common practice with him to print other men's copies and he is frequently entered as fined for that offence in the Stationers' Registers. He printed up to the year 1566, after which his name is not found. His printing office was first "by the hospital in Little St Bartholomew's Smithfield" and then at the Spread Eagle, "near Great St Bartholomew's gate."

ROOD (THEODORIC), printer in Oxford, was a native of Cologne and set up a press in Oxford in 1478. He made use at first of a very distinctive Cologne type used previously in that city by Gerard ten Raem de Bercka, and with it printed three books the famous *Expositio in simbolum apostolorum* of Rufinus with the misprinted date 1468, the *Aegidius de peccato originali* of 1479 and the *Textus ethicorum Aristotelis* of the same year. In 1481 he issued a work of Alexander of Hales upon the *De anima* of Aristotle, and in this for the first time his name is given. About 1483 he appears to have gone into partnership with an Oxford stationer named Thomas Hunte and as a result some new founts of type very much more English in appearance were used. The last book issued was an edition of the *Liber Festivalis* of 1486. It has been suggested that Rood returned to Cologne and was identical with a Theodoricus who printed there in 1486, but this has been disproved. [Madan, *Oxford Press.* Duff, *Early Printed Books*, pp. 147–155.]

ROSS (ANDREW), bookseller in Edinburgh, is mentioned in an Act of the Privy Council passed January 14th, 1509–10, prohibiting him or any other bookseller from selling Sarum service books, or any book which Walter Chepman had caused to be printed. [Dickson and Edmond, p. 84.]

ROUX (JEAN and NICHOLAS LE) *see* Le Roux (J. and N.).

ROWE (JOHN), bookbinder in London, is mentioned by Foxe as having done penance in 1531 for selling *New Testaments* in English which he had bought from one Christopher [van Ruremond] a Dutchman. In 1541 he is mentioned in the Subsidy Rolls as a servant to Henry Harman, who was factor for Arnold Birckman and kept his shop in St. Paul's Churchyard. [R. of A., I, p. 67.]

ROWSE (JOHN), *see* Le Roux (J.).

ROYE (CYBRYKE VAN), stationer in London, was a brother of the Stationers' Company before its incorporation, and is mentioned in the list of subscribers for the house of Bridewell in 1555–6. [Arber, I, 48.]

RUE (ANDREW and JOHN), *see* Ruwe (A. and J.).

RUPIUS (HENRY), *see* Starkerfelser (H.).

RUREMOND, RÉMONDE, or ENDHOVEN (CHRISTOPHER VAN), printer in Antwerp, began to work about 1523. He was a relation, probably a brother of Hans van Ruremond. Christopher was also known as Christopher van Endhoven, which is the name engraved on his device and under which he was entered in the Registers of the St. Lucas Gilde. Many have thought that Van Ruremond and Van Endhoven were two different people, but as all the books in the two names have the same type and woodcuts and in three cases at least we find the device of Van Endhoven with the name of Van Ruremond we may take them as the same. Besides were they two men it would be curious that they should die at the same time, and their widows simultaneously begin to carry on their businesses. In 1523 Christopher began to print, issuing two Sarum service books ; in 1524 he issued four more, and in 1525 five. Until after February 6th, 1525, all these were printed for Peter Kaetz, who appears to have been his London agent, but the later books were printed for Byrckman. At the beginning of 1526 he printed a Sarum *Breviary* and also set to work to print an edition of the English *New Testament*. When copies of this had found their way into England vigorous attempts were made to have the books suppressed and the printers punished. On November 24th, 1526, Hackett the active agent at Antwerp wrote to Wolsey, saying there were two printers who printed them and a proclamation against them would shortly be issued. On the 12th January following he again wrote that the Margrave declared that according to the Emperor's last mandate these English books must be condemned to be burnt, the printer Chr. Endhoven banished and the third part of his goods confiscated. The prisoner's attorney however fought against this judgment, denying that the books were heretical and saying that the Emperor's subjects ought not to be judged by the laws of other countries. This plea seems to have been successful, for there is no sign of the printer having been banished, nor did he cease to print. Between 1527 and 1530 he printed six Sarum books, two *Missals*, two *Horae*, a *Processional* and a *Hymni cum notis*, as well as an *Almanack* in English. In 1530-1 he seems to have come over into England in connexion with the sale of *New Testaments*, and there can be little doubt that he is the person referred to by Foxe under the year 1531, "An Antwerp bookseller named Christopher, for selling certain New Testaments in English to John Row, bookbinder, was thrown into prison at Westminster and there died."

Catherine the widow of Christopher succeeded to his business which she carried on for a number of years, issuing many books, including *New Testaments*, for the English market. A son, Hans van Ruremond, began to print at Antwerp about 1530 and continued long in business. The device of Christopher van Ruremond consisted of a shield suspended from a tree and supported by two lions. The shield contains three fleurs-de-lys and below them the printer's mark and initials C.E. Above the tree is a half-length Virgin and Child. In the base of the device is a space pierced for type, in which the name is printed sometimes Christophorus Endoviensis and sometimes Christophorus Ruremundensis.

RUREMOND, RÉMONDE, RAIMUND (HANS VAN), printer and stationer in Antwerp and London, is first mentioned in 1525, when in partnership with Christopher van Ruremond, probably a brother, he printed an edition of the Dutch *Bible*. On October 30th, 1525, Hans was brought before the town council of Antwerp and accused of printing a heretical Lutheran book. He was sentenced to leave the State immediately and perform a pilgrimage to the Holy Blood of Wilsenaken in Prussia and was forbidden to return without a certificate that he had performed it. He apparently fled to London where he began to take an active part in publishing the English *New Testament*. In 1527 Christopher was brought up, in Antwerp, for printing *New Testaments* but apparently escaped punishment, but Hans was not so fortunate. Foxe in his list of persons forced to abjure in the diocese of London in 1528 mentions "John Raimund a Dutchman: for causing fifteen hundred of Tyndale's New Testaments to be printed at Antwerp and for bringing five hundred into England." Christopher died in London in 1531 and John returned to Antwerp at the beginning of the same year, for the town archives contain an entry dated March 29th, 1531, that letters of his pilgrimage having been presented he was free to re-enter the City and district. He does not appear to have been long in Antwerp, but returned to London and may with great probability be identified with the following who took out letters of denization on February 24th, 1535, "John Holibusche alias Holybusche of London, stationer otherwise bokebynder, born in Ruremond under the obedience of the Emperor." As an assistant to John Nicholson, another Dutchman and a printer in Southwark, he edited an edition of the English *New Testament* printed in 1538 and also translated the *Exposition on the song of the Blessed*

Virgin Mary. After this nothing is known of him, and he must not be confused with his nephew and namesake Hans van Ruremond, the son of Christopher who began to print at Antwerp about 1530, and continued in business for many years.

RUWE or RUE (ANDREW), stationer in London, carried on business in St. Paul's Churchyard with his brother John. His will dated October 10th, 1517, was proved on November 24th. He left bequests to his sister Katherine at Frankfort, his wife Joane and his daughter Katherine. To Thomas Wallis and David Owen priests of St. Faith's he left copies of the *Sermones Dormi Secure* and Quentin's sermons. John Reynes and Joyce Pelgrim were two of his executors. [Plomer, Wills, p. 2.]

RUWE or RUE (JOHN), stationer in London, was in business in St. Paul's Churchyard with his brother Andrew. He was a native of Frankfort. His will dated December 23rd, 1492, was proved January 15th, 1493. He desired to be buried in the Pardon churchyard, and bequeathed his goods to his brother. A blank space is left for the name of one of the executors who is described as a printer of Westminster. [Plomer, Wills, p. i.]

RYCARD (HANS), printer in London, was an assistant to Anthony Scoloker in 1549 when he lived in the Savoy Rents without Temple Bar. He is entered in the Subsidy Roll as "With Anthony Scolyca, Hance Rycard" and was valued at twenty shillings and taxed one. [R. of A., I, 151.]

RYCHARD (THOMAS) printer in Tavistock, was a monk of the exempt monastery. The first book he issued was a translation of *Boethius* printed in 1525 at the request of Robert Langdon. The only other book known from this press is the *Statutes of the Stannary* of which a unique copy is in Exeter College, Oxford. [*Bibliographica*, vol. ii, pp. 29, 30.]

RYPPE (ALAN), stationer in London, is mentioned in the Records in the Guildhall as entering into recognizances December 12th, 1532, along with three other stationers, Lewis Sutton, John Gough and Henry Tabb. [Journal 13, p. 291.]

S. (I.), for bindings with these initials, *see* Siberch (J.).

S. (N.), for bindings with these initials, *see* Speryng (N.).

SALISBURY (JOHN), *see* Byddell (J.).

SAINCT DENIS (JEAN DE), stationer in Paris, began business about 1510 and died in 1531. He lived at the sign of St. Nicholas in the Rue Neuve Notre Dame. [Renouard, p. 336.] He issued, apparently about 1520, an undated book entitled *Les faictz merveilleux de virgille*, of sixteen leaves in 8vo, in which Wynkyn de Worde appears to have had some interest. The colophon on the recto of the last leaf runs " Cy finissent les faictz merueilleux de virgille. Imprimees nouvellement a Paris pour Jehan sainct Denis Libraire demourant en la Rue neufue Nostre Dame a Lenseigne sainct Nycolas." On the reverse of the leaf is W. de Worde's device 9 [Bibl. Soc. Handlists] in a more damaged condition than in 1511. This volume was described by Brunet [II, p. 1167], who has added to his notice a facsimile of a device of De Worde's different from the one occurring in the book.

SALT (HENRY), printer in London, is mentioned in the returns of 1571 " Henry Salt borne in Deluke, printer, came into this realme about xxx yeares past." [R. of A., II, 29.] In the other return of 1571 he is called a bookbinder. He was apparently only an assistant to some other person for in the Subsidy Roll of 1576 he pays only a poll-tax of four pence. [R. of A., II, 170.] He lived in the Parish of All Hallows Staining.

SAMPSON (JOHN), *see* Awdley (J.).

SAWYER (THOMAS), stationer in London, was an original member of the Stationers' Company. He is only once mentioned later in the Registers as presenting an apprentice in 1559.

SCAPULYS (PHILIPPE), stationer in London, was a brother of the Stationers' Company before the incorporation and is entered as a subscriber to the house of Bridewell in 1555–56 when he gave six pence. [Arber, I, 48.] His will dated 1590 was proved in the Prerogative Court of Canterbury. [36 Drury.] He is described as "Philipp Scapulis, par. holie trinitye in Brustoe ; borne in cittie of Trier in Germany."

SCARLETT (JOHN), stationer in Cambridge, is only mentioned in 1551, the year of his death, when he rented a little house at the west end of St. Mary's Church. His will was made July 13th, 1551, and proved on August 1st. In it he mentions his wife Elizabeth and a son, Philip and Thomas his brothers, his sisters and an apprentice named Rowland. [Gray, *Cambridge Stationers*, pp. 66, 67.]

SCHOEFFER (PETER), printer in Mainz, Worms and Strassburg, commenced to print at the first-named town in 1512. By 1525 he was settled at Worms and by 1530 at Strassburg. At Worms he printed Tindale's octavo *New Testament* of 1525-6 and also his *Prologue to the Romans*. [Bodl.]

SCHOTT (JOHN), printer in Strassburg, was born June 19th, 1477. He was the son of Martin Schott, and grandson of John Mentelin, both famous Strassburg printers. He was educated at the universities of Freibourg and Basle and commenced to print in 1500, immediately after his father's death, continuing to print up till 1545. [Schmidt, *M. & J. Schott*, Strassburg, 1893.] In 1528 he printed Roye's *Rede me and be not wroth*. Hermann Rinck writing to Wolsey on October 4th, 1528, said "In the presence of the consuls, judges and senators of Frankfort I compelled John Schott the printer, on oath to confess how many books of that sort he had printed in the English, German, French or any other language. And on taking the oath he acknowledged that he had only printed one thousand copies of six signatures, and in addition a thousand of nine signatures in the English language, and this by the orders of Roye and Huchyns; who being in want of money were not able to pay for the books that were printed and much less to procure their being printed in other languages." [Demaus, *W. Tyndale*, pp. 162-3.]

SCOLAR (JOHN), printer in Oxford, was at work during the years 1517-18, carrying on business in St. John's Street near Merton College. He printed altogether five books and a broadside prognostication. He was perhaps officially recognised by the University since several of his books were issued "Cum privilegio" and he used the University arms as his device. Part of his materials were obtained from W. de Worde. Since he does not occur in the lists of inhabitants paying taxes in 1524 he had probably left the town. In 1528 he seems to have worked for a while at Abingdon where he printed a *Breviary* for the use of the Abbey of which the only copy known is in Emmanuel College Cambridge. [Madan, p. 263.]

SCOLOKER (ANTHONY), printer in Ipswich and London, was an Englishman by birth and not as Herbert suggested a foreigner. He began to print at Ipswich in St. Nicholas' Parish about 1547 and after printing some four books moved in 1548 to London, where he settled in St. Botolph's Parish without Aldersgate. There he printed about ten books, the majority being issued in partnership with William Seres, and the three which are dated being all of 1548. After that year he moved to the Savoy Rents in the Strand and his assistant is mentioned in the Subsidy Roll of 1549 "With Anthony Scolyca, Hance Rycard." [R. of A., I, 151.] At this new address he printed about six books, all undated, and one at least with W. Seres. The two editions of Hans Brinklow's *Complaint of Roderyck Mors* which are said in their colophons to have been printed at Geneva in Savoy by Michael Boys are in Scoloker's type and were perhaps printed in the Savoy Rents. Several books which he printed were translations of his own from French and German. He used as a device a hand rubbing a coin on a touchstone inscribed "Verbum Dei" with the text "Prove the spyrites whether they be of God." In his edition of the *Ordinary of Christians* is a good woodcut illustration of a printing press. [D.N.B.]

SCOTT (JOHN), *see* Skot (J.).

SEDLEY (JOHN), stationer in London, was at one time Warden of the Craft of Stationers. His will dated February 23rd, 1531, was proved on November 15th, 1532. [Arber, II, 8.]

SERES (GYLES), bookbinder in London, was a Frenchman who came to England about 1554. In March, 1562, he took out letters of denization. [Pat. 4 Eliz., p. 11, m. 7.] In 1567 he occurs in a list of aliens in Aldersgate Ward and is said to have been in London thirteen years. [R. of A., I, 326.] In the two returns of 1571 he is described as "bookebinder and denizein, of the Frenche nacion, hath byn here xvi yeares." [R. of A., I, 435; II, 47.] In 1576 he was still in St. Anne's Parish, Aldersgate Ward and paid a poll-tax of four pence. [R. of A., II, 186.] In 1582 he is entered as a bookbinder. In 1583 and 1585 he is entered very fully amongst the strangers in the liberties of St. Martin Le Grand and is mentioned as paying tribute to the Company of Stationers. [R. of A., II, 349, 392.] He is last found in 1595 noted as one of those who had not paid his tax of eight pence, being too poor. [R. of A., II, 477.]

SERES (WILLIAM), printer in London, commenced work about the year 1546. At first he appears to have joined with other printers, Anthony Scoloker, William Hill and especially John Day. His addresses at first also varied but he seems to have lived first in Ely Rents, Holborn, then at

N

Peter College, finally settling before 1553 at the Hedgehog in St. Paul's Churchyard. In 1553 Seres obtained a privilege for printing service books but on the accession of Mary this privilege was withdrawn, the printer imprisoned and many of his books confiscated. [*Egerton Papers*, p. 140.] In the charter granted to the Stationers' Company in 1557 Seres' name occurs twenty-first in the list and he was evidently a man of much importance, having been elected Master no less than five times. The privilege of printing service books which Seres had lost was re-granted to him and his son by Queen Elizabeth, a valuable concession which gave rise to much contention amongst the stationers. Seres seems to have printed steadily during Elizabeth's reign up to about 1577, after which time his name is not found. [D.N.B.]

SERO (JOHN), sealmaker in London, was admitted a brother of the Stationers' Company on November 5th, 1555. He may be identical with the John de Sheron who was an assistant to Thomas Hacket the bookbinder in 1565.

SETH (JOHN), stationer in Cambridge, is mentioned in the accounts of St. Mary's Church as supplying books in 1550-1. [Gray, *Cambridge Stationers*, p. 68.]

SEYGAR (PAUL), printer in London, was an assistant to Edward Whitchurch and is entered in St. Bride's Parish in the Subsidy Roll of 1549 with goods valued at four pounds. [R. of A., I, 180.] In 1550, October 29th, he took out letters of denization. [Pat. 4 Edw. VI, p. 4, m. 4.] In 1551 we find him in a list of members of the Dutch Church "Paulus Seghers, met Margareta, een drucker, met Nicolais" [R. of A., I, 213], so that he had then left Whitchurch and joined Nicholas Hill.

SHEDMORE (ROGER) was apparently an assistant to Henry Pepwell as we learn from an inscription in a book in the library of Corpus Christi College, Oxford, "Roger Shedmore s'uaunte wᵗ Hary Pepwell at the sine of the trinite."

SHEFELDE (JOHN), bookseller in London, commissioned Nicholas Hill to print for him John Chrysostom's *Sermon of pacience* in 1550. The colophon runs "Imprinted at London . . . by Nicolas Hyll, for John Shefelde, dwelling in Pauls church yarde." He probably died before 1557 for his name does not appear in the list of members of the Stationers' Company.

SHEREMAN (JOHN) was an original member of the Stationers' Company and was made free on October 8th, 1555. He is entered several times as subscribing to the Company and was twice fined, once for misnaming a brother, William Hill and again for printing a ballad without license. He is last mentioned in 1559.

SHERES (JAMES), bookbinder in London, came to England about 1535. He took out letters of denization October 29th, 1550. [Pat. 4 Edw. VI, p. 4, m. 5.] He is entered in the two Returns of Aliens of 1571 as "bokebynder, borne in Andwerpe, denizon, in this realme 38 yeares and in the saide warde 22-yeares" and "bookebynder, borne in Anwarpe, came into this realme to his brother about xxxv yeares past, and is a denizen." [R. of A., I, 411; II, 12.] He lived in Paul's Churchyard, St. Faith's Parish.

SHERES (PETER), stationer in Cambridge, was appointed by the University, February 5th, 1545, to succeed Nicholas Pilgrim. In 1550 he was one of the witnesses to the will of John Scarlett, who left him a coat. From 1553–8 he occurs several times in the accounts of St. Mary's Church as binding or supplying books, and was, during the same period one of the Masters of the Sepulchre light. In 1557 he appeared before the University Commissioners and is mentioned in Mere's diary "Peter Sheres had his iiij colloquies promised hym agayne by the vysytors to redelyver to his merchawnte allthowghe thei were by them condempned." He lived in the Parish of St. Mary the Great and was buried in that church August 20th, 1569. [Gray, *Cambridge Stationers*, p. 68.]

SIBERCH (JOHN), printer in Cambridge, was a native of Siegburg near Cologne his proper name being John Laer. He was probably settled in Cambridge by 1520 and in that year an edition of Croke's *Introductiones in rudimenta graeca* was printed for him in Cologne by Eucharius Cervicornus. During 1521 and 1522 Siberch printed nine different books in his house with the sign of the Arma Regia, which stood near Caius College between the gates of Humility and Virtue. In some of these he used two wood blocks of the Royal Arms and also his own initials and mark showing white on a black ground. After 1522 he is not known to have printed anything, though references in a letter written to him by Peter Kaetz would make it appear that he had at any rate such intention. At Christmas, 1525,

Erasmus sends greetings to him. In the Grace book of the University he is mentioned in 1538-9 as "dominus Johannes law [laer in later entries] presbiter alienigena" owing a debt of twenty pounds to the University, and this is repeatedly entered up to 1553. It would seem from these entries that Siberch had given up his business as a stationer and joined the Church. Siberch was also a bookbinder and used a handsome roll containing three fleurs-de-lys, a Tudor rose, a turreted gateway and a pomegranate and the binder's initials I.S. [D.N.B. Gray, *Cambridge Stationers*, pp. 54-61.]

SIMON, printer in London, was an assistant to W. de Worde who left him in his will twenty shillings in books. [Plomer, Wills, p. 4.] He may perhaps be the same as Simon Martynson.

SINGLETON (HUGH), printer in London, commenced work about 1548 at the sign of St. Augustine in St. Paul's Churchyard. In 1553 he had moved to the Double Hood in Thames Street. What he was doing for the next few years is not known, but he issued a number of books with the colophon "Rome, before ye castle of S. Angel at the sign of St Peter" and though without his name they contain his rebus or a copy of it. Some books in his type were issued at "Strasburg at the sign of the golden Bibel." He was an original member of the Stationers' Company, though not mentioned in the charter, and it is probable that when it was passed he was in disgrace abroad. In 1579 he was prosecuted for printing Stubbs' *Discoverie of a gaping gulf*, but was pardoned, and soon after was made Printer to the City of London. By 1578 he worked at the Golden Tun, Creede Lane, and in 1588 at the North door of Christ's Hospital. He gave up business in 1593. He used as a device a rebus with his initials and mark and a single tun. He was also a bookbinder and his mark is found on a binding roll which passed later to an Oxford binder who made considerable use of it.

SKEREWE (THOMAS), stationer in London, was made free October 8th, 1555, and his name occurs in the original list in the Stationers' Company's charter of 1557. He is entered in the Registers, once as taking an apprentice, twice as being fined, but his name is not found after 1563.

SKOFELD (JOHN), stationer in York, was admitted a freeman by patrimony in 1551-52. He is entered as "Johannes Skofeld, stacyoner, fil. Hugonis Skofen (*sic*) skryvener." [*Freemen of York*, p. 272.]

SKOT (JOHN), printer in London, issued his first dated book, *The Body of Policy*, in May, 1521. His first address was in the Parish of St. Sepulchre outside Newgate, and there he printed altogether six books with his name, though it is clear that he also printed some for W. de Worde. In these early books occurs his first device, having his mark and initials on a shield surmounted by a helmet and supported by two dragons. In 1528 he was settled in St. Paul's Churchyard where he printed eight books, two only bearing dates 1528 and 1529. One book is known, an edition of Stanbridge's *Accidence*, printed "Without Bishopsgate in St. Botolph's Parish at George Alley gate," but whether before or after this date cannot be determined. While at St. Paul's Churchyard he began to use another device, an exact copy, down to the mistake in the motto, of that used at Paris by Denis Rosse, but so carelessly has it been engraved that both his name and monogram are printed backwards. He also used his first device with a slight alteration, the mark has been cut out of the shield and a monogram inserted. In 1531 an edition of the *Gradus comparationum* was issued, said in the colophon to have been printed by John Toye, but it has Skot's device at end and he was probably the real printer. Skot was implicated in the troubles connected with the impostures of Elizabeth Barton, the maid of Kent, and printed a book about her which has now absolutely disappeared. Among the documents connected with the case in 1533 was the confession of the printer and Cranmer entered among his notes "to remember that Dr. Bokking did put unto Skotte all the Nun's book to print and had five hundred of them when they were printed and the printer two hundred." [*Letters and Papers of Henry VIII*, vol. vi, p. 648.] Skot's last move was to Fauster Lane in St. Leonard's Parish where he printed one dated book of 1537 and five undated books. [D.N.B.]

SKOT (JOHN), printer in Edinburgh and St. Andrews, first appeared in Edinburgh in 1539 when he rented two rooms in a house in the Cowgate. For the next few years he lived in Edinburgh, though nothing printed by him at this early period is known. In 1547 a warrant for his arrest was issued by the Privy Council to John Scrymgeour, Constable of Dundee, so that Skot was apparently at that time resident there. Soon after he was at St. Andrews and probably printed there some tracts now lost which gave offence to the Government and called forth the Act of Parliament of February, 1551-2, against printing books without license. In 1552 Skot issued his first dated book, the *Catechism* of Archbishop Hamilton. He printed on to 1562 when his materials were seized by the magistrates of Edinburgh while he was engaged in printing Ninian Winzet's *Last blast of the trompet.* Skot's materials were given over to Thomas Alexander, a creditor of Skot's and were handed on to Thomas Bassendyne a printer, who however did not retain them long, as Skot printed again in 1567 probably for Bassendyne. Skot's last book is dated 1571 and during his career he printed some fourteen known books including the various works of Sir David Lindsay. Skot used as a device a small block with a figure of Hercules striking a centaur. Much of his material was obtained from England, some having been used earlier by Lawrence Andrewe. Though he has been often confused with the English printer John Skot, there seems to have been no connexion between them. [Dickson and Edmond, pp. 150–97. Edinb. Bibl. Soc., 1893–4, No. 1. D.N.B.]

SMITH (ANTHONY), stationer in London, is mentioned in an edition of the *Psalter or boke of the Psalmes* printed for him in 1548 by Roger Car. [B.M.] He received along with three other stationers forty shillings under the will of Robert Toy, proved March, 1556, as payment for making a valuation of his stock. His name occurs in the first list of the Stationers' Company. He lived in the Parish of St. Faith's London and his will dated 1560 was proved in the Prerogative Court of Canterbury. [39, Mellershe.]

SMITH (HENRY), printer in London, was son-in-law to Robert Redman and is mentioned in his will dated 1540. He appears to have printed only in the years 1545 and 1546 and to have issued nothing but law-books. He lived at the sign of the Trinity, outside Temple Bar in St. Clement's Parish. He died in 1550 and his will was proved in December of that year. [Herb., II, 706–7.]

SNOW (JOHN), printer in London, was an apprentice to Richard Pynson who bequeathed him six shillings and eight pence in his will.

SNOW (THOMAS), bookbinder in Oxford, rented "selda secunda occidentalis cum sellario ibidem [Wodcokhall]" in 1458 from Oseney Abbey. [Gibson, *Oxford Bindings*, p. 46.]

SOULL (HENRY), printer in London, is mentioned in the Subsidy Roll of 1549 as an assistant to R. Grafton. [R. of A., I, 159.]

SPENCER (R.), bookbinder, made use of a diamond-shaped die with his name upon it. The date of the die is probably about 1500.

SPERYNG (NICHOLAS), stationer in Cambridge, was a member of a large family of that name who were stationers and bookbinders in various Low Country towns. He probably came from Antwerp and was settled in Cambridge before 1514, when he is mentioned in the parish book of St. Mary the Great as supplying ironwork for a window. In 1517 he was made a churchwarden and was closely connected with the church during his life. In the Subsidy Roll of 1523-4 his goods were valued at twenty-five pounds and in 1534 he was appointed one of the three official University stationers. His will dated August 20th, 1545, was proved January 27th, 1546. He left bequests to his wife Anne, his son William and his grandson Nicholas, also to Katherine and Anne Spyrynke, whose relationship is not specified. As a bookbinder he made use of two panel stamps. On one is the Annunciation, on the other St. Nicholas raising the three children from the tub, with the name below, Nicolaus Spiernick (*sic*). He also used several rolls which contain his mark and initials. [Gray, *Cambridge Stationers*, pp. 43-53.]

SPILMAN (SIMON), bookbinder in London, was an original member of the Stationers' Company. He is mentioned by Foxe [viii, p. 724] as having been brought before Bonner for binding a Bible and service book for W. Gie. He was sent to the Tower, but escaped. He is mentioned several times in the Stationers' Company's Registers as taking apprentices, the last entry of his name being under the year 1569.

SQUIRE (WILLIAM), stationer in Cambridge, was the official "stationarius" to the University from 1482 to 1486 and received a yearly fee of thirteen shillings and four pence. He occurs in several accounts as having bound and mended books. [Gray, *Cambridge Stationers*, p. 12.]

STARKERFELSER, alias RUPIUS (HENRY), stationer in London, was entered and sworn a brother of the Stationers' Company, February 22nd, 1557. [Arber, I, 43.]

STEELSIUS (JEAN), printer in Antwerp, was born at Brusthem, and married in 1535 Margaret daughter of Michael Hillenius the printer. She died in 1540 and he married again in 1542 Anne van Ertborne. Steelsius was admitted a member of the St. Lucas Gilde in 1559 and died in March, 1562. He lived first in the House of Delft in the Cammerstraet and in 1537 at the Shield of Burgundy in the same street. He used several devices in all of which appear two birds standing on either side of a sceptre on a frame or altar, with the motto "Concordia res parve crescunt." [Van Havre, p. 351.] In 1556 he printed the *History of Aurelio and Isabella* in four languages, French, Italian, Spanish, English.

STEWARD (WILLIAM), stationer in London, is first mentioned in 1545 when he acted as overseer to the will of James Gaver whose daughter Mary he had married. He was an original member of the re-founded Company of Stationers and up to 1564 appears in their books where he is entered as taking apprentices though he does not appear to have printed on his own account.

STODARD (WILLIAM), stationer in London, was made free on the 26th April, 1534. [Bibl. Soc. Trans., VI, 24.]

STOKE (THOMAS), bookbinder in London, is mentioned with others in January, 1527, as having been granted pardon. [*Letters and papers of Henry VIII*, IV, pt. ii, p. 1270.]

STONDO (BERNARD VAN), stationer in London, was in partnership with Henry Franckenbergk. Together they took a lease in 1482 of a house in St. Mark's Alley off St. Clement's Lane, a street running out of Lombard Street. [*Descriptive Catalogue of Ancient Deeds in the Public Record Office*, I, p. 491, C. 1058.]

STORY (JOHN), printer in Edinburgh, is only known as the printer of a small supplement to the Aberdeen *Breviary* containing the *Compassio Beate Marie* and the account of the advent of the relics of St. Regulus. It has no date but was probably printed about 1520, and the colophon runs "Impressum Edinburgi per Johannem Story nomine et mandato Karoli Stule." [Dickson and Edmond, pp. 100-102.]

STOUGHTON (ROBERT), printer in London, seems only to have printed between the years 1548 and 1551 during which time he issued about fourteen books. His place of business was in Ludgate at the sign of the Bishop's Mitre. The will of a Robert Stoughton dated 1553 was proved in the Prerogative Court of Canterbury.

STUFFOLDE, bookbinder in Oxford, is mentioned in the college accounts of Balliol and Magdalen as having bound books for the libraries in 1553–60. [Gibson, *Early Oxford Bindings*, p. 47.] His name occurs as early as 1539 in the University Archives, and as a name occurring singly is generally a Christian name it is not improbable that this name is a corruption of Stoffel the usual Dutch short form of Christopher.

SUETHON (LEWIS), stationer in London, is known only from the occurrence of his name in one book. This was a very fine folio edition of the Sarum *Gradual* printed at Paris in 1527 by Nicholas Prevost, "impensis ac sumptibus honestorum virorum Wynkyn de Worde, Joannis Renis, et Ludovici Suethon." [Bodl.] The name Suethon is unknown but it might possibly be a mistake or mis-spelling for Sutton, and a Lewis Sutton was Warden of the Company of Stationers in 1526.

SUTOR (RADULPHUS), *see* Cousturier (R.).

SUTTON (EDWARD), printer in London, was an apprentice to John Reynes who left him five pounds in books, and afterwards to Lucy Reynes who left him one pound. [Plomer, Wills, pp. 6, 8.] His first printed book, the *Treatise of the New India*, was issued in 1553 from his house in Lombard Street with the sign of the Cradle. On the incorporation of the Stationers' Company he appears fifty-second on the list and was taken into the livery in 1561. He printed up to 1568, though he did not issue many books. He was also a bookbinder, as we learn from the accounts of St. Mary Woolnoth [Registers, p. xxi] "1557 Item paide Edward Sutton bookbinder for twoo bookes called the twoo Antisymes xls." He died at the beginning of 1569–70 and was buried on January 30th at St. Mary Woolnoth. He had seven children Rose, John, Henry, Jane, Mary, Thomas, Lewis, several of whom died young. His will dated 1569 was proved in the Prerogative Court of Canterbury [23, Sheffeld] and in it his address is given as "Frier Lane otherwyse grenewiche lane."

SUTTON (HENRY), printer in London, commenced business about 1552, when he issued several ballads on the controversy between Churchyard and Camell. During Mary's reign he was associated with Kingston for the production of service books. On the incorporation of the Stationers'

Company his name appears thirty-sixth on the list. He printed continuously up to 1563 and his address was the Black Boy or Moryan, sometimes described as in St. Paul's Churchyard, sometimes as in Paternoster Row. As a device he had a picture of two naked children seated on the ground.

SUTTON (LEWIS), stationer in London, was Warden with Henry Pepwell of the Stationers' Company in 1526. [Arber, I, xxi.] He is mentioned in the Records at the Guildhall as having entered into recognizances along with Alan Ryppe, John Gough and Henry Tab on December 12th, 1532. [Journal 13, fol. 291.] In 1534–5 he was defendant in an action brought by John Gough and John Rastell relating to the house with the sign of the Mermaid used as a printing office. [*Bibliographica*, II, 438.] The name of Ludovicus Suethon, who in partnership with W. de Worde and John Reynes had a Sarum *Gradual* printed at Paris in 1527, may very probably be a foreign mis-spelling of Sutton. The last mention of Sutton is in the *Letters and papers of Henry VIII* [Vol. xiv, pt. ii, p. 11.] "Aug. 12 1539 Receipt by Lewys Sutton, bookbinder of London of 5 mks from Wᵐ Hatton of Haldenby for lands in Northamptonshire sold to him." The will of a Lewis Sutton, perhaps this stationer, dated 1541, was proved in the Prerogative Court of Canterbury.

SUTTON (NICHOLAS), stationer in London, died some time before April 30th, 1531, for in that year his widow Elizabeth took a lease from the college of the petty canons of St. Paul's of a shop on the North side of St. Paul's Churchyard for 60 years at four marks a year. This lease was surrendered and a new one taken for 70 years by Humphrey Toy. Nicholas Sutton was probably the stationer mentioned as Nicholas the bookseller in St. Paul's Churchyard who sold prohibited books to Antony Dalaber. [v, Nicholas.] Two panel stamps on bindings are known [Westm. Abbey] with medallion heads and the initials N.S, followed by a tun, which may be ascribed to him.

SYM (WILLIAM), bookseller in Edinburgh, was prohibited by an Act of Council passed January 14th, 1509–10, from selling Sarum service books, or causing to be printed any books which had been already produced by Walter Chepman. [Dickson and Edmond, p. 84.]

SYMONDS (PETER), stationer in London, is mentioned in the Subsidy Roll of 1549 as an assistant to Andrew Hester in St. Paul's Churchyard. [R. of A., I, 159.]

SYMONDS (THOMAS), stationer in London, carried on business in St. Paul's Churchyard. He was a witness in a case mentioned by Foxe under the year 1514 and his deposition is given. [Foxe, vol. iv, p. 193.] In 1525–6 he is mentioned in the accounts of London Bridge "for binding in boards 17 quires in parchment containing 17 accounts of the bridge works, 6.s." The binding of these volumes is ornamented with a roll containing a castle and portcullis, a fleur-de-lys, a trotting horse, a rose, a pomegranate and the Royal Arms, and between the horse and rose are Symonds' mark and initials. [Welch, *History of the Tower Bridge*, p. 46.]

SYSAY (ROBERT), stationer in London, was a member of the Stationers' Company before 1557 though he is not found in the list in the charter. He presented apprentices in 1559 and 1561 and paid a fine in 1562. After this his name is not found in the Registers.

TAB or DABBE (HENRY), stationer in London, is first mentioned in a letter written in October, 1539, by Richard Stevenage, abbot of St. Albans to Cromwell about John Hertford the printer. "Sent John Pryntare to London with Harry Pepwell, Bonere and Tabbe of Powlles churchyard, stationers, to order him at your pleasure." [*Letters and papers of Hen. VIII*, xiv, pt. ii, No. 315.] In 1540 he was summoned before the Privy Council as suspected of having printed an edition (of which no copy is now known) of the *Epistle of Melanchthon to Henry VIII* for the revoking and abolishing of the six articles, but he was declared innocent of the matter, and dismissed. [*Acts of the Privy Council*, vol. vii, pp. 100–101.] In 1541 he issued, with Richard Banks, the *Questionary of Cyrurgyens*, translated by Robert Copland and printed by Robert Wyer. He is spoken of in the colophon as "the ryght honest parsone Henry Dabbe stacyoner and byblyopolyst in Paules churche yarde." R. Lant printed for him an edition of Skelton and he also issued according to Herbert the *Book of hawking and hunting* and the *Treasury of poor men*. In 1545 he was "overseer" of the will of Edward Ylle, stationer, for which he received six shillings and eight pence. His place of business was in Paul's Churchyard at the sign of Judith. He died in 1548 and his will was proved in the Prerogative Court of Canterbury.

TABBE (RICHARD), stationer in London, was party to a Chancery suit brought in 1472–75. [Early Chancery Proceedings, Bundle 47, No. 77.]

TAVERNER (JOHN), stationer in London, is mentioned in 1521 in the accounts of Henry VIII "April. To John Taverner, stationer of London, by the serjeant of the vestry for binding, clasping and covering 41 books for the King's chapel 4£." [*Letters and papers of Henry VIII*, vol. iii, pt. ii, p. 1545.] His will dated November 27th, 1529, was proved on November 30th, 1531.

TAVERNER (NICHOLAS), stationer in London, is first mentioned in a deed of March, 1538, "License to Sir Thomas Audeley to alienate a tenement with a little garden, shop, cellars etc in the parish of St. Katherine Christ Church within Aldgate London to Nicholas Taverner of London and Mary his wife." Taverner occurs in the original list of Stationers in the charter of 1557 but is nowhere else mentioned in the Registers.

TELOTSON (WILLIAM), bookseller in London, had a shop at the west door of St. Paul's. Two books were printed for him by Edward Whitchurch in 1543 and 1544 [Sayle, I, p. 149], and a Sarum *Breviary* in 1544 by Whitchurch and Grafton. [Herbert, I, 519.]

THOMAS, bookbinder in Oxford, occurs frequently in entries of the fifteenth century and the name may refer to Thomas Hokyn, Thomas Snowe, Thomas Uffyngton, and perhaps others.

THORNE (JOHN), *see* Dorne (J.).

TIRER (RANDALL), stationer in London, is mentioned by Foxe as having been imprisoned for selling books sent into England by the preachers who had fled abroad, in October, 1554. [Foxe, vol. vi, p. 561.] He was an original member of the Stationers' Company and died in 1558-9.

TISDALE (JOHN), printer in London, commenced business about 1554 in partnership with J. Charlewood "In Holburne nere to the Cundite at the signe of the Sarsins head." On October 8th, 1555, he became a freeman of the Stationers' Company, and is entered in the list in their charter in 1557. In 1558 he printed Fisher's *Dialogues* "in Smithfield at the signe of the Mytre." From 1560 onwards till 1563 he continued to print and is frequently mentioned in the Registers as entering copies and taking apprentices. His residence and printing office were in Knight Riders Street near the Queen's Wardrobe, and he had also a shop in All Hallows Churchyard, Lombard Street, near Gracechurch. [D.N.B.]

TOLNA (ADRIAN DE), *see* Turner (A.).

TORRENTINI (LORENZO), printer in Florence from 1547 to 1563 obtained a privilege from Edward VI in April, 1551, giving him the sole right of printing the *Pandects of Justinian*. [Rymer's *Foedera*, vol. xv. Herbert, III, pp. 1569–70.] The work was issued in three volumes in 1553 with Edward's privilege printed on the verso of the sixth leaf.

TOTTELL (RICHARD), printer in London, is supposed to have been third son of Henry Tottell of Exeter. In 1552 he received a patent for printing law-books of which he issued large numbers. He was an original member of the new Stationers' Company and was Master in 1579 and 1584. In 1573 he made an effort to start a paper mill in England, but the matter meeting with no encouragement from the Government, the scheme was allowed to drop. Towards the close of his life Tottell retired to Wiston in Pembrokeshire where he died in 1593. He left a son William born in 1560 and a daughter Anne who married December 18th, 1594, William Pennyman. [Plomer, Wills, pp. 33–35. *English Printing*, pp. 113–116. D.N.B.]

TOURNES (JEAN DE), printer in Lyons, was at work between the years 1540 and 1564. He printed in 1553 Peter Derendel's *True and lyuely historyke purtreatures of the woll bible*, with woodcuts by Bernard Salamon.

TOY (ELIZABETH), stationer in London, was the widow of Robert Toye and carried on his business for a short time after his death. Her maiden name was Elizabeth Scampion and she was Toy's second wife, having married him in January, 1546. She was a generous benefactor to the Company of Stationers and is entered several times in the Registers as entering copies of ballads, or taking apprentices. She died in 1565 and left most of her property to her husband's family. [Plomer, Wills, pp. 15, 16.]

TOY (JOHN), printer in London, appears to have printed only one book. This was an edition of the *Gradus comparationum* [Bodl.] which has the following colophon " Imprinted at London in Poules chyrche yard, at the sygne of saynte Nycolas, by me John Toye. The yere of our lorde God M.D.XXXI . the xxx day of May." At the end is John Skot's device so that the book may have been really printed by him. In 1534 an edition of

Stanbridge's *Shorter Accidence* [U.L.C.] was printed for Toy by Martin de Keyser at Antwerp. There is a letter in existence [*Letters and papers of Henry VIII*, vol. vii, p. 252] written in 1534 from Leonard Cox to "The Goodman Toy at the sign of St Nicholas in Powles Churchyard" concerning some translations of Erasmus' paraphrases to be printed, doubtless the paraphrase of the Epistle to Titus which Cox translated. There are some reasons for believing that Toy married Elizabeth, the widow of Nicholas Sutton, whose house in Paul's Churchyard afterwards belonged to Humphrey Toy. He apparently died in 1535 and his will was proved in that year. [P.C.C., 23, Hogen.]

TOY (ROBERT), printer in London, must have been free of the Stationers' Company before 1534, since his son was made free by patrimony in 1558. He was in business from 1542 up to 1555 issuing about twenty-six books, most of which were printed for him by others. He lived in St. Paul's Churchyard next to Thomas Petyt at a house with the sign of the Bell. His first wife by whom he had two children, Robert and Rose, died before 1546, for on January 22nd of that year he married a second wife Elizabeth Scampion of St. Margaret's Westminster. [Marriage Licenses, Faculty Office, p. 6.] Toye died at the beginning of 1556 and his will dated February 5th was proved March 4th. [Plomer, Wills, pp. 12, 13.] He had considerable property in St. Paul's Churchyard which he left to his wife and children. His daughter Rose afterwards married Arthur Pepwell. [D.N.B.]

TRAUTH (THOMAS), pseudonym. This name is found in the colophon of *The lamentacion of a christian against the citie of London made by Roderigo Mors, anno domini 1542*, which runs "Prynted at Jericho in the Land of Promes by Thome Trauth." [B.M.]

TREVERIS (PETER), printer in London, may have been, as Herbert suggests, a native of Treveris or Triers in Germany. His first dated book was the *Syntaxis* of Whitinton issued in 1522 and the majority of books printed by him were grammars. He printed for Reynes and for Lawrence Andrewe, and his last book, Fisher's *Two fruytfull sermons*, was printed for him in 1532 by Rastell. Some of his books, as for example the *Handywork of Surgery*, 1525, are remarkable for their woodcuts, and the *Polycronicon* which he printed in 1527 for John Reynes is a very fine specimen of printing. His more ordinary work was not good. During the ten years of his work he printed at least thirty-six books. He lived over the bridge in Southwark at the sign of the "Wodows" or woodhouses. His device consisted of a shield suspended from a tree and supported by a wild man and woman, the wodows, carrying bows and arrows. On the shield are his initials and mark while below all is a ribbon with his name and before the centre of it a cross-bow leaning against the tree. [D.N.B.]

TROOST (JAN), pseudonym, occurs as the printer of an edition of *The defence of the marriage of preistes* by James Sawtry, printed at Auryk by Jan Troost in 1541. [Herbert, III, p. 1833.] The type however is that of J. Oswen of Ipswich, so that the book was very probably printed by him.

TRUTHEALL (CHRISTOPHER), pseudonym. This name is found in the colophons of two books professing to have been printed at Southwark in 1556, *Antichrist* by Rodolphus Gualtherus and John Olde's *Confession of the catholike belefe*. [Herbert, III, p. 1451.] An account of the sale of the first named book in England will be found in Foxe's Book of Martyrs. [Vol. viii, p. 521].

TURKE (JOHN), stationer in London, published several ballads about the year 1540 relating to Cromwell, printed by Richard Bankes. Before this date he is mentioned by Foxe as one of those compelled to abjure. [Vol. iv, p. 585-6.] In April, 1543, he was brought before the Privy Council "for delivering off a certeyne erroneows booke named a Postilla upon the Gospelles to be printed" and committed to the Fleet. On May 11th he was bound over in £40 with two sureties to come up. [*Acts of the P. C.*, vol i, p. 120, etc.] About 1547 he issued *A lamentation of the death of Henry VIII*. [U.L.C.] Herbert mentions besides these an *Almanack* in 1550, a *Commentary on the 82nd Psalm*, and an undated book by Thomas Lancaster. On the granting of the Stationers' Company's charter in 1557 Turke is tenth on the list, and he must have been a freeman before 1537 as his son Isaac became free in 1561 by patrimony. He was Warden in 1558. He entered the copy of only one book, the *Kinge's and Queene's Psalms*. His first place of business was in Pater-noster Row at the sign of the Rose, but he afterwards moved to the Cock in St. Paul's Churchyard.

TURNER or DE TOLNA (ADRIAN), printer in London, was a refugee from the Low Countries. In the Subsidy Roll of 1549 he is entered as an assistant to Walter Lynne living at St. Mary-at-Hill in Billingsgate Ward and is taxed eight pence. [R. of A., I, 161.] In the Registers of the Dutch Church he is entered as "Adrianus de Tolna familus Gualtery Lyns." [R. of A., I, 202.]

TURONA (FRANCIS DE), pseudonym. This name is found in the colophon of *The Complaynt of Roderyck Mors* which runs "Imprinted at Savoy per Franciscum de Turona." The book may have been printed at Zurich. [Sayle, III, p. 1416. Herbert, III, p. 1563.]

TURONENSIS (PETRUS), bookseller in Oxford, is mentioned in the Oxford Univ. Archives between 1502 and 1507. In December, 1502, he is spoken of as "librarius" in a suit between himself and Robert Capp. [Univ. Reg., Cl, f. 176.] He died in Oxford in 1507 and his goods were valued by George Chastelayn and William Howberghe, both stationers, and Egidius Stephenson. [Univ. Reg., F., f. 22.]

TWONSON (NICHOLAS), pseudonym. This name is found in the colophon to *The Souper of the Lorde*, "Nornburg by Niclas Twonson. 5 April. An 1533." [Sayle, III, p. 1513. Herbert, III, pp. 1540–41.]

TYLLAM VAN HAMBOURGH, printer in London, is entered on the Subsidy Roll of 1544 in St. Botolph's Parish, Aldersgate Ward as "servaunt with the Printer." [R. of A., I, 84.]

TYLLY (WILLIAM), printer in London, is known only from one book which he printed in 1548-9, an edition of the *New Testament*. [B.M.] He lived in the Parish of St. Anne and St. Agnes, Aldersgate, and in 1549 had an assistant named William Bole. [R. of A., I, 173.] As his servant is entered in the Subsidy Roll next the servants of John Day, the two printers may have been near neighbours.

TYNNER (ROBERT), stationer in London, was made free on the 28th September, 1535. [Bibl. Soc. Trans., VI, 24.]

TYPLADY (JOHN), stationer in York, was admitted a freeman in 1542–43. [*Freemen of York*, p. 263.]

TYSE, printer in London, is entered on the Subsidy Roll of 1549 as an assistant to Richard Grafton. [R. of A., I, 159.] The Roll is mutilated at this place and the surname obliterated. The name Tyse is the Dutch abbreviation for Matthys, Matthew.

UFFINGTON (THOMAS), bookbinder in Oxford, had a shop in 1479 in part of Haberdashers' Hall in St. Mary's Parish for which he paid twenty shillings a year. In 1482, 1494 and 1495 he bound books for the library of Magdalen College. [Gibson, *Oxford Bindings*, p. 46.]

URBANUS VAN CUELEN, printer in London, is given in the Registers of the Dutch Church as a book-printer living in Smithfield. [R. of A., I, 209.] It is just possible that he may be identical with Urban Lynyng. [*q.v.*] On the accession of Mary he probably fled the country and is found at Emden in 1557. Later on he appears to have been employed by Christopher Plantin who gave him a certificate. [*Certificats delivrés aux imprimeurs des Pays-Bas par Chr. Plantin.* Publ. par Ph. Rombouts. *Maatschappij der Antwerpsche Bibliophilen*, Uitgave 10, 1881, p. 54.]

VALENTIN (FLORENCE), stationer in Rouen, was the son of Robert Valentin and he entered into partnership with his father about 1555.

VALENTIN (ROBERT), stationer in Rouen, commenced business about the year 1524 and about 1555 took his son Florence into partnership. Besides being a publisher he was also a wood engraver and the cuts which were used in the *Horae* printed for him are mostly his work and are signed R.V. He worked with his son at the sign of the Virgin Mary and both had shops at the "Portail des libraires." They issued a large number of service books during the reign of Mary, printed for them by Hamillon and others. Valentin's device consisted of a shield suspended from a tree and supported by two unicorns. The shield contains the emblems of the passion and the initials R.V. [Frère, *Livres de Liturgie ; L'Imprimerie à Rouen*, p. 45.]

VAN METEREN (JAMES), *see* Cornelii (J.).

VEALE (ABRAHAM), printer in London, was a member of the Drapers' Company and also admitted a brother of the Stationers' Company. He began to print about 1548 and issued a considerable number of books. In 1566 he turned over his printing office to William How who continued to print for him, and confined his attention to publishing and bookselling up to the year 1586, after which date he is not heard of.   His place of business throughout his career was at the sign of the Lamb in St. Paul's Churchyard.

VÉRARD (ANTOINE), stationer in Paris, was at work from 1485 to 1513. He was a publisher in a very large way of business and was especially noted for his lavish use of illustrations.   He lived first on the Pont Nostre Dame at the sign of St. John Evangelist but after the bridge was burnt down in 1499 he moved his sign to the Petit-pont près du carrefour St. Severin.   He had besides these several other shops.   [Renouard, pp. 361–4.]   Vérard issued several Sarum service books between 1501 to 1508.   In 1503 he issued two extraordinary books in the Scottish language *The Kalendayr of Shyppars* and the *Traytte of god lyuyng and good Deyng* and also the first edition of Barclay's translation of the *Castle of Labour* by Gringore.   He was also probably the publisher of *The passion of our lord Jesu Christ with the contemplations* a curious translation by a foreigner issued about 1508 and illustrated with a remarkable series of woodcuts copied from a series engraved by Urs Graf.   Vérard died in 1513 leaving three sons and two daughters.   [Macfarlane, *Antoine Vérard.*]

VIOLETTE (PIERRE), printer in Rouen, was a student in the University of Caen in 1480.   In 1486–87 he worked with Jean du Pré and P. Gerard at Abbeville.   In 1489 he went to Rouen and worked with Noël de Harsy and P. Regnault and in the early years of the sixteenth century by himself. In 1517 he was in Paris and printed for F. Regnault.   [Renouard, pp. 367–8.] It was in his workshop that Andrew Myllar, the first Scottish printer, learned the art and Violette printed for him an edition of the *Equivoca* in 1505 and of the *Expositio Sequentiarum* in 1506.   In the same year he printed a Sarum *Breviary* for Bienayse and about the same time an undated Stanbridge's *Accidence*.   In 1507 he printed a series of York books for Gachet, *Hymns and Sequences*, *Breviary*, *Missal* and *Directorium*, and in 1509 a Sarum *Missal* for Guil. Candos.

VOLCKWINNER (COLLINUS), printer in London, was probably a refugee from the Low Countries.   His name is found in a book by Marten Mikroen *De Christlicke Ordinancien der Nederlantscher Ghemeynten Christi, die vanden Christelicken Prince Co. Edewaerdt den VI. in't iaer 1550, te Londen inghestelt was.*   The colophon runs "Ghedruckt buyten Londen, doer Collinus Volckwinner, anno 1554."

VORSTERMAN (WILLEM), printer in Antwerp, began to print about 1511. In 1512 he was admitted a member of the S. Lucas Gilde of which he was head in 1527 and 1542. His place of business was at the sign of the Golden Unicorn by the Cammerpoorte, and the six devices he used were all varieties of the double-eagle, generally supporting a coat-of-arms. He died July 23rd, 1543, and his wife Marie Slichten May 4th, 1544. [Van Havre, p. 377.] He is generally supposed, probably erroneously, to have been the printer of one or two early editions of the English *New Testament*.

VOSTRE (SIMON), stationer in Paris, was at work between the years 1486 and 1520 and is famous for the very large number of beautifully ornamented books of hours which he issued. At least eight editions of the Sarum *Horae* were printed by him between 1498 and 1520. His shop was situated in the Rue Neuve Nostre Dame at the sign of St. John Evangelist. In the Bodleian is an imperfect copy of a little tract entitled *Psalterium beate marie virginis* which has the colophon "Imprynted at London in Flete aley the .xxi daye of October by Simon Voter." This may perhaps mean that he had a shop in London for the sale of his books. [Edinburgh Bibliographical Society, 1894–5, No. I.] Vostre's device consisted of a shield hanging from a tree and supported by two leopards on which are engraved his initials, and his name in full below. [Renouard, pp. 369–71.]

VRANKENBERGH (HENRY), see Franckenbergk (H.).

VYKE (JOHN DE), bookbinder in London, was a Frenchman from Rouen who came to England about 1551. In 1562 he took out letters of denization "9 March John De Visque from the dominion of the King of France." [Pat. 4 Eliz., p. 11, m. 6.] In 1567 he was living in Aldersgate Ward but in the returns of 1571 is entered in the Tower Ward "John de Vyke, bokebynder, Frenchman, denizen and haith byne here xx ty yeres." [R. of A., I, 454.]

W. (L.), bookbinder, used two panel stamps. One contains the vision of Ara coeli, the other two apostles standing before a tree. At the foot of the second panel is a shield with the binder's initials. [Weale, *Bookbindings*, p. 114.]

W. (R.), bookbinder, made use of a roll with renaissance ornament and his initials. [Weale, *Bookbindings*, p. 141.]

WAAKE (GERARD), see Wake (G.).

WAEN (JOHN), bookseller in Louvain, was a native of Scotland. He was sworn bookseller to the University and carried on business between 1549 and 1554 in which time four books were issued in his name. Of these three were connected with England being works by Richard Smith and Bishop Gardiner. He lived "ad intersignium Castri Angelici." [Maittaire, *Index*, I, 5, 246 ; II, 249. Herbert, III, p. 1576.]

WAKE or WAAKE (GERARD), stationer in Cambridge, is mentioned as binding books as early as 1454. He was the official "stationarius" of the University and as such is mentioned several times in the Grace book. [Gray, *Cambridge Stationers*, pp, 10, 11.]

WALKER (PETER), stationer in London, was apparently a freeman of the Stationers' Company before 1557, though he is not mentioned in the list. In 1559–60 he was licensed to print a ballad called *King Salamon*, but he is nowhere else mentioned in the Registers. [Arber, I, p. 127.]

WALLEY (CHARLES), stationer in London, is mentioned in the original list of the Company of Stationers, but beyond this nothing is known of him.

WALLEY (JOHN), printer in London, began business about 1546 at the Hart's Horn in Foster Lane. On the incorporation of the Stationers' Company in 1557 he appears sixteenth on the list, so must have taken up his freedom at an early date. He was Renter from 1554 to 1557 and three times Warden. He printed a large number of books up to 1585. He died in 1586 and his will was proved on April 28th. [Plomer, Wills, p. 26.] He left bequests to his wife Agnes, his son Robert, also a stationer, and his grandchildren.

WALLYS (RICHARD), stationer in London, was made free on May 9th, 1555, and is included in the original list of the Stationers' Company. Beyond being entered in some subscription lists his name does not occur again in the Registers. He moved to Oxford and was admitted a bookseller there August 11th, 1556. [Clark, I, p. 321.]

WALTER, printer in London, is entered on the Subsidy Roll of 1541 in St. Olave's Parish, Southwark as "Water Prynter, master in goodes x^{li}" and is taxed ten shillings, and his servant Mychell van Antwarpe pays a poll tax of four pence. No Southwark printer of that date with the Christian name Walter is now known. [R. of A., I, 35.]

WANDSFORTH or FREEZ (FREDERICK), stationer in York, was a native of the Low Countries, his original name no doubt was Vries or De Vries. In 1495-96 he became a freeman of the City, being described as a "bookbynder and stacioner." He is elsewhere described as a printer and though nothing remains of his work he may have practised the art. In 1500 he was admitted along with Johanna his wife into the guild of Corpus Christi. On March 20th, 1506, he was granted by the Corporation a house called the Rose, otherwise the Bull, in Conyngestrete, for ten years at three pounds rent. In 1510-11 he was engaged in a lawsuit respecting his brother's property. In 1515 he was living in the Parish of St. Helen's super Muros. Frederick Freez had two sons, Valentine and Edward, both of whom were burnt for heresy. [Davies, *York Press*, pp. 7, 8. Bibl. Soc. Trans., V, pp. 89-95.]

WANDSFORTH or FREEZ (GERARD), stationer of York, was a brother of Frederick Freez. In 1507 he issued the first book with a York imprint, an edition of the *Expositio Hymnorum et Sequentiarum* printed at Rouen by Pierre Violette. Violette printed about the same time a York *Missal* and *Breviary* most probably also for Wandsforth. In 1510 Wandsforth was admitted into the guild of Corpus Christi, but his name is not found in the City Registers, since as he lived in the liberties of St. Peter he could carry on business without being a freeman. He died in October, 1510, at Lynn in Norfolk and his will dated October 3rd was proved on October 24th at York. He left bequests to Ralph Pulleyn a goldsmith, his brother Frederick, Richard Waterson of London, probably a stationer, and Wynkyn de Worde. After Gerard's death a suit was instituted against Pulleyn who together with a Mr. Mayner Weywick had gone shares with him in purchasing books, by Frederick Freez as to the ownership of the large stock left by Gerard. The report of this case furnishes a considerable amount of information on the trade of a bookseller at that period. [Davies, *York Press*, pp. 8-15, 341. Bibl. Soc. Trans., V, pp. 89-95.]

WAPULL (ROBERT), stationer in London, though not entered in the charter list must have been an original member of the Stationers' Company. He is mentioned in 1558 as presenting an apprentice for his freedom. [Arber, I, pp. 94, 99.]

WARD (JOHN), stationer in Cambridge, was the official "stationarius" of the University from about 1468 to 1475.

WARE (ROBERT), is mentioned as binding a MS. presented to St. Alban's Abbey in the latter part of the fifteenth century. [James, *Sources of Archbp. Parker's MSS. at C.C.C., Cambridge*, p. 16.]

WARWYKE (JOHN), stationer of York, was admitted a freeman by patrimony in 1529–30. He is entered as "Johannes Warwyke, stacyoner, fil. Ed. Warwyke, merchaunt." [*Freemen of York*, p. 250.]

WATERSON (RICHARD), stationer in London, was a member of the Stationers' Company at the time of its incorporation, having taken up his freedom in December, 1555, but he is not mentioned in the original list. He was apparently an assistant to Thomas Duxwell as we learn from the following passage in Foxe's Book of Martyrs [VIII, p. 724] "One W. Gie servant with master Revet, merchant, bought a Bible and service book of Richard Waterson who then dwelt with master Duixile in Paul's churchyard." For this offence Bonner ordered Gie and Waterson to be beaten. Waterson is several times mentioned in the Registers as taking apprentices, and was frequently punished for keeping open his shop on Sundays. He married Alice, daughter of Simon Burton and had a son Simon Waterson, the well-known printer. He died in 1563 [Dugdale, *Hist. of St. Paul's Cathedral*, p. 128] and his widow married successively two stationers Francis Coldock and Isaac Byng.

WATKINS (RICHARD), printer in London, was an apprentice to William Powell and was made free on April 27th, 1557. He served the Stationers' Company in various capacities, twice as Renter, four times as Warden and twice as Master. He began to print in 1561 when his address is given as St. Paul's Churchyard; at a later date he was in Cheapside near the little Conduit. In 1569 he married Katherine daughter of Richard Jugge. [*London Marriage Licenses*, p. 42.] He printed a large number of books up to about 1598 when he appears to have been reduced to poor circumstances. As an apprentice of his, Thomas Grantham was transferred to George Bishop in June, 1599, it is probable that he died in that year.

WATSON (HENRY), printer in London, was an apprentice of W. de Worde as may be seen from the prologue to *Oliver of Castyle*, 1518, "J Henry Watson apprentice of London trustynge in the grace of god, hathe enterprysed for to translate this present hystorye out of frensshe into

Englysshe, oure moders tonge, at the comaundement of my worshypfull mayster Wynkyn de Worde." He translated a number of books for De Worde, amongst others the *Ship of Fools*, 1509, *The Church of evil men and women*, 1511, *The Gospel of distaves* and *Valentine and Orson*, both without date. Bagford [Harl MS., 5974] has noted a book *Donatus cum remigio*, " Impressus Londiniis juxta Charing Crosse per me Hugonem Goes et Henery Watson," with the printer's device H. G. The only book now known printed by Goes is the *Directorium* of 1509 printed at York with W. de Worde's type who in the same year printed the York *Manual*. If the colophon quoted by Bagford is correct it is quite probable that the Henry Watson mentioned in it is the same as W. de Worde's workman.

WATSON (SIMON), stationer in Cambridge, may very probably have been one of the London family of printers named Waterson. He is mentioned first in the accounts of St. Mary's Church as supplying books in 1553–54 and was still living in 1564. In 1557 he was summoned before the University Commissioners and entries in Mere's diary on the subject refer to his mother Mrs. Watson in London and his own visits there. [Gray, *Cambridge Stationers*, pp. 70, 71.]

WATTES (THOMAS), stationer in London, is mentioned in 1488 in a deed. [*Calendar of Inquisitions post mortem, Hen. VII*, vol. I, p. 161.]

WAYE (RICHARD), stationer in London, must have been of considerable standing and importance in the trade. In the charter of 1557 he stands fourth, and succeeded Thomas Dockwray as Master of the Stationers' Company in 1558–59 and again in 1563–64. He was most liberal to the Company but does not seem to have been engaged in business, for he is not mentioned either as taking apprentices or registering copies. His will, dated 1577 was proved in the Prerogative Court of Canterbury. [18, Daughtry.] He is described as " citizen and stacioner of London, St Michaell, Croked Lane : Skydbrooke, Lincoln."

WAYLAND (JOHN), printer in London, began his business in 1537 in which year he printed three books, two by Richard Whitford and one by Erasmus. In 1539 he printed several issues of Bishop Hilsey's *Primer* or had them printed for him by John Mayler : they were sold also by Andrew Hester and Michael Lobley. Wayland was then living in Fleet Street at the sign of the Blue Garland. After this time for several years we know nothing of his work, though Herbert ascribes some unsigned books to him in 1542, 1545 and 1550. Apparently at the beginning of Mary's reign E. Whitchurch, who had got into trouble, gave up his shop in Fleet Street at the sign of the Sun and this was taken by Wayland who, in October, 1553, procured a patent for the sole printing of all primers and manuals of prayers howsoever denominated, as likewise for all such books as he should first print for and during the term of seven years from the date thereof. For the next three years he was busy and printed about twelve books, but his work seems to have brought him little success. In his will dated 1556 he left nothing but "desperate debts." He is mentioned by Foxe [VIII, 521] as having brought his servant Thomas Greene before Dr. Story for having in his possession a book named Antichrist, for which the servant was put in the stocks.

WAYTE (NICHOLAS), stationer in London, was apparently made free on December 11th, 1556, but nothing further is known of him in London. He was admitted as a bookseller in Oxford in August, 1556. [Clark, I, p. 321.]

WELLES (JOHN), bookbinder in York, was admitted a freeman by patrimony along with his brother Thomas in 1518-19. He is entered as "Johannes Welles, bookbynder, fil. Ricardi Welles, caryer." [*Freemen of York*, p. 241.]

WENNSLER (MICHAEL), printer in Basle, worked in that city from before 1474 up to 1490. He printed after this at Cluny, Mâcon and Lyons. About 1488-9 he printed an edition of the Sarum *Missal*. [Cop., ii, 4225. Proctor, 7519.]

WHAPLANE (DUNSTAN), stationer in London, though not mentioned in the charter of 1557 was apparently a member of the Stationers' Company before that date. He was taken into the Livery in 1571. He published in 1566-7. He was still alive in 1577 when his wife Joan Sutton took an apprentice. Joan Sutton was the widow of either Henry or Edward Sutton and married Dunstan Whaplane in June, 1571. [*London Marriage Licenses*, p. 48.]

WHEXLAY (THOMAS), stationer of York, was admitted a freeman in 1549-50. [*Freemen of York*, p. 269.]

WHITCHURCH (EDWARD), printer in London, was a member of the Haberdashers' Company.   He was much interested in the printing of the English *Bible* in which he was associated with Richard Grafton and Anthony Marler, and superintended on the Continent the preparation and printing of the *Bibles* of 1537 and 1539.   On coming to England Whitchurch printed for a time with Grafton in the Grayfriars, and together in January, 1544, they obtained an exclusive patent for printing service books.   About 1541 Whitchurch parted from Grafton and in the following few years is found at various addresses "Jn the olde Jewery," "on the south side of Aldermary Church" and, according to Herbert at the Well and two Buckets in St. Martin's.   About 1545 after the death of Byddell Whitchurch succeeded him at the Sun in Fleet Street, W. de Worde's old printing office.   From this time up to 1553 Whitchurch was very busy issuing such important books as the *Prayer-book* and the *Paraphrases of Erasmus*.   In 1549 he had five foreign assistants who are quoted in the Returns of Aliens. [R. of A., I, 180.] Under Queen Mary Whitchurch was in trouble and was excluded from pardon in the proclamation at her coronation, and during her reign he ceased to print.   Some time after 1556 Whitchurch married Margaret, niece of Osiander, pastor of Nuremberg and widow of Archbishop Cranmer.   One book dated 1560 printed by Whitchurch is mentioned by Herbert, but this appears to be the only book he issued after 1553.   He died in 1562 and his will dated November 25th was proved December 3rd. [Plomer, Wills, pp. 14, 15.]   He leaves legacies to his children and stepchildren and to his wife who after his death took as her third husband Bartholomew Scott of Camberwell.   Whitchurch used as a device his monogram in an oval frame. [D.N.B.]

WHITE (HENRY), stationer in London, appears to have been a freeman of the Stationers' Company in 1557 although not entered on the list. The following is the only entry relating to him in the Registers "Roberte Wapull present John Fyldynge his apprentes and sett over to Henry White to be made fre of this howse.   1558–59." [Arber, I, p. 99.]

WHITNEY (JOHN), stationer in London, was an original member of the Company of Stationers and was for a time Renter.   He appears to have married Elizabeth Pickering in 1559.

WIGHT (JOHN), bookseller in London, was not a member of the Stationers' Company but belonged to the Drapers. He began business about 1551 issuing a *Bible* in that year. Like all booksellers he was under the jurisdiction of the Stationers' Company and is frequently entered in the Registers sometimes as entering copies and sometimes as being fined. He issued books regularly up to 1589. In 1585 a book which he issued, Bunney's *Booke of Christian exercise appertaining to resolution*, was reprinted at Oxford by Barnes the University printer which led to considerable friction between the Stationers' Company and the University Press. Wight died in 1589 and his will dated May 25th was proved on July 16th. He left legacies to various relations and to the Drapers' and Stationers' Companies. His executor was his son Thomas Wight who though not a member of the Stationers' Company, published from 1590 to 1608. [Plomer, *Wills*, 29, 30.] Wight's place of business was in St. Paul's Churchyard at the sign of the Rose and he used as his device a woodcut portrait with his initials I. W. surrounded by the motto "Welcom the Wight that bringeth such light."

WILCOCK (WILLIAM), publisher (?) in London, is mentioned in the colophons to the two books printed in London by John Lettou in 1480 and 1481. It is not known whether he was a publisher or a private patron.

WILLEMS (CONRAD), printer at Münster, pseudonym. This name occurs in the colophon to *A book made by John Frith prisoner in the Tower*, which runs "Imprintid at Monster, Anno 1533 By me Conrade Willems." [Herbert, III, p. 1540.]

WILLIAM, bookbinder in Oxford, is mentioned as a witness when MS. Merton Coll. 135 was given to the college in 1459. His name occurs in the same year in the Oxford University Archives. [Madan, *Oxford Press*, p. 272.]

WILLIAM, bookbinder in London, is entered on the Subsidy Roll of 1544 in the Parish of St. Anne and Agnes, Aldersgate Ward with goods valued at forty shillings. [R. of A., I, 83.]

WILLIAM (GARRET), printer in London, is entered on the Subsidy Roll of 1549 in St. Faith's Parish as an assistant to Robert Holder. [R. of A., I, 159.] He took out letters of denization in 1562 "24 Feb Garrett Williams from the dominion of the Dukes of Cleves." [Pat. 4 Eliz., p. 11, m. 3.]

WILMOTT (JOHN), stationer in London, died in 1535 and his will is preserved in the Registers of the Commissary of London. [Plomer, Wills, p. 55.]

WILSON (THOMAS), was an assistant to John Rastell who left him in his will in 1536 the sum of twenty shillings. [Plomer, Wills, p. 5.]

WISLYN (JOHN), was an assistant to W. de Worde who bequeathed him twenty shillings in books. [Plomer, Wills, p. 4.]

WITHERS (RICHARD), printer in London, was an apprentice of Richard Pynson, who bequeathed him forty shillings on condition that he served out his time as an apprentice. [Plomer, Wills, p. 3.]

WOLFE (REYNER), printer in London, was in business as a bookseller as early as 1530 and in 1533 took out letters of denization in which he is described as a native of Gelderland. [Pat. 24 Henry VIII, p. 1, m. 31.] Another Reginald Wolff from the dominion of the Emperor was denizened 8th February, 1542. [Pat. 33 Henry VIII, p. 5, m. 26.] Early in 1536 he was specially admitted a freeman of the Company of Stationers. He apparently went backwards and forwards to the Frankfurt fairs and served as a messenger. Partridge writing to Bullinger in 1538 says "Our friend Rayner did not come to this fair by reason as I understand of the recent death of his wife." [*Original Letters relating to the Reformation.*] In 1539 we find a payment of a hundred shillings to Rayner Wolf for conveying the King's letters to Christopher Mounte. [*Letters and Papers of Henry VIII*, xiv, II, 781.] In 1542 Wolfe commenced to print, issuing some works of Leland printed in Roman and Italic type probably obtained abroad and identical with some used by John Wolf at Frankfurt. In these he used a device of children throwing sticks at an apple tree, with the motto "Charitas." In 1547 he was appointed King's printer in Latin Greek and Hebrew, with an annuity of twenty-six shillings and eightpence. From Henry VIII he purchased the chapel or charnel house in St. Paul's Churchyard, which he cleared away and replaced by shops. His own shop in the Churchyard had the sign of the Brazen Serpent and one of his devices had a serpent on a rod as its subject. On the incorporation of the Stationers' Company Wolfe's name occurs seventh on the list and he was elected Master on four occasions in 1560, 1564, 1567 and 1572. During the reign of Mary he produced little, but after Elizabeth succeeded his patents were renewed and his business became more active. During the later years of his life he appears to have collected materials for a chronicle which he intended to have published and which was afterwards prepared by Holinshed. In 1571 he is entered in the Returns of Aliens as "denizen, Douchman, came into this realme about xxv yeares past fre of the companye of Stacioners" [R. of A., II, 12] though this might refer to Reginolde Wolfe the younger, who was made free of the Company May 17th, 1565. Wolfe died at the end of 1573 and his will was proved January 9th, 1574. It was a very short document leaving some property to his wife Joan and everything else to his children. His widow died in 1574 and her will, an elaborate and lengthy document, contains much information both about the family and about other London stationers of the period. [Plomer, Wills, pp. 19–23.] She made arrangements for the publication of Holinshed's Chronicle, which was printed by John Harrison her son-in-law and published in 1577. [Plomer, *English Printing*, pp. 103-108. Timperley, 353. D.N.B.]

WOLFROTE (JAMES), printer in London, is mentioned in 1550 in the register of the Dutch Church as a type setter in the employment of Richard Grafton [R. of A., I, 207] and he is no doubt one of the two Jacobs mentioned in a mutilated portion of the Subsidy Roll of 1549 as assistants to Grafton and as being taxed eight pence. In 1571 he is entered in the Returns under Aldersgate Ward "James Wolforte booke printer, borne in Clevelande, who hath dwelt in London synce the first yeare of K. Edwarde the sixte, and Katheryne his wyfe, borne in the countrye of Horne, hath byn here about xiiij yeares." [R. of A., II, 45.] In 1582–83 he was living in Cripplegate Ward. [R. of A., II, 268.]

WOOD or BOYS (MICHAEL), printer in Geneva and Rouen. In 1545 an edition of Bale's *Mysterye of inyquyte* professed to be printed by "Michael Woode" at Geneva, but the type of the book appears to be Wyer's. In 1548 "Michael Boys" issued two editions of *The complaint of Roderick Mors* by Hans Brinkelow at Geneva, but these appear to have been printed by Scoloker. In 1553 and 1554 some six or more books were printed, some also translated by Michael Wood at Rouen, but whether this name is fictitious or not is not at present known.

WORDE (WYNKYN DE), printer in London, was a native of Wörth in Alsace and thus by birth a German and not, as usually stated, a native of the Low Countries. He was settled in Westminster as early as 1480, in which year his wife is mentioned in a deed, so that he probably came to England with Caxton as an assistant in 1476 or joined him immediately on his arrival. Nothing is heard of him until 1491 the year of Caxton's death, when he took over his late master's house and was duly entered in the rent roll of Abbot Esteney as the tenant. In this he was entered by some unexplained error as Jan Wynkyn and it has been hastily assumed that his name must have been John, which must obviously be a mistake. Wynkyn is itself a Christian name and like many other printers De Worde used his Christian name in conjunction with the name of his native town or country. Jan Wynkyn could only mean John the son of Wynkyn, and as neither in his many hundred colophons, his patent of denization, or his will does De Worde give any hint of such a name as John, it may safely be assumed that it was not his name. Caxton apparently left no son and all his printing materials passed to De Worde, who at first made little use of them, issuing but five books in two years. In 1493 he started a type of his own and in 1494 his name is first found in a printed book. On April 20th, 1496, he took out letters of denization granted "Winando de Worde de ducatu Lothoringie oriundo, impressori librorum." In this same year also he began to make use of paper made in England by John Tate, though its use was soon given up. Up to the end of the year 1500 De Worde continued to live in Caxton's house at Westminster and in the nine years of his tenancy printed at least one hundred and ten different books. There can be little doubt that could Caxton's will be found, De Worde would prove to be one of the executors. In the registers of St. Margaret's Westminster is an entry in 1506 "Item four printed books, ii of them the Lyfe of St Kateryn and other ii of the Birth of our Lady of the gift of the executors of Caxton." [Nichols, *Illustrations*, p. 5.] Now the *Life of St. Katherine* is one of the books printed at Westminster by W. de Worde after Caxton's death. At the end of 1500 De Worde moved into Fleet Street, where he rented two houses, a dwelling-house and a printing office, at the rental of three pounds six shillings and eight pence. His printing office with the sign of the Sun was situated on the south side of the street, close to the Conduit, opposite the entrance to Shoe Lane, the abode of many bookbinders. In 1502 De Worde issued an edition of the *Manipulus Curatorum*, one single copy of which [Bodl.] differs from other known copies in containing a device of the printer used nowhere else. It most resembles No. 7 [Bibl. Soc. *Handlist*] but the C has been engraved backwards. In 1504 De Worde began to use his most ordinary device No. 5 which was replaced in 1519 by an almost exact copy, No. 10, which itself gave way in 1529 to a third variety No. 14. Towards the end of 1508 when Pynson was appointed printer to the King, De Worde seems to have received some sort of official appointment as printer to the Countess of Richmond, which he notified in all his colophons up to her death in 1509: calling himself printer to the King's mother, and after the death of Henry VII, to the King's grandmother. About this time De Worde had another shop in St. Paul's Churchyard with the sign of Our Lady of Pity and made use sometimes of a woodcut of Our Lady of Pity in place of his ordinary device. About 1522 we find that De Worde was employing other presses, and it is clear that several books were printed for him by John Skot. In 1533 and 1534 De Worde in his turn printed several books for John Byddell. The last book which De Worde issued was *The Complaint of the too soon maryed* of 1535. He died at the beginning of that year for his will dated June 5th, 1534, was proved January 19th following. [Plomer, Wills, pp. 3, 4.] To his servants Robert Darby, Robert Maas, John Barbanson, Hector, Simon [Simon Martynson?], John Wislyn and Alard, a bookbinder he left bequests; also to John Butler, James Gaver and John Byddell, described as late servants. Besides these legacies were left to Henry Pepwell, John Gowghe, Robert Copland, and Nowell [Noël Havy]. Byddell and Gaver were made executors and continued to carry on business in the same house. The trustees were ordered to purchase land in or near London which should produce at least twenty shillings a year, to be given to St. Bride's Church to keep an obit for his soul, and we learn from the survey of chantries made in February, 1547, that the sum thus expended was thirty-six pounds. De Worde printed altogether nearly eight hundred books, and made use of at least seventeen varieties of devices, in all of which Caxton's initials and device are prominent. [D.N.B. Bibl. Soc. *Handlists*. Duff, *Early Printed Books*, pp. 137–143.]

WRAITH (THOMAS), stationer in York, was admitted a freeman in 1556. [*Freemen of York*, p. 277.]

WRENNE (PHILIP), stationer in London, was party in an action for debt at an uncertain date before 1500. [Early Chancery Proceedings, Bundle 74, No. 50.]

WRIGHT (EDWARD), printer in London, was an apprentice to John Reynes and had served his full time before 1542. Reynes left him ten pounds in books in his will and requested him with Robert Holder "to helpe their Mistress two yeres long after my departing." He probably gave up business or died shortly after as he is not mentioned in Lucy Reynes' will in 1548. [Plomer, Wills, pp. 6, 7.]

WRIGHT (JOHN), stationer. Herbert [III, p. 1821] under the year 1508 inserts " *Liber Theodoli sive Theoduli cum commento.* Lond. 1508. Impress. pro Johanne Wright." No such stationer is known, but the edition appears to be that issued by Pelgrim and Jacobi at the Trinity in Paul's Churchyard. This may be a copy with a variation in the colophon.

WYER (JOHN), printer in London, lived in Fleet Street, a little above the Conduit. He printed only one book, Bale's *Ymage of both Churches*, which was issued in 1550. [Herbert, II, 712–13.]

WYER (RICHARD), printer in London, issued in 1548 *The Rekenynge and declaration of the fayth of Huldrike Zwyngly* and in 1550 the *Debate betwene the heraldes of Englande and Fraunce.* A work by Bale mentioned by Ames under the same year seems doubtful. He printed one work without date *A christen sentence and true judgement of the sacrament* [Caius Coll., Camb.] which has been wrongly entered by Herbert [I, 376] under Robert Wyer. His shop was in St. Paul's Churchyard. In the Archives of the City of London he is twice mentioned once as "stationer" and once as "boke prynter." On one occasion he was bound over to keep the peace as regards Guylam Peltere, a Frenchman; on the other he deposed that he was drinking in a tavern called the Three Cups, and was witness to a quarrel between the landlord and a "costard monger" over a game of dice. [Bibl. Soc. Trans., VI, 23.]

WYER (ROBERT), printer in London, is supposed by some to have been an assistant to John Butler, but for this there is no direct evidence, and it is rendered improbable by the fact that when Wyer commenced to print, about

1529-30, at Charing Cross he was of sufficient importance in the Parish of St. Martin-in-the-Fields to be a churchwarden. His shop was at the sign of St. John the Evangelist in the Bishop of Norwich's Rents which were known after the sale in 1536 as the Duke of Suffolk's Rents. This change of name is very valuable as dating many of Wyer's books before or after 1536. Wyer printed a very large number of small popular books, though he also issued a few important works such as the *Defence of Peace* printed for W. Marshall. Wyer's wife Jane or Joan died in 1559 and the last notice of Robert Wyer is found between 1559 and 1561 in the registers of the church of St. Martin-in-the-Fields where very numerous entries of the Wyer family occur. He was succeeded at the sign of St. John the Evangelist by Thomas Colwell in 1560. Wyer's device was a representation of St. John seated, writing, on the island of Patmos while at his side an eagle holds his inkhorn. Of this device he had several varieties. [Plomer, *English Printing*, pp. 57–60. *The Library*, 1891, pp. 6–11. *Accounts of the Churchwardens of St. Martin-in-the-Fields.* D.N.B.]

WYNKYN (WILLIAM), stationer of London, was made free on the 2nd July, 1534. [Bibl. Soc. Trans., VI, 24.] It has been suggested that he was a son of Wynkyn de Worde but this is extremely improbable. He may be the person mentioned in a Subsidy Roll of 1525 as dwelling in Tower Ward "Wyllyam Wynkyne, stranger, for hys goodes, xls. ij.s." [R. of A., I, p. 11.]

YLLE (EDWARD), bookbinder in London, is known only from his will which was proved on April 20th, 1545. He was apparently in the employment of Lucy Reynes, the widow of John Reynes, and several of the people mentioned in the will were or had been her assistants. Thomas Barthelet was executor and W. Bonham and H. Tab overseers. Bequests were left to Lucy Reynes and her former assistants R. Holder, E. Sutton and J. Cawood, to Gyles Lauret and Nowell [Havy] bookbinders, while to John Nowseley was left "my hole harnyse." [Plomer, Wills, p. 8.]

APPENDIX I.

INDEX OF CHRISTIAN NAMES.

P

INDEX OF CHRISTIAN NAMES.

DESIDERIUS. Maheu.
DUNSTAN. Whaplane.

EDMUND. Campion, Hawley.
EDWARD. Browne, Cater, Huby, Sutton, Whitchurch, Wright, Ylle.
EGIDIUS, *see* Giles.
EHERET. Harkes.
ELIZABETH. Pickering, Toy.
EUCHARIUS. Cervicornus.
EUSTACE. Hardy.

FELIX. Baligault.
FLORENCE. Valentin.
FRANCIS. Birckman, Foxe, Frost, Regnault, Turona.
FREDERICK. Egmont, Wandsforth.

GARBRAND. Harkes.
GARRET, *see* Gerard.
GEORGE. Chastelain, Joy, Meryson, Oliver.
GERARD, GARRET. Barrevelt, Cluen, Garret, Godfray, Harris, Leeu, Pilgrim, Wake, Wandsforth, William.
GERMAIN. Hardouyn.
GILES, EGIDIUS. Chandler, Erve, Giles, Godet, Heerstraten, Huke, Lauret, Seres.
GODFREY, GODFRIED, GOTTFRIED. Haeghen, Hatsoo, Kempen, Midilton.
GREGORY. Brodehead.
GUILLAUME, *see* William.
GYSBERD. Geyson.

HANS, *see* John.
HARRY, *see* Henry.
HECTOR. Hector.
HEINRICH, *see* Henry.
HENRY, HARRY, HEINRICH. Arnoldt, Birckman, Coke, Cooke, Fleteman, Franckenbergk, Gastus, Hammande, Harman, Harmanson, Harry, Henry, Houdouin, Jacobi, Marshall, Mylward, Nicholson, Norton, Pepwell, Quentell, Renkens, Salt, Smith, Soull, Starkerfelser, Sutton, Tab, Watson, White.
HERMAN, HORMAN. Evans, Men.
HUBERT. Danvillier.

HUGH, HUGO. Cottesford, Goes, Meslier, Singleton.
HUMPHREY. Powell.

INGELBERT. Haghe.
ISAAC. De Bruges.

JACOB. Aurik, Jacob, Meteren, Pieter.
JACOBUS, *see* James.
JACQUES, *see* James.
JAMES, JACOBUS, JACQUES. Coiplett, Cornelii, Cousin, Ferrebouc, Foxe, Gaver, Gonneld, Holyland, Nicholson, Picory, Poulain, Ravynell, Sheres, Wolforte.
JAMET. Loys.
JAN, *see* John.
JASPER. Ferrall, Hallyar.
JEAN, *see* John.
JOANNES, *see* John.
JOHN, JEAN, JOANNES, JAN, HANS. Adam, Allde, Amazeur, Antoine, Awdley, Baker, Bale, Barbanson, Barbier, Barlow, Bars, Benet, Bienayse, Bignon, Birckman, Boeidens, Bonham, Borrell, Brachius, Bray, Brygges, Burtoft, Butler, Byddell, Caillard, Case, Cawood, Charlewood, Childryn, Clarke, Cockes, Crespin, Day, Doesborch, Dorne, Dowghton, Droseler, Dupré, Fayreberne, Ferrom, Foxe, Franckine, Frellon, Fylkyn, Gachet, Gore, Gowghe, Gowthwaite, Graphaeus, Growte, Gryphius, Gybkyn, Hacket, Harrington, Harrison, Harvey, Haukyns, Heron, Hertford, Hertzog, Hewtee, Higman, Hill, Hitprik, Hochstraten, Hollinder, Holyland, Horspath, Hothersall, Hulton, Hunsworthe, Hurson, Huvin, Jaques, Jehannot, Joannes de Aquisgrano, Judson, Kele, Kempen, Kerbriant, Kevall, King, Kingston, Le Blanc, Le Prest, Le Roux, Lettou, Longe, Lorraine, Low, Loye, Lufft, Marchant, Mardeley, Mather, Mauditier, Mayler, Meguissher, Meltynbe, Messyngham, Mockyll, More, Mychell, Nicholson, Nowseley, Oryns, Oswen, Overton, Pennowe, Pennys, Petit, Philippe, Philoponos, Pietersz, Poitevin, Pole, Pollard, Powell, Rastell, Redman, Reynes, Richard, Richardson, Rivery, Rogers, Rowe, Ruremond, Ruwe, Rycard, Sainct Denis, Scarlett, Schott, Scolar, Sedley, Sero, Seth, Shefelde, Shereman, Siberch, Skofeld, Skot, Snow, Steelsius, Story, Taverner, Tisdale, Tournes, Toy, Troost, Turke, Typlady, Vyke, Waen, Walley, Ward, Warwyke, Wayland, Welles, Whitney, Wight, Wilmott, Wislyn, Wright, Wyer.

JOYCE. Badius, Pelgrim.
JUDOCUS, *see* Joyce.
JULIAN. Notary.

KATHERINE, *see* Catherine.

LAMBERT. Brey.
LAWRENCE, LAURENTIUS. Andrewe, Hostingue, Torrentini.
LEONARD. Andrewe, Leonard.
LEWIS, LUDOVICUS. Kemmyse, Suethon, Sutton.
LUDOVICUS, *see* Lewis.
LUKE. Harrison.

MADELEINE. Boursette.
MARCUS. Constantius.
MARTIN. Caesar, Coffyn, Dature, Morin.
MATTHEW, TYS. Crom, Tyse.
MICHAEL. Fawkes, Hillenius, Lendon, Lobley, Michael, Morin, Paule, Wenssler, Wood.

NEWELL, *see* Noel.
NICHOLAS, CLAES. Berghe, Bourman, Cleston, Dixon, Dorcaster, England, Grandysshe, Grave, Higman, Hill, Leblonde, Lecomte, Le Roux, Marcant, Nicholas, Pilgrim, Prevost, Roddon, Speryng, Sutton, Taverner, Twonson, Wayte.
NICODEMUS, Nicodemus.
NOËL, NOWELL, NEWELL. Havy, Morres.

OLIVER. Jacobson, Lyghtes.
OWEN. Rogers.

PATRICK. Lowes.
PAUL. Seygar.
PETER, PIETER, PETRUS, PIERRE. Actors, Breynans, Bright, Chaunter, Cupere Dathenus, Frenche, Guerin, Kaetz, Legraunde, Levet, Mighen, Moreux, Olivier, Post Pascha, Quentell, Schoeffer, Sheres, Symonds, Treveris, Turonensis, Violette, Walker.
PHILIP, PHILIPPE. Coste, Cowelance, Cuttier, Pigouchet, Scapulys, Wrenne.
PIERRE, *see* Peter.

PIERS. Bauduyn.

PIETER, *see* Peter.

RADULF, *see* Ralph.

RALPH, RADULF, RANULF. Bonifante, Cousturier, Ranulf.

RANDALL. Tirer.

RANULF, *see* Ralph.

REGINALD, REGNAULD. Chaudière, Oliver.

REINARDT, REYNALDUS. Ae, Novimagio, Wolfe.

RICHARD. Adam, Applay, Baldwyn, Bankes, Charlton, Crosse, Faques, Foster, Fydlynge, Garnett, Goupil, Grafton, Grene, Hamillon, Harrison, Harvey, Hill, Jugge, Kele, Kevall, Lant, Lynnell, Macé, Nele, Noke, Paffroed, Paget, Pynson, Richard, Richardson, Tabbe, Tottell, Wallys, Waterson, Watkins, Waye, Withers, Wyer.

ROBERT. Aylton, Blythe, Broke, Burton, Caly, Colson, Copland, Crowley, Darby, Fryer, Holder, Loksmith, Maas, Massellin, Redborne, Redman, Stoughton, Sysay, Toy, Tynner, Valentin, Wapull, Ware, Wyer.

ROGER. Car, Ireland, Lathum, Madeley, Shedmore.

ROMYN. Maynmour.

ROWLAND. Beken, Hall.

SEBASTIAN. Actors.

SEGAR. Nicholson.

SIBERTUS. Roedius.

SIMON. Cock, Coston, Martynson, Simon, Spilman, Vostre, Watson.

STEPHEN. Kevall, Mierdman.

THEODORICUS, THIERRY. Martens, Plateanus, Rood.

THEOPHILUS. Emlos.

THIELMAN. Kerver.

THIERRY, *see* Theodoricus.

THOMAS. Baker, Bedford, Berthelet, Boyden, Bylton, Cole, Cots, Davidson, Devell, Dockwray, Duxwell, Gaultier, Gee, Gemini, Gibson, Godfray, Grey, Hacket, Harris, Hert, Holwarde, Hunte, Jones, Kele, Knight, Lawe, Mannyng, Marshe, Maskall, Messyngham, Myles, Newell, Nicholl, Parker, Pattinson, Petyt, Powell, Purfoot, Pursset, Raynald, Richardson, Rychard, Sawyer, Skerewe, Snow, Stoke, Symonds, Thomas, Trauth, Uffington, Wattes, Whexlay, Wilson, Wraith.

APPENDIX II.

INDEX OF LONDON SIGNS BEFORE 1558.

INDEX OF LONDON SIGNS
BEFORE 1558.

*[Similar Signs occurring in Paternoster Row and St. Paul's
Churchyard may refer to the same house.]*

———

A.B.C.   St. Paul's Churchyard.
  Richard Faques.

ANNE (Saint).   St. Paul's Churchyard.
  Joyce Pelgrim.

AUGUSTINE (Saint).   St. Paul's Churchyard.
  Unknown stationer [1520].
  Hugh Singleton.

BALL.   Peter College Rents, St. Paul's Churchyard.
  John Case.

BELL.   St. Paul's Churchyard.
  Robert Toy.

BIBLE.   St. Paul's Churchyard; north door of St. Paul's.
  Richard Jugge.

BISHOP'S HEAD.   St. Paul's Churchyard.
  Unknown stationer [1553].   *See* CALY (R.).

BISHOP'S MITRE.   Within Ludgate.
  Robert Stoughton.

BLACK BOY.   Paternoster Row.
  Henry Sutton.

BLACK BOY. Joining to the middle North door of Paul's.
William Martyne.

BLACK ELEPHANT. Fleet Street.
Henry Wykes.

BLUE GARLAND. Fleet Street: next Temple Bar.
John Wayland.

BRAZEN SERPENT. St. Paul's Churchyard.
Reyner Wolfe.

COCK. St. Paul's Churchyard.
John Turcke.
Robert Redborne.

CRADLE. Lombard Street.
Edward Sutton.

CRANE. St. Paul's Churchyard.
Luke Harrison.

CROWN. Fleet Street; next to White Friars' Gate.
John Bale.

DOUBLE HOOD. Thames Street.
Hugh Singleton.

DURHAM RENTS. Strand.
Richard Faques.

EAGLE. Lombard Street, near the Stocks Market.
Richard Kele.
William Riddell.
John Tisdale.

FALCON. Fleet Street, against St. Dunstan's Church.
William Gryffyth.

FOX UNBOUND. Cheapside, against the great Conduit.
Unknown stationer [1548].

GEORGE (Saint). Fleet Street: next St. Dunstan's Church.
    Richard Pynson.
    Robert Redman.
    William Middleton.
    William Powell.

GEORGE (Saint). Outside Temple Bar.
    Robert Redman.

GEORGE (Saint). St. Paul's Churchyard.
    John Reynes.
    William Riddell.

GOLDEN CROSS. Fleet Street.
    Lawrence Andrewe.

GOLDEN TUN. Creed Lane.
    Hugh Singleton.

GREEN DRAGON. Royal Exchange.
    Thomas Hacket.

GREEN HILL. St. Paul's Churchyard: west door of Paul's.
    William Hill.

GREYHOUND. Paternoster Row.
    John Harrison.

GRIFFIN. Fleet Street; a little above the Conduit.
    William Gryffyth.

HALF EAGLE AND KEY. Gutter Lane.
    Rowland Hall.

HALF EAGLE AND KEY. Barbican.
    John Charlewood.

HAND AND STAR. Fleet Street; within Temple Bar.
    Richard Tottell.

HART'S HORN. Foster Lane.
    John Walley.

HEDGEHOG.   St. Paul's Churchyard : west end.
William Seres.

HOLY GHOST.   St. Paul's Churchyard.
John Cawood.

JOHN BAPTIST (Saint).   Within Paul's Chain.
John Bale.

JOHN EVANGELIST (Saint).   Fleet Street.
John Butler.

JOHN EVANGELIST (Saint).   Beside Charing Cross.
Robert Wyer.
Thomas Colwell.

JUDITH.   St. Paul's Churchyard.
Henry Tab.

KATHERINE (Saint).   St. Paul's Churchyard.
Unknown stationer [1515].   *See* COWELANCE.

KEY.   St. Paul's Churchyard.
Thomas Hacket.

KING'S ARMS.   St. Paul's Churchyard.
William Bonham.
William Norton.

KING'S ARMS.   Fleet Street : near St. Dunstan's.
Thomas Marshe.

LAMB.   Lombard Street.
John Harvey.

LAMB.   St. Paul's Churchyard.
Abraham Veale.

LONG SHOP in the Poultry, by St. Mildred's Church.
Richard Bankes.
John Mychel.
Richard Kele.
John Allde.

LUCRECE. St. Paul's Churchyard.
Thomas Purfoot.

LUCRETIA. St. Nicholas shambles within the New Rents.
Thomas Purfoot.

LUCRETIA ROMANA.   Fleet Street ; by the Conduit.
Thomas Berthelet.
Thomas Powell.

MARK (Saint). St. Paul's Churchyard.
Julian Notary.

MAIDEN'S HEAD. St. Paul's Churchyard.
Richard Faques.
Thomas Petyt.

MERMAID. Paul's Gate, next to Cheapside.
John Rastell.
William Bonham, ⎫
John Heron,   ⎬ Sub-tenants.
Thomas Kele,   ⎪
John Gowghe,   ⎭

MERMAID. Lombard Street ; against the Stocks Market.
John Gowghe.

MICHAEL (Saint). St. Paul's Churchyard.
Michael Lobley.

MITRE. Smithfield.
John Tisdale.

NICHOLAS (Saint). St. Paul's Churchyard.
Nicholas Lecomte.
John Toy.

OUR LADY OF PITY. St. Paul's Churchyard.
Wynkyn de Worde.

APPENDIX III.

CHRONOLOGICAL INDEX OF FOREIGN PLACES,
PRINTERS AND STATIONERS.

CHRONOLOGICAL INDEX OF
FOREIGN PLACES, PRINTERS AND STATIONERS.

[The dates refer only to the period of their connexion with the English book trade. Fictitious names are printed in Italics.]

BRUGES [1474–1476].
Mansion (Colard) with W. Caxton [1474–1476].

COLOGNE [1475]–1547.
Unknown printer [1475].
Quentell (Heinrich) [1492].
Cervicornus (Eucharius) 1520.
Quentell (Peter) [1525].
Kempen (Johann and Gottfried von) 1546, 1547.

VENICE 1483–1551.
Novimagio (Raynaldus de) 1483.
Hertzog (Joannes) 1493–1495.
Gryphius (Joannes) 1551.

ANTWERP 1486–1556.
Leeu (Gerard) 1486–1493.
Martens (Thierry) 1493.
Berghen (Adrian van) [1503]–1529.
Doesborch (Jan van) [1505–1521].
Grave (Nicolas de) 1516.
Hillenius (Michael) [1518]–1531.

ANTWERP—*continued.*
Ruremond (Christopher van) 1523–1531.
Ruremond (C. van) Widow of, 1531–1545.
Caesar (Martin) [1531–1535].
Graphaeus (Joannes) 1534.
Haeghen (Gottfried van der) 1534, 1535.
Cock (Simon) 1536.
Haeghen (Angell van der) [1536].
Crom (Matthew) 1538, 1539.
Steelsius (Jean) 1556.

LOUVAIN [1486]–1499.
Heerstraten (Egidius van der) [1486].
Martens (Thierry) 1499.

PARIS 1487–1557.
Maynyal (William) 1487.
Baligault (Felix) 1494.
Levet (Pierre) 1494.
Hopyl (Wolfgang) 1494–1519.

PARIS—*continued.*

Pigouchet (Philippe) 1495–1502.
Kerver (Thielman) 1497–1522.
Philippe (Jean) 1497–1501.
Jehannot (Jean) 1498.
Poitevin (Jean) 1498.
Rembolt (Berthold) [1498]–1523.
Vostre (Simon) 1498–1520.
Dupré (Jean) 1500.
Higman (Jean) 1500.
Vérard (Antoine) 1501–1508.
Bocard (André) 1502.
Badius (Jodocus) 1504–1511.
Barbier (Jean) 1504–1512.
Bienayse (Jean) 1506–1521.
Ferrebouc (Jacques) 1510–1516.
Petit (Jean) 1510–1530.
Cousturier (Raoul) 1511.
Chevallon (Claude) [1512]–1531.
Cowelance (Philippe de) 1515.
Adam (Jean) 1516–1521.
Kerbriant (Jean) 1516.
Higman (Nicholas) 1519.
Regnault (François) 1519–1538.
Sainct Denis (Jean de) [1520].
Bignon (Jean) [1521].
Bonhomme (Yolande) 1523–1534.
Maheu (Desiderius) 1526.
Prevost (Nicholas) 1527–1532.
Plomier (Alard) 1528.
Hardouyn (Germain) [1528–1533].

PARIS—*continued.*

Boursette (Madeleine) 1541–1556.
Chaudière (Regnauld) [1550].
Massellin (Robert) 1553.
Amazeur (Jean) 1555.
Merlin (Guillaume) 1555–1557.
Le Blanc (Jean) 1556, 1557.

BASLE [1488].
Wenssler (Michael) [1488].
Emlos (Theophyll) [*1550*].
Edmonds (Alexander) 1553.

DEVENTER 1489.
Paffroed (Richard) 1489.

ROUEN [1490]–1557.
Le Talleur (Guillaume) [1490].
Morin (Martin) 1492–1517.
Ravynell (James) 1495.
Richard (Jean) 1496–1510.
Lorraine (Jean de) 1500, 1501.
Olivier (Pierre) 1500–[1520].
Huvin (Jean) 1501–1508.
Mauditier (Jean) 1502.
Violette (Pierre) 1505–1509.
Bernard (Guillaume) 1506–[1517].
Coste (Philippe) 1506.
Loys (Jamet) [1507]–1508.
Hostingue (Lawrence) [1507].
Goupil (Richard) 1510.
Cousin (Jacques) 1512–1537.

ROUEN—*continued.*
  Macé (Richard) 1515.
  Caillard (Jean) 1517–1522.
  Daubet.   1517.
  Guerin (Pierre) [1517].
  Hardy (Eustace) 1518.
  Le Roux (Nicholas) 1533–1557.
  Marchant (Jean) 1536, 1537.
  Marshall (Henry) [1539].
  Wood (Michael) 1553, 1554.
  Le Prest (Jean) 1554, 1555.
  Hamillon (Richard) 1555–1557.
  Valentin (Florence) 1555–1557.
  Valentin (Robert) 1555–1557.

WORMS [1525–1526].
  Schoeffer (Peter) [1525–1526].

MARBURG.
  Lufft (Hans) 1528–1535.
  Philoponos (Joannes) 1538.

STRASSBURG 1528–1530.
  Schott (Johann) 1528.
  Foxe (Francis) 1530.
  Beckeneth (Balthasar) 1531.

MALMOE 1533.
  Hochstraten (John) 1533.

MUENSTER.
  Willems (Conrad) 1533.

NUREMBERG.
  Twonson (Nicholas) 1533.

EMDEN 1534.
  Aurik (Jacob) 1534.

ZÜRICH 1535–1555.
  Froschauer (Christopher) 1535–
    1555.
  Jacobson (Oliver) 1543.
  Fries (Augustine) 1547.

AURICH.
  Troost (Jan) 1541.

LEIPZIG.
  Hoffe (Ubright) 1541.

AUGSBURG.
  Anonimus (Adam) 1545.

GENEVA 1556, 1557.
  Wood or *Boys (Michael) 1545–*
    1548.
  Crespin (Jean) 1556.
  Poulain (Jacques) 1556.
  Rivery (Jean) 1556.
  Badius (Conrad) 1557.

WESEL 1548.
  Nicholson (Henry) 1546.
  Plateanus (Theodoricus) 1548.

LYONS 1549–1553.
  Frellon (Jean) 1549.
  Tournes (Jean de) 1553.

AMSTERDAM [1550].
  Pietersz (Jan) [1550].

"SAVOY."
   Turona (*Francis de*) [*1550*].

FLORENCE 1553.
   Torrentini (Lorenzo) 1553.

WITTENBERG.
   Dorcaster (*Nicholas*) *1554.*

ROME.
   Constantius (*Marcus Antonius*) *1555.*